SPITFIRE
GLORY

SPITFIRE GLORY

THE WARTIME FLYING LIFE OF LEIF LUNDSTEN

TOR IDAR LARSEN

FONTHILL

With special thanks to Knut Åshammer,
Antoine Crespin, and A. C. Evans

Fonthill Media Language Policy

Fonthill Media publishes in the international English language market. One language edition is published worldwide. As there are minor differences in spelling and presentation, especially with regard to American English and British English, a policy is necessary to define which form of English to use. Tor Idar Larsen was born and educated in Norway; therefore British English has been adopted in this publication.

Fonthill Media Limited
Fonthill Media LLC
www.fonthillmedia.com
office@fonthillmedia.com

First published in the United Kingdom and the United States of America 2016

British Library Cataloguing in Publication Data:
A catalogue record for this book is available from the British Library

Typeset in 10.5pt on 13pt Sabon
Printed and bound by CPI Group (UK) Ltd, Croydon, CR0 4YY

Contents

'Lest We Forget'

Lest we forget the boys who died,
That we—in peace—might live.
Lest we forget the boys who gave,
The most that they could give

Lest we forget the boys who gave
An eye, a leg, an arm,
Who lived with pain and suffering,
Who kept us free from harm

The boys in khaki, and navy blue
And the blue to match the sky,
Who volunteered for freedom's cause,
Who volunteered to die.

They do not ask for monuments
Whilst they're resting above,
They only wish to be remembered
In the hearts of those they love.

Dedicated to all Spitfire pilots, the young who fought and died in the Second World War, the test pilots who worked tirelessly to develop it, the veterans who survived and sadly are now leaving us, the aviators, restorers, and owners who have thrilled and entertained the public for seven decades since the war, the RC scale pilots who immaculately construct and fly their priceless possessions, and the simulator pilots who spend countless hours online creating great communities.

Introduction

It all started with a logbook. It came into my hands by pure chance. The old and frail artefact had been digitally copied by someone who was willing to invest time and money in photographing Second World War logbooks. The original was in the possession of a museum that (in my eyes at least) would rather not let it out for public viewing. I convinced this individual to send me a copy of Leif Lundsten's logbook, although he was reluctant. It is, perhaps, understandable to see the man's reluctance to share, and the museum's reluctance to accept these logbooks to be shared freely online. But, I got the logbook and I looked at it with amazement.

I knew Leif Lundsten had been a test pilot, but the sheer amount of Spitfires he flew overwhelmed me. I started to Google a few of them to see what had happened to some of these birds. It became somewhat of an obsession—after that it became a book. I hope that I can somewhat show both the hesitant individual and the museum that, despite the reluctance of both parties, something good has come out of it.

This is a detailed and in-depth look into one of Norway's greatest Spitfire pilots' career in the Second World War. Hundreds and hundreds of hours on Spitfires, and about 300 different Spitfires flown—from Seafires to Spitfires I, II, III, V, VII, VIII, IX, XII, and XIV—with well over 100 operational sorties to his name, countless take-offs and landings, and four (plus one shared) victories to his name. He was a part of a group of relatively few pilots who spent their rest period testing brand-new Spitfires, thus actively taking part in keeping the Spitfire technologically up to date as the war progressed. It was essential work.

The book has four different sections. First, an introduction to Leif Lundsten's life as a young boy to his first days of training to become a pilot at Kjeller Aerodrome and onwards to Canada and Britain. Second, his first 'tour' with 331 Squadron from August 1941 (he flew his first Spitfire in September) to June 1943 when he went on his rest period. Third, his rest period as a Vickers-Armstrongs test pilot at Worthy Down and Chattis Hill. The fourth section deals with his return to 331 Squadron as a major and squadron leader for 331 Squadron, leading them on D-Day and the first days after the invasion up until his disappearance 9 June 1944.

The book has been written almost as a diary, with the date, Spitfires (with serials) flown, where it was built, hours flown, and information about each sortie, and the history of each Spitfire. Not one take-off he took part in has been ignored, which gives the reader an insight into just how much flying Leif Lundsten did during the Second World War.

I decided to drop the hours flown each day during his test period July 1943—February 1944 due to space issues. There are instead summaries added (when possible) at the end of each month. For his operational periods, the hours flown each day are listed and documented if they are known.

The first period focuses on his operations with 331 Squadron. The fate and history of the Spitfires he flew during the period are added to the text, but it is not the main focus; this is only natural. The two periods with 331 Squadron obviously relies heavily on the 331 Squadron Operational Record Book (in the book shortened to ORB), Lundsten's own logbook, and one essential, secondary source, Cato Guhnfeldt's *Spitfire Saga I-V* books, released between 2009 and 2014. These five massively researched books are often (shamelessly) quoted in the book, but the option to leave it out or refrain from using them feels somewhat counterproductive to the cause. Arguably the most controversial mentions in this book would be the rumoured Burma Spitfires—Spitfires crated and buried in Burma and rumoured to still be there. The Spitfires in this case connected to Leif Lundsten are just loosely mentioned online by enthusiasts, but I decided to add them to the text, if only because everyone likes a good mystery. It's also a good way to show how the past connects to the present.

Other books have also been used as sources, including biographies by fellow pilots Tarald Weisteen, Svein Heglund, Kristian Nyerrød, and Birger Tidemand-Johannessen—all 331 Squadron pilots. You will find a complete listing at the back of the book, including all ORBs used to gather information.

Since Leif Lundsten never could tell his own story, I have let his friends and colleagues do it for him by using translated quotes from mentioned books. I have also added comments directly from 331 Squadron pilots' logbooks. One individual often quoted during Lundsten's first tour in the book is Reidar Haave-Olsen, who more often than not added cheeky and keen comments to his sorties. It makes it all livelier.

For the third part of the book—his time as a test-pilot—everything changes drastically. Here, the fate and story of the Spitfires takes over as the main focus. Secondary sources from books released as far back as the

1980s have been added. Relatively few books have been written about Worthy Down and Chattis Hill, but some interesting quotes can be found. ORBs from respective squadrons in question have been obtained from the National Archives (UK) in large numbers. It is my hope to bring some new information to the table in this section, and to shed light on many sad endings to brave young pilots from around the world coming together for a common cause.

A Spitfire went through many stops during its career, Maintenance Units to name but one. I hope you can forgive me when I say I have ignored most of these stops along the way and focused on the squadrons each Spitfire served with, but there are exceptions. Considering the amount of Spitfires he flew, Lundsten was bound to have made mistakes in his logbook. I have relied heavily on www.airhistory.org.uk/spitfire/ as the primary source, in addition to using books, archives, and the internet to track down these Spitfire stories. Surprisingly, many of them have been of interest to others in the past years, and several have been photographed during the Second World War. I have managed to purchase (mostly from eBay) or obtain many photographs of the Spitfires he flew. For the rest of them, I hope the correct source have been listed, but do get in touch if there are photographs that are credited to the wrong individuals. It is my experience that people often want to take credit of rare photographs, which originally do not belong to them (after all, it's been seventy years), which makes everything very confusing for someone who struggles to do it right. I hope anyone offended can forgive my ignorance, and instead focus on the goal: to shed light on a forgotten hero.

The fourth part of the book brings him back to 331 Squadron, taking charge of 331 Squadron. Here, I follow the same plan as his first period with the squadron, using the same sources of information. The last day, 9 June 1944, has already been researched heavily by Cato Guhnfeldt, collecting memories from these pilots for several decades. I am forever grateful for the work done, this book would suffer greatly without this research. Nevertheless, it is my hope that I have taken a step further into the career of Leif Lundsten, corrected a couple of misunderstandings, and added a bit of information along the way.

Also added to the book is information on airfields Lundsten came to know and operate from, as well as a special chapter on his fiancée, Miss Sheila Lee.

Sadly, there's an obvious part that is often missing in this book: a look into Leif Lundsten's personal life, his character, his thoughts and opinions, hopes and dreams. In 2015, at the time of writing this, almost all of those who knew him have left us and those very few that are left find that their memories of lost comrades fade as time goes by. I can only agree with what his friend from middle school once told me when I said I was writing a book about Leif Lundsten. He said: 'You are too late.' However, he is only partly right. Ironically, this book would never have come to fruition thirty, forty, or fifty years ago. All this information about these Spitfires would have been virtually impossible to obtain. Simply flying to London to research ORBs would have been economically impossible in the long run. Just getting one ORB needed for a specific Spitfire would have been a struggle. Not now though, thanks to the internet and online archives. So, while it may be too late to find his fiancée Sheila Lee or add 100 pages of great stories about him from his friends that were there with him, thanks to modern technology it is exactly the right time for everything else.

It has been a privilege to work on this book. The further I got with this project, the more I understood just how much Leif Lundsten had done for the war effort and for our freedom. I am absolutely without doubt when I say Leif Lundsten's name deserves to be mentioned alongside the absolute greatest Spitfire pilots in history—past or present.

A Boy from Toten: May 1917–June 1938, Gjøvik and Toten, Norway

Toten, Norway, is a place of peace and serenity. It is quiet and calm with little crime. The seasons vary greatly from mild summers to cold winters. In English terms, it was and still is sparsely populated. It makes for peace, people busy making a living and spending their lives in peace.

Toten is divided into two municipalities, the eastern and the western part. In 2015 the population was about 26,000, divided almost identically between the two. The population having only marginally increased since the 1980s, but still considerably larger than in the 1920s and '30s. The soil is very fertile, making Toten the perfect place for farming with its almost English-looking large, waving fields. The inhabitants, both present and past, mostly rely on farming, however the western part has developed an industrial stronghold going back to before the Second World War started. The eastern part also has a developing industry.

In 1902, a train line from Oslo (then called Kristiania) was built through tough terrain, stretching from the capital to the small town of Gjøvik. Along the train line, small villages slowly developed. Just a few stops south of the town of Gjøvik, in a tiny village called Reinsvoll, a train line was developed to a village in the eastern part of Toten, Skreia. At the peak of its operations, the train line to Skreia had thirteen stops including the connection point at Reinsvoll station. Toten was suddenly connected to Norway's largest city.

It was at one of these stations that Otto Lundsten found work. Between the small towns of Lena and Skreia a small village called Bilitt was situated. A post office opened almost simultaneously with the train station in 1902. Close by the train station, a liqueur distillery was situated between the large farms and farming fields. Otto's brother found work at the neighbouring station at Kraby, just slightly closer to the village of Lena to the west. Otto and his wife Laura (originally from a farm called Heggernes in neighbouring village Bøverbru) moved into a house a short walk from the train station at

Bilitt, on the (in 2015) other side of the road going to Skreia. The house still stands today. In 1918, their first child was born. He was given the name Leif, a popular name in Norway at the time (1.6 per cent of all boys were given the name Leif in 1918). The name is from Norse mythology and means descendant or heir. A few years later, Laura gave birth to their second son, Bjarne. Later on, a third child was born. A girl. They became a family of five.

> You could tell he was Lundsten. He looked like a Lundsten through and through.
>
> Olav Gundersen, conversation with the author in 2011.
>
> Those boys [Lundsten sons] were very bright. Leif was very bright indeed.
>
> Erna Johansen, conversation with the author in 2015.

Leif grew up in a part of Norway slowly adjusting and developing alongside the changing times. Travelling to Oslo could suddenly be done within a day. The railway naturally had a massive impact on the area, but work was still mainly found in farming or in the growing factories in the western part of Toten or in the bigger town of Gjøvik and its industrial Mustad factory (producing mainly special nails for horse shoes and fish hooks).

Most boys in Toten adapt to the changing seasons, historically picking their activities mostly from the outdoors. For Leif Lundsten, he took up the art of ski jumping in the winter. Without knowing it, he had picked a sport that army air officials looked upon as essential if one were to be a skilled pilot. His first step towards his ultimate character had already been taken. During Easter time, usually in Toten a time of a warming sun, but still plenty of snow on the ground, ski jumping competitions were held in the mountains to the south (you may see them or even fly over them on your way into Oslo Airport Gardermoen). The mountains, only known to Norwegians as a hill (called Totenåsen) with its highest peak at 841 metres above sea level, give plenty of options to go skiing. It was in the hills close to a lake in Totenåsen called Skjeppsøen that Lundsten won his medals in ski jumping. Today, the lake is used as a source of drinking water. The restrictions due to this have made swimming illegal, and no ski jumping competitions are held any more in the area. To this day, Toten has provided Norway with several excellent ski jumpers, some reaching the very top of international competitions.

With the snow usually gone by mid-April or early May, Lundsten shifted his focus to a more English type of sport—football. Alongside football, he quickly developed a talent for building model cars. He soon had a reputation to his name as a talented constructor. In 1937, aged nineteen, he constructed a model truck for his cousin Roald. Roald still remembered getting the truck almost seventy years later. Lundsten went to the middle school in Kraby, not far from his home. Progressing through the school system with excellent grades, he went to Gjøvik to study for his *Examen artium*, the Norwegian-Danish name of academic certification, qualifying the student for university. Today, these school years would be defined as high school. The curricula Lundsten studied included Latin, mathematics, physics, English, French, biology, and chemistry.

It was at Gjøvik (Tranberg high school) that Lundsten met Olav Gundersen from Kapp (a village between Bilitt and Gjøvik). They soon became friends. Gundersen also visited Leif's home at Bilitt on several occasions.

We had different ideas about what we wanted to do after high school. I wanted to join the army, but Leif was adamant he wanted to join the army air force. He was a good student, very good in mathematics. He applied and was accepted.

Olav Gundersen, conversation with the author in 2011.

It is not known where Leif got his interest in flying from. Perhaps from his ski jumping or simply because of this new and exotic form of activity that fascinated him. Flying in Toten in the 1920s and 1930s was simply non-existent, until the first steps towards a local Flying Club was developed when Lundsten had already gone to Kjeller for his training.

2

Learning to Fly:
1938–1939, Kjeller Aerodrome,
Akershus, Norway

With good grades and a keenness to fly, Leif Lundsten was accepted to Army Air Force Training at Kjeller Aerodrome (close to Lillestrøm) in the summer of 1938. His first instructor was Jens S. Hertzberg, a first-class teacher according to fellow pilot Tarald Weisteen. Leif Lundsten's first solo flight in a Tiger Moth happened sometime in August–September 1938.

On 20 February 1939, Lundsten and his friends left Kjeller for a winter exercise at Tisleia between the villages of Gol and Fagernes. They used Tisleia as their airfield, and they used the Tislefjorden Lake for target practice. The pupils lived at the Oset Hotel. Navigational flights as far as Gardermoen (now Oslo Airport Gardermoen, OSL) were also among their tasks. After a month or so, they returned to Kjeller in their Fokker C.V-Ds & -Es and de Havilland DH 82 Tiger Moths.

In parallel with their pilot training, they also took part in long marches lead by Lt. Jean-Hansen. According to Tarald Weisteen, these marches were very unpopular until Jens S. Hertzberg took charge of them. Hertzberg took his fair share of the load on his back, just as the boys did, and he also carried the loads of others if they got tired. The marches actually became popular after the change of leadership.

After graduation from Kjeller, Leif left Norway for Gothenburg, in Sweden, to study at a technical school of excellence. It didn't take many months before he was called back in Norway for neutrality service with the military. Leif was ordered north together with several other future big names from the RAF—for example, Wing Commander Rolf Arne Berg. Lundsten was still up north when the Germans invaded Norway.

Invasion and Escape: 1939–1941, Northern Norway, Scotland, Toronto, Aston Down, and Catterick

For the entire winter of 1939 to 1940, Leif was in northern Norway. He was at Banak on 9 April 1940 (invasion of Norway), and arrived at Bardufoss on 13 April, and then to Kirkenes the day after.

While 331 Squadron was based at Skeabrea in 1941–42, several pilots wrote down their experiences of 9 April 1940 and the following days. Leif wrote the following:

On 9 April 1940 I was at Banak at Finnmarksvidda for neutralityservice, close to the border to Finland. I left from there on 10 April with S/S *Ingøy* to Målselv and from there by car to Bardufoss airfield. Moved from here to Kirkesnes in the valley of Målselv the same day. From here, daily and nightly bombing operations against German positions by Narvik was undertaken. I crashed during a landing after a bombing operation and stayed in the hospital for a couple of days.

Leif Lundsten, personal account.

On 7 May, Leif mentioned in his writings that he ran into serious trouble. Rundhaug, close to Kirkenes, was not an airfield, but just a farmer's field, which they used as best as they could. From Rundhaug, they kept flying recce missions, photographing the German lines when they could find them. The men also invented something they called the 'Halling Throw'. This included manoeuvring the Fokker to drop bombs by hand in a particularly effective way.

Morten Ree recalled the incident with Lundsten years later:

Leif Lundsten had a terrible crash at Rundhaug. He put the Fokker C.V 1 down too far into the field and overshot, ending up on a fairly steep hill approaching the river. The Fokker went right up on its nose and was reduced to a pile of scrap in the subsequent crash. Both Lundsten and his scout, Mensen, were stuck in their cockpits, and the aircraft caught fire. Mensen eventually got out on his own, but we had to break Lundsten free using a saw. He was badly injured, and the Fokker was a write-off.

Morten Ree, Våre flygere i kamp, 1962, p. 90

Lundsten stayed in a hospital for a few days; however, he decided to leave on 11 May, and travelled by car and boat to Harstad.

At the beginning of May some aircraft arrived from the south, but these were in such a poor shape that most of them were written-off on the spot. The flying school's leader on those long marches at Kjeller, Jean-Hansen, showed up at Rundhaug with a Fokker that had a piece of cut timber in place of one of the undercarriage wheels. The conditions at Rundhaug deteriorated significantly when the snow started to melt.

On 18 May 1940, Lundsten and fourteen other pilots escaped Norway with the Polish ship *Batory*. This after first being on board *Chobry*, which was bombed and sunk. He arrived in Greenoch, Scotland, on 23 May 1940. Leif Lundsten and most of the Norwegian Army Air Force personnel were quickly sent to Dumfries. After three weeks in Dumfries, he boarded the Norwegian steamer *Lyra* departing Glasgow to Montreal. He arrived in Canada on 3 August 1940. Leif recalls the events leading up to his arrival in Canada:

During 11 May, sixteen pilots left Kirkesnes for Harstad to go England to bring back Hawker Hurricanes. On 12 May I boarded S/S *Chobry*. Was bombed in Vestfjorden outside Bodø. I was picked up by two destroyers. Came back to Harstad and then boarded S/S *Batory* on 18 May after crazy drunken party in Harstad 17 May accompagnied by a thunderous salute from fifty air defence cannons. Arrived in Greenock on 24 May. After eight days in Glasgow I left for London. No aircraft available for us. Then left for Canada in the middle of July and came back from there at the end of May 1941 with the 1st Fighter Wing.

Leif Lundsten, personal account

With Leif's valuable experience, he quickly became an instructor at their base in Canada. Now legendary Ole Reistad was in command of the base, and the construction of a more permanent establishment was completed in record time. It was officially opened on 10 November 1940, very close to where the Maple Leaf baseball stadium once stood. The Norwegians used

Fairchild Cornells, Douglas 8A-5s, and Curtiss Hawk 75A-8s, the bomber pilots concentrating on the Douglas. Leif stayed on as an instructor for six months, in addition to taking an advanced class on fighters before he left Canada on 10 May 1941, as part of what was called the 1st Fighter Wing.

Leif left Halifax onboard a merchant vessel called *Aurania* and arrived in Iceland on 23 May. The journey was eventful; several ships in their convoy were sunk by German submarines.

Thirteen men from *Aurania*, among them Lundsten, arrived at Operational Training Unit 52 at Aston Down. On 5 August 1941 he arrived at the newly formed 331 Squadron at Catterick, Yorkshire. The squadron started out with Hawker Hurricanes before converting to the Supermarine Spitfire in early September 1941. Prior to their switch to Spitfires, Lundsten experienced a mid-air collision with Jens Müller, which nearly killed him. He landed the Hurricane at Castletown with hardly any elevator or rudder control at his disposal. He crashed into a 124 Squadron Spitfire due to having no ground control over the stricken Hurricane.

First Flight:
September 1941, 331 Squadron,
Castletown, Skeabrea, and Orkneys

Date: 06.09.1941 (first Spitfire flight)
Spitfire: Ia, ON-A
Built: Unknown
Length: 1:00
Where: Castletown, Scotland

This day (6 September 1941) proved to be a most historic day for Leif Lundsten. It was his first time flying a Supermarine Spitfire. The Norwegians had heard plenty about the already famous fighter, and they were all keen on making the change from their old and frail Hurricanes to brand-new Spitfires.

For his first flight, Leif Lundsten borrowed one of 124 Squadrons Spitfire Ias, with squadron code ON-A, for an hour of flying over Castletown and the local area. He does not list the serial number in his logbook, and 124 Squadrons own operational record book does not list their squadron codes assigned to each Spitfire. No. 124 Squadron operated Mk Ia Spitfires at this point after they had reformed at RAF Castletown in May 1941 to provide air defense for Scapa Flow, much like 331 Squadron was doing from Skeabrea later the same year. At the end of July 1942 the squadron was operating altitude Spitfire VIs, and at one point operated from North Weald, in Essex, the same airfield that the Norwegians would operate from later on. The squadron received Spitfire VIIIs in March of 1943 with detachments being sent to airfields in the West Country for high-altitude interceptions. In March 1944 they joined No. 141 Airfield at Church Fenton as part of Second TAF, and flew escort missions for American bombers over France until the invasion. In July 1944 they converted to Spitfire IXs, and in August returned to Fighter Command for escort duties from the UK. In February they attacked V-2 sites in Holland as well as shipping recces. In April 1946, the squadron was renumbered to 56 Squadron at Bentwaters.

It was nevertheless Leif Lundsten's first Spitfire flight. It would be the first of many.

RAF Castletown and RAF Skeabrea

RAF Castletown was located in the north of Scotland, slightly south-east of the village of Castletown. It opened in 1940, planned as a satellite airfield for RAF Wick, but also used to protect Scapa Flow. No. 504 Squadron first took up residency, flying Hawker Hurricanes. Other RAF fighter (and Fleet Air Arm) squadrons followed after 504 moved down south to participate in the Battle of Britain. The airfield had three runways at its disposal. Castletown was located in a rough landscape with weather being one of its primary enemies. No. 331 Squadron arrived in August 1941, replacing 607 Squadron. No. 331 Squadron moved to Skeabrea, in the Orkneys, a month or so later.

RAF Skeabrea, situated on the north-west side of Mainland, served as the Norwegians home until they moved south in May 1942. The airfield served as protection for Scapa Flow, as well as catering to aircraft operating over Norway. It was first opened in August 1940, but the airfield was largely unfinished and needed much attention and work in the coming months. The airfield (at its peak) had two runways, twelve hangars, as well as a cinema (still standing as of 2015). During 331 Squadrons stay at Skeabrea, 801 Squadron arrived with their Hawker Hurricanes. In February 1942, 132 Squadron also operated from Skeabrea. Several squadrons had durations of stay at Skeabrea during the war. Post Second World War, the airfield gradually went back to its natural grassland and there's little left of Skeabrea today.

Battle of Britain Spitfires: November 1941, 331 Squadron, Skeabrea and Orkneys

Our stay at Skeabrea brought the squadron together, and prepared us for what would come. Our task was to protect the Royal Navy and their base at Scapa Flow, as well as giving protection for convoys sailing up and down the coastline and to the north of the Scottish islands. Convoy patrols were dull and did not do any favours for a fighter pilots natural talents. Usually, German reconnaissance aircraft flew over with great speed and height to keep an eye on ship traffic and the navy base. We went quickly up after then, but they were usually all gone when we reached their height.

Svein Heglund, *Høk over Høk*, 1997, p. 42

Date: 15.11.1941
Spitfire: IIa, FN-L P7366
Built: Castle Bromwich
Length: 00:25, 00:25
Where: Skeabrea, Orkneys

Lundsten simply wrote 'Test Spitfire' in his logbook for his two test flights on 15 November 1941. He also listed L.S as the squadron letter, which makes little sense. An educated guess is that the 'S' stands for Spitfire, since he had been flying Hurricanes up until this point and wanted to point out the change of equipment.

P7366 certainly had combat history to its name before it arrived at 331 Squadron. On 5 February 1941, legendary John Freeborn of 74 Squadron shot down a Dornier 215 flying P7366. No. 74 Squadron's Red Section, led by Adolph 'Sailor' Malan, attacked it first before Yellow Section and John Freeborn roared in from the left, attacking the bomber from the side. The Dornier crashed into the sea. John Freeborn in P3766 fired 1,360 rounds, all together 6,541.

Another pilot flying P7366 on an occasion, but under less stressful surroundings, was Pilot Officer Peter Chesters from Thorpe Bay, in Essex. Chesters joined 74 Squadron at Coltishall on 29 September 1940, and practised circuits and landings in P7366, much like Lundsten would do about a year and two months later in the same Spitfire.

John Freeborn survived the war and he passed away peacefully in 2010. Peter Chesters died on 10 April 1941. He shot down a Messerschmitt 109 over Canterbury, and could not resist a victory roll when he returned to Manston. He misjudged it, and crashed onto the parade ground, killing himself instantly.

Date: 24.11.1941
Spitfire: IIa, FN-L P7366
Built: Castle Bromwich
Length: 0:55
Where: Skeabrea, Orkneys

Lundsten took P7366 up for an hour of aerobatic flying over Skeabrea.

Date: 28.11.1941
Spitfire: Ia, FN-C X4622
Built: Eastleigh
Length: 0:25
Where: Skeabrea

Aerobatics in Spitfire Ia, X4622. This Spitfire first flew in October 1940, and shortly thereafter joined 222 Squadron. X4622 was a presentation Spitfire. The idea was that an individual, organisation, or town could present the cost of an airframe (£5,000 for a Spitfire) and the aircraft would be allocated to bear the name of the donor or any other caption they chose. Many towns had their own Spitfire fund. The Falkland Islands were the presenters of X4622. The Spitfire was struck off charge at the very end of 1944.

Date: 29.11.1941 to 03.12.1941
Spitfire: QV-A
Built:
Length: 1:30, 0:40, 0:55, and 0:30
Where: Skeabrea–Inverness–Skeabrea

Lundsten lists QV as a squadron letters, which belongs to 19 Squadron. In November 1941, 19 Squadron was down south and not anywhere near northern Scotland.

Lundsten flew QV-A around Inverness on 1 and 2 December. On 3 December, he brought the Spitfire to Prestwick and found other means of transportation (flights in a Wellington, a Rapid, and a Botha) back to Skeabrea on 5 December.

Because the squadron being so far away the action, there was a bit of arguing and complaining going around the base. It didn't take long until I started to get unhappy myself. I was almost longing for the days in Trondheim working for the underground resistance. Fellow pilot Fredrik Fearnley voiced a critical opinion of the Defence Ministry High Command since they had to be blamed for us ending up in the middle of nowhere.

Tarald Weisteen, *Nattjager*, 2004, p. 85

'A' is for Bad Luck:
December 1941, 331 Squadron,
Skeabrea and Orkneys

Date: 05.12.1941
Spitfire: IIa, FN-A P7377
Built: Castle Bromwich
Length: 0:35
Where: Skeabrea

On 5 December, Lundsten was up in the air test flying P7337 over Skeabrea. P7377 was another Spitfire with combat history to its name prior to joining up with the Norwegians.

In the afternoon of 8 November 1940, twenty-two Italian Fiat G.50s flew an offensive patrol between Dungeness, Canterbury, and Margate. The Fiats got tangled up with legendary Squadron Leader Brian John Edward Lane flying P7377 alongside three other Spitfires. Lane later reported he was bounced by a Hurricane and had to make an emergency landing with damage inflicted on his Spitfire. It might have been one of the Fiats that attacked Lanes Spitfire as one of the pilots claimed a Spitfire shot down.

With 331 Squadron, in 1941, P7377 was also flown by Helge Mehre, later Wing Commander Flying and Group Captain.

Brian Lane died while serving as a squadron leader for 167 Squadron on 13 December 1942. He was last seen chasing two Focke-Wulf 190s and never returned from the sortie. It was his first with 167 Squadron. P7377 was struck off charge on 20 August 1945.

The squadron code, FN-A, was to become known as bad luck for 331, with several Spitfires coded 'A' being lost in the coming months and years. Tarald Weisteen, on the other hand, picked 'A' as his squadron letter deliberately. The 'A' was in honor of his girlfriend back home in Norway, named Anne. Weisteen himself never had any bad luck with the 'A' and kept the letter when he started to fly Mosquitoes with 85 Squadron in 1944—he survived the war.

Date: 12.12.1941
Spitfire: Ia, FN-B
Built: TBC
Length: 0:40
Where: Skeabrea

Cine-gun test in a Spitfire Lundsten listed as FN-B, but the correct serial number remains unclear. Per 'James' Svanøe Endresen flew the Spitfire on 18 November 1941—John Nordmo the following day. Endresen also flew it on 22 November. Helge Sognnæs flew it a month later (20 December 1941).

Date: 16.12.1941
Spitfire: Ia, FN-C X4622
Built: Eastleigh
Length: 0:30
Where: Skeabrea

Formation flying with the rest of the squadron, flying X4622. Lundsten shortened it to 'Form' in his logbook.

Date: 17.12.1941
Spitfire: Ia, X4622, FN-C
Built: Eastleigh
Length: 0:50
Where: Skeabrea–Sule Skerry–Skeabrea

Lundsten flew out to Sule Skerry, a remote Scottish island located 60 kilometres west of Skeabrea. Lundsten most likely brought newspapers and other artefacts to the two men in charge of the lighthouse. The journey was usually flown 'on the deck' and pride was taken in getting the navigation spot on.

Date: 19.12.1941
Spitfire: FN-D?
Built: TBC
Length: 1:00
Where: Skeabrea

Formation flying in Spitfire FN-D. Serial number remains unclear. Both Ias lettered 'B' and 'D' were used for practice flying, but not listed on operational sorties.

Date: 19.12.1941
Spitfire: IIa, FN-F P8729
Built: Castle Bromwich
Length: 0:40

Lundsten's first night-flying exercise in a Spitfire was on 19 December 1941. He flew P8729 on this occasion. For the rest of the year, and the first month of 1942, Leif Lundsten stayed at Peterhead, mostly flying what seems to be previous 303 or 310 (Polish) Squadron Hurricanes. He was back with 331 Squadron by February 1942.

> The landscape at the Orkneys is flat and with no vegetation. When the storms came in, as they often did, we had to tie everything down. In the air, the aircraft flew with the wind, and took off and landed vertically. We lived in barracks made of wood as well as Nissen Huts. More than once we had to start the day shoveling snow off the floors, and use a knife to cut through the ice in our drinking water. This hard and ever changing climate gave us good practice in instrument flying and in navigation.

> Svein Heglund, *Høk over Høk*, 1997, p. 43

Scrambles and Dawn Patrols: February 1942, 331 Squadron, Skeabrea and Orkneys

Date: 15.02.1942
Spitfire: Ia, FN-C X4622
Built: Eastleigh
Length: Unknown
Where: Skeabrea area

Arnt Hvinden and Leif Lundsten on a dawn patrol (listed as a night patrol in the ORB). On this day, Leif wrote his short account of the time from 9 April 1940 to his arrival back in England via Canada as told earlier in this book. Arnt Hvinden came from Brandbu, by modern standards just an hour's drive south of Toten.

Date: 16.02.1942
Spitfire: IIa, FN-Y P7886; IIa, FN-S P7388; IIa, FN-T P7616
Built: Castle Bromwich
Length: Unknown
Where: Skeabrea area

More test flights on 16 February. P7886 was an ex-Polish 308 Squadron Spitfire. On 2 July 1941, Sgt Stanislav Widlarz claimed a Bf 109 in the area of Lille, France. He also claims a probable on the day. With 308, the Spitfire have the squadron codes ZF-B. Just a week later, on 7 July, Sgt John Kremski claimed another Bf 109 as destroyed, while flying P7886. It had previously been with 611 Squadron before moving on to 308, and then to 331 on 2 November 1941. It stayed with 331 Squadron until 17 April 1942, and is then transferred to 58 OTU. The Spitfire kept flying until 1944.

For P7388, see 09.03.1942.

P7616 was a IIa that first went to 91 Squadron as DL-B. In early 1941, it was transferred to 609 Squadron before moving onwards to 616 Squadron six months later. Then onwards to 234 Squadron in the summer of 1941 before it finally arrived at 331 Squadron in September 1941. It did not stay long with the Norwegians though. The Spitfire stopped by several OTUs before being written-off in the summer of 1944.

Lundsten's flight in FN-T on 16 February was a scramble. The Norwegians were often scrambled from Skeabrea, but not once did they locate any German aircraft that far up north during their stay.

Date: 17.02.1942
Spitfire: IIa, FN-X P7929
Built: Castle Bromwich
Length: 0:30
Where: Skeabrea

Another scramble from Skeabrea, and Lundsten took P7929 to the air. The Spitfire had the letters FN-X. A year before Lundsten flew the Spitfire, it suffered an engine failure in mid-flight, and the pilot made a wheels-up landing at Beeston Farm, Ternhill. It was transferred from 331 to 58 OTU in May 1942. It was eventually struck off charge 30 December 1944.

Date: 18.02.1942
Spitfire: IIa, FN-P P7759
Built: Castle Bromwich
Length: Unknown
Where: Skeabrea

Lundsten took P7759 up for an air-firing test on this day. P7759 is the Spitfire that Ulf Wormdal flew when he crashed into the sea, 3 miles west of Brough Head, Orkney Islands, while attempting a mock attack at a group of Swordfish torpedo aircraft from the Fleet Air Arm. Wormdal either misjudged his height or he blacked out from the heavy g he pulled when he passed (or tried to pass) underneath the slow Swordfish aircraft.

Wormdal came from Hamar, Norway, and had a talent for drawing and artistry. According to Svein Heglund, Wordmal was perhaps 'a bit too nice for a fighter pilot'.

Date: 19.02.1942
Spitfire: IIa, FN-U P7366
Built: Castle Bromwich

Length: 0:20
Where: Skeabrea

Another air-firing test in John Freeborns old Spitfire. Lundsten listed it as FN-L for his first flights, but it was either later painted FN-U or Lundsten listed it in error. Most likely it was a repaint, but since Lundsten does not list these specific Spitfires' serial numbers in his logbook, it could very well also have been a different Spitfire.

It was noted in the Squadron Operation Book that spare parts for their Spitfires were delayed by several months. This made the operation of the squadron on a day-to-day basis very challenging. Considering Freeborns Spitfire P7366, a Battle of Britain combat veteran, and far from factory fresh at this point, the Norwegians had a valid point indeed.

Date: 22.02.1942
Spitfire: IIa, FN-Y P7366
Built: Castle Bromwich
Length: Unknown
Where: Skeabrea

Written in Lundsten's logbook as a dawn patrol, but not listed in the ORB.

Date: 23.02.1942
Spitfire: IIa, FN-N P7357
Built: Castle Bromwich
Length: Unknown
Where: Skeabrea

The whole squadron took off for a convoy patrol. The convoy consisted of one battle cruiser, one cruiser, one aircraft carrier, and seven destroyers. The ORB stated that the squadron got a message from the admiral of the fleet thanking the squadron for the fighter escort. A job well done indeed.

Date: 26.02.1942
Spitfire: IIa, FN-X P7929
Built: Castle Bromwich
Length: Unknown
Where: Skeabrea

Scramble with Arnt Hvinden flying P7886, FN-Y at 10.30 a.m. They both landed back at Skeabrea 11.10 a.m. with nothing to report.

Combat Veteran Spitfires: March 1942, 331 Squadron, Skeabrea and Orkneys

Date: 01.03.1942
Spitfire: IIa, FN-A P7377
Built: Castle Bromwich
Length: Unknown
Where: Skeabrea

The first Spitfire flight of the month, an air-firing test in P7377.

Date: 09.03.1942
Spitfire: IIa, FN-S P7388
Built: Castle Bromwich
Length: 0:15
Where: Skeabrea

A short flight in Spitfire P7388. The Spitfire arrived with 331 on 2 February 1942, and stayed with the Squadron until 17 April 1942 when it was transferred to 58 OTU. This was most likely in relation to the Norwegians getting factory fresh Spitfire Vbs. By 1 March, new Spitfire Vbs had already started to arrive. As an example of the tough Orkney weather, they suffered through snow, hail, and rain—all during the same day.

Date: 10.03.1942
Spitfire: IIa, FN-H P8199
Built: Castle Bromwich
Length: Unknown
Where: Skeabrea

Another standard routine patrol out of Skeabrea in FN-H P8199. The Spitfire was delivered to 331 Squadron on 26 November 1941 after a spell with 74 Squadron in 1941. It was transferred to 58 OTU on 4 April 1942 before it was finally scrapped in 1944.

Date: 12.03.1942
Spitfire: IIa, FN-A P7377
Built: Castle Bromwich
Length: 1:15
Where: Skeabrea

Another Hvinden/Lundsten sortie. Lundsten flew P7377; it was the first patrol by the squadron done this day in March. The squadron flew a total of twenty-one hours and ten minutes this day, which makes it a very busy day in the cold, clear skies over the Orkneys.

Date: 16.03.1942
Spitfire: IIa, FN-T P7616
Built: Castle Bromwich
Length: 0:45
Where: Skeabrea

Almost an hour's worth of aerobatics over the airfield in P7616. The weather must have been showing its good side on this day.

Date: 16.03.1942
Spitfire: IIa, FN-C P7963
Built: Castle Bromwich
Length: 0:30 and 0:20
Where: Skeabrea

An air-firing test in FN-C (now P7963). P7963 is another combat veteran, previously flown by Robert Finlay Boyd in 54 Squadron. Almost to the day, eleven months before Lundsten's aerobatics over Skeabrea, Boyd had fired P7963's guns in anger (17.03.41). In Boyd's sights was a Messerschmitt 110, which he claimed as destroyed. According to the 602 Squadron Museum website, he claimed the Me 110 while operating out of Catterick, in Yorkshire, with 54 Squadron where 331 Squadron first formed (and 332 formed in January 1942). Boyd later took command over the Kenley Wing. He finished the war with twenty-two confirmed kills (although other sources state it was twenty-one). Boyd passed away in 1975.

Date: 20.03.1942
Spitfire: IIa, FN-T P7616
Built: Castle Bromwich
Length: 0:40
Where: Skeabrea

Lundsten simply wrote 'lowflying exersice' in his logbook, flying P7616.

Date: 21.03.1942
Spitfire: IIa, FN-J P7384
Built: Castle Bromwich
Length: 1:10
Where: Skeabrea

A dusk patrol with Tim Heiberg flying P7963 on Lundsten's wing. P7384 arrived from 19 Squadron on 6 November 1941—it had also previously been with 64 Squadron in late 1940—and it left 331 Squadron on 17 April 1942. It was later transferred to Central Gunnery School at Sutton Bridge. When the school was moved to RAF Catfoss in 1944, it followed suit. On 25 April 1944, P7384 blew a tyre during take-off from the airfield, resulting with the aircraft overturning and it was ultimately written-off; there were luckily no fatalities.

Date: 22.03.1942
Spitfire: IIa, FN-P P7759
Built: Castle Bromwich
Length: 0:40
Where: Skeabrea

Something different was scheduled for this day, an Army co-operation exercise flying P7759. It was to be another busy day for 331 Squadron, with bright sunshine and calm weather. Thirty hours of operational patrol (shipping protection) was undertaken. It would be the last business done for a while. Lundsten would get some well-deserved leave in the upcoming weeks.

From 26 to 28 March, he flew one of 331 Squadrons old Hurricanes via several stops down to RAF Charmy Down, in Somerset (via Dyce, Peterhead, Usworth, Catterick, Peterborough, Wittering, and finally Charmy Down). One squadron at Charmy Down was 533 Squadron, which operated Hawker Hurricanes at the time. Charmy Down would perhaps be the Hurricanes new home. It also gave Lundsten the possibility of coming rather close to London and everything it had to offer. It looks like the return trip was done by railroad and ferries.

Mk V Spitfire:
April 1942, 331 Squadron,
Skeabrea and Orkneys

Leif Lundsten returned from leave on 9 April 1942. He would be back in the air the following day.

Date: 10.04.1942
Spitfire: Vb, FN-P AD509
Built: Castle Bromwich
Length: Unknown
Where: Skeabrea

According to Lundsten, this was a search mission for a PRU Spitfire, a high-altitude reconnaissance version of the Spitfire. Lundsten flew the search mission with Martin Gran in BL821.This was Lundsten's first operational sortie in the Mk Vb version of the Spitfire.

What Lundsten and Gran were looking for could have been Spitfire PR MK. IV AA797, belonging to No. 1 PRU. It was flown by F/S Jones of C-Flight. He was plotted on the radar between the Shetlands and Orkneys before he disappeared without a trace. Several PRU Spitfires were downed during their trade that day—a dangerous search for the German battleship *Tirpitz*. Jones disappeared on 3 April—seven days before Lundsten and Grans search mission, which is quite some time after the event had taken place. Considering the amount of days gone, it could very well be Lundsten and Gran looked for another PRU Spitfire of unknown origin.

AD509 stayed with 331 for quite some time. Tarald Weisteen claimed a Fw 190 damaged as early as 19 May 1942 flying this Spitfire. The Norwegians claimed two 190s damaged that day, the first claims done by the Norwegians while operating from North Weald, in Essex. Fredrik Fearnley claimed a probable when flying AD509 during the Dieppe landings. Erik Fossum claimed a Dornier 217 damaged on the same day flying AD509. According to the production lists, it was damaged on operations in October 1942, but nothing was found in regards to the Norwegians on this day. AD509 was transferred to 416 Squadron a month later, then onwards to 411 Squadron in March of 1943. It was written-off in early January 1944.

Date: 11.04.1942
Spitfire: Vb, FN-V BL821
Built: Castle Bromwich
Length: Unknown
Where: Skeabrea

Air-firing and a cine-gun test flying BL821. BL821 was ordered as a Mk III, but the Spitfire was converted to a Vb before delivery. On 16 May 1943, BL821 made a heavy landing at Southend causing failure of the starboard oleo leg-locking unit. It was classified category 'A', and repairs were carried out by personnel of 331 Squadron (this according to Peter Browns book *RAF Southend*). There is nothing in 331 Squadrons ORB about the heavy landing. No. 331 Squadron did not go on any operations until 19 May, and BL821 was flown by Anton C. Hagerup on this sortie. Either Southend personnel got it wrong, or repairs had been done already.

The Spitfire had spells with 443 Squadron, 58 OTU, and 61 OTU before being transferred to Portugal in 1947. It most likely ended its days there.

Date: 15.04.1942
Spitfire: Vb, FN-S BL891; Vb, FN-O AR328
Built: Castle Bromwich, Westland
Length: 0:20, 0:50
Where: Skeabrea

A scramble with Kristian Nyerrød flying in AR298, and ten minutes later Tarald Weisteen took off in BL673—the third Spitfire to the party. They returned empty handed twenty minutes later.

BL891 stayed with 331 until 24 September 1942 when it was transferred to the Fleet Air Arm. For 331 Squadron, the Vb was replaced by new IX models. BL891 received several updates and modifications during the next years. On 6 June 1944, BL891 was received by 719 Squadron at St. Merryn. It stayed with 719 until Squadron Leader J. E Jones undershot and hit a barbed wire fence just outside the runway during landing. The barbed wired fence protected an ammunition deposit. A lucky escape on his part.

Leif Lundsten took AR328 up for the first time on the same date (15 April), after the scramble. AR328 would become his 'personal' Spitfire. He would fly the Spitfire on many sorties to come. However, it was another pilot who made claims flying AR328—Fredrik Fearnley. On 31 May 1942, he claimed a Bf 109 destroyed together with Martin Gran. It was 331 Squadron's first victory in the air, and when the news came in from Gran and Fearnley that they had been successful, the squadron—especially the ground crew—went wild with joy. Finally their hard work was paying off. During the Dieppe landings, Fearnley claimed a shared Dornier 217 flying 'Lundsten's Spitfire'.

AR328 first flew on 11 February 1942 and arrived with the Norwegians on 15 March 1942. After a long and successful spell in the hands of Leif Lundsten, the Spitfire left the Norwegians on 25 October 1942 (being replaced by Spitfire IX). It had its fuel systems upgraded and modifications done to its wing in the spring of 1943, before being sent back with operational squadrons. No. 308 Squadron (Polish) was the first to receive the Spitfire in the summer of 1943. It went to 349 Squadron the same year, and onwards to 222 Squadron in the spring of 1944. It stayed just a month or so with 222 before transferred to 322 (Dutch) Squadron. A month later, the Spitfire found its way to 345 Squadron before it was delivered to de Havilland for repairs and service. The last trace of the Spitfire can be found in April 1945 when *Armée de l'Air*, the French Air Force, took charge of AR328. It most likely ended its days in France.

Date: 16.04.1942
Spitfire: IIa, FN-Y P7886; Vb, FN-S BL891
Built: Castle Bromwich
Length: 0:54 and 0:55
Where: Skeabrea

Squadron formation flying in P7886. The squadron still had some of the older Spitfires left, and Lundsten flew one of the remaining ones during this formation exercise. The Spitfire would leave 331 Squadron the day after, heading for 68 OTU.

Date: 17.04.1942
Spitfire: Vb, FN-O AR328; Vb, FN-T AB794
Built: Castle Bromwich
Length: 0:35
Where: Skeabrea

Air-firing practice in Lundsten's now 'personal Spitfire', AR328.

AB794, on the other hand, shared a very similar fate to Lundsten's own tragic end. Three days after Lundsten perished on 9 June 1944, the Spitfire was lost to friendly fire over Normandy. AB794 belonged to 130 Squadron at the time of the incident. On 12 June 1944, nine Spitfires of 130 Squadron took off at 4 a.m. to patrol the western area of the invasion, and encountered heavy flak. Flight Sergeant Brown in AB794 got hit, and called on the radio to say he had to make a forced landing. Nothing was heard from the pilot after that. The rest of the squadron was back at 6.05 a.m. The ORB does not state if the Spitfire was indeed lost to friendly fire, but the production list does—even if it states the Spitfire belonged to 322 (Dutch) Squadron at the time.

Date: 18.04.1942
Spitfire: Vb, FN-O AR328; FN-S BL891
Built: Westland, Castle Bromwich
Length: 0:45, unknown, 0:40
Where: Skeabrea

Flight formation in AR328, a cine-gun test in BL891, and then a dusk patrol in AR328. No. 331 Squadron had two dusk patrols up this evening, taking off in pairs, only five minutes apart. First to take-off was Stein Sem (AR297) and Erik Fossum (BL891) at 9.15 p.m., followed by Tarald Weisteen (AB794) and Lundsten in AR238 at 9.20 p.m. It was a rather short patrol, as Lundsten and Weisteen returned twenty minutes later.

> There was very little to do in our spare time. Kirkwall was not very exciting, and you were quickly done with your business there. There was no local pub there either. So, instead, we often took long nature walks in the surrounding areas. We brought our Smith & Wesson revolvers, and shot at seagulls. Birds in free flight are difficult targets, and it was only the master shooter Svein Heglund who managed to get one. It was good practice for those of us who would later shoot at Germans instead. There were rabbits up there too, but we left them alone. We had enough with the ones being served in the mess for lunch and dinner. Rabbit stew and rabbit pie every other day was not something to easily look forward too. The fact that there were other ways to cook these poor animals seemed to have gone over the cooks head. Sometimes we suspected that the rabbits had been stewed with the hairs still on them.
>
> Kristian Nyerrød, *En av de mange*, 1995, p. 73

Date: 20.04.1942
Spitfire: Vb, FN-T AB794
Built: Castle Bromwich

Length: Unknown
Where: Skeabrea

An unknown length of flying in AB794. Not listed in Operations Record Book, and therefore not an official sortie.

Date: 21.04.1942
Spitfire: Vb, FN-V BL821
Built: Castle Bromwich
Length: 1:10
Where: Skeabrea

Dawn patrol in BL821 with Kristian Nyerrød flying AR298.

After the dawn patrol was over, Lundsten flew a passenger in a Miles Magister down to Inverness. They returned back to Skeabrea the same day. It is not known who the passenger was.

The squadron lost Per Svanøe Endresen on this day in AR291. It is not known what happened to Endresen, as he simply disappeared somewhere over the cold sea. Svein Heglund later speculated he was shot down by a German tail gunner.

Date: 23.04.1942
Spitfire: Vb, FN-O AR328; Vb, FN-Z AR297
Built: Westland
Length: Unknown
Where: Skeabrea

A convoy patrol in AR328 and then air firing in AR297 later the same day. AR297 stayed with the squadron when it left for North Weald a month later. Martin Gran made claims for the squadron flying this Spitfire. Flying as Red 2, he was flying home after attacking a trawler when two Bf 109s attacked from behind. Together with Red 1, Rolf Arne Berg, they turned into the attackers. One passed underneath Gran, the other turned and climbed. Gran decided to follow the second one, climbing after him. He fired three short bursts from underneath astern. He observed bullet strikes on the fuselage, just behind the cockpit. It dived down with black smoke from the engine. Gran then broke away. He claimed half a damaged with Berg.

AR297 would come to have a very interesting career. When Lundsten flew it on 23 April it had only just arrived with 331 (10 April). It was category 'B' damaged on 4 September 1942, then with 885 Squadron (Fleet Air Arm) at Lee-on-Solent. It was fitted with a hook for carrier landings the same year. AR297 was now converted to a Seafire. With 788 Squadron, it was damaged during landing at Machrihanish and it was also damaged during a landing incident on HMS *Furious*. Yet more damage to the fighter happened on 4 October at Machrihanish, flown by Squadron Leader J. Davies. From June 1944 (after several small mishaps during the next two years) it was put into storage August on 1944 at Evanston.

Date: 25.04.1942
Spitfire: Vb, FN-Z AR297
Built: Westland
Length: 0:20
Where: Skeabrea

Another air-firing test in AR297.

Date: 27.04.1942
Spitfire: Vb, FN-O AR328
Built: Westland
Length: 1:00
Where: Skeabrea

Formation flying exercise. Lundsten flew his regular AR328.

10

Baptism of Fire:
North Weald Airfield, May 1942,
331 Squadron, North Weald, Essex

Things were about to change for the Norwegians. Their (almost) solitary presence at the Orkneys would soon be replaced with something very different. They were about to go into the heat of the battle where the Germans would be ready to fight them from their bases across the Channel.

North Weald would be their next stop, and Leif Lundsten would, in all sense of the word, lead the way. On 1 May 1942, he embarked on a seven-hour flight from Skeabrea to North Weald with the squadron's adjutant, Erik Lynneberg, in a Miles Magister. Lynneberg would be making the necessary arrangements for the squadron's arrival. The rest of the pilots would fly down to North Weald in their Spitfires, while six Harrow transport planes would take care of their equipment. While not the first Norwegian to set foot at North Weald (fellow pilot John Nordmo had stopped by in the summer of 1941), Lundsten was definitely one of the first.

> I joined in getting the cargo into the transports. The fuselages were covered in fabric, and some of the pointy corners on the boxes penetrated the fabric so you could look outside [from inside the Harrows]. We loaded them pretty heavy. I don't think anyone weighed anything. It was a bit of a 'wild west' situation.
>
> Per Sundsbakk via *Spitfire Saga I*, p. 171

The rest of the squadron arrived at North Weald on 4 May 1942, three days after Lundsten's arrival. Until AR238 left the Norwegians on 25 October 1942, Lundsten would use this Spitfire on seventy sorties of a total of eighty-seven, the last with AR238 on 4 October 1942.

RAF North Weald

North Weald was a pre-war aerodrome. In 1942, it had the capability to house at least three fighter squadrons. Located in Essex, just a short drive from the town of Epping, it had been heavily damaged during the Blitz of 1940. Since the Battle of Britain, North Weald had undergone several repairs to its infrastructure, but some hangars still had scars of the dark days of 1940. When Lundsten arrived at North Weald, just prior to the rest of his squadron mates, the airfield was inhabited by three other Spitfire squadrons, 222 (Natal) Squadron, 242 Squadron, and 121 (Eagle) Squadron. Nos 121 and 222 would operate together with the Norwegian squadrons the same year. When the other squadrons subsequently left North Weald, and also with the other Norwegian squadron (332) present, the Norwegians (with some exceptions) had North Weald to themselves until they left for Bognor Regis on 31 March 1944.

When the Norwegians arrived in 1942, North Weald had one runway facing the most common wind direction, and a slightly shorter runway for those times when the winds were facing from other directions—the shorter runway was later extended to a full runway. The Norwegians often used the grass to take off from. Until 1941, North Weald had four grass runways. It was one of the first airfields to have non-grass runways.

The Norwegians, having arrived from their solitary stay in the Orkneys, were given housing at Hill Hall, south-east of Epping, about half-an-hour's drive from the airfield itself. The building had the appearance of a castle with several posh rooms inside. A German bomb had struck the building in 1940, but it did not damage the building extensively. The Norwegians lived at Hill Hall until there were rooms available in the North Weald Officers Mess. No. 331 Squadron pilots, as sergeants, were given housing inside the airfield boundaries. Lundsten was promoted to lieutenant on 1 June 1942. He was a second lieutenant before this date, and, as such, was given a room at Hill Hall. Lundsten and his fellow officers moved to the Officer's Mess at North Weald when it became available to them in August 1942.

East of North Weald, there were about twenty tall radio and radar masts. Most of them were 250 feet tall, and stayed in operation throughout the war. It was usually what pilots flying to North Weald could spot first when they were coming back to their base of operations. Many pilots welcomed the sight of the masts in good weather, but feared them when the clouds were low and visibility restricted.

At Hill Hall, Philip Yatman wrote of his first day:

The garden was just the place to come back to after a day's work on the 'drome'; the trees and fields seemed to merge into it. The arrival at this big house was as though a lot of school boys had gathered together.

Confusion reigned supreme! Of course, there was one mad scramble to get the best rooms. Then nearly everyone seemed to have lost at least one piece of luggage, consequently after a little while the corridors and rooms became full of very angry people wandering about with dark looks on their faces and swearing that they had been robbed. The place rang with agonizing shouts such as 'Who has taken my boots?', 'Get out of my cupboard!', 'No it's not it's mine!' This was largely due to people changing their rooms, but in a short time things sorted themselves out, pandemonium gave way to quietness and eventually all that could be heard were the snores and regular breathing of the first night at Hill Hall.

Philip Yatman, 331 Squadron adjutant, Operations Record Book, 5 May 1942

Yatman continued:

We go to the station intelligence office and listen to the briefing of the pilots who are making a sweep over France. The Wing Commander Flying [David Scott-Malden] gives us a talk on R/T procedure and tactics when going over France. We feel we are beginning to get near serious operations.

331 Squadron, Operations Record Book, 5 May 1942

It would still be a few days until Lundsten and 331 Squadron would head for the enemy coast, but his first flight after his arrival happened the next day.

Date: 06.05.1942
Spitfire: Vb, FN-O AR328
Built: Westland
Length: 1:15
Where: North Weald

Lundsten listed it as sector reconnaissance. A local flight around the North Weald/Epping/Ongar area to get acquainted with the surroundings. Things to take special notice for was the mentioned large radio and radar masts not far from the airfield. Other landmarks of interest would be the North Weald church, Epping and its church spire, Ongar village, and Toot Hill. Of course their close proximity to London would also be of interest. Wing Commander Scott-Malden wouldn't just be showing Lundsten and his fellow Norwegians the local sights though. He led them, in formation, over the Channel to observe operations by other squadrons. The ORB noted they looked well, all taking off together. For Lundsten, it was 'so far, so good'.

Date: 07.05.1942
Spitfire: Vb, FN-O AR328
Built: Westland
Length: 1:10
Where: North Weald

Formation flying around the Essex countryside with 331 Squadron in the morning and a wing-formation exercise in the afternoon.

Date: 09.05.1942
Spitfire: Vb, FN-O AR328
Built: Westland
Length: Unknown
Where: North Weald

The Squadron's first Rodeo to France was on this day, coming in over Calais and going out over Boulogne. This was 331 Squadron and Leif Lundsten's first real sortie from North Weald. Much excitement could be seen among the Norwegians. They went together with 121 Eagle Squadron and 222 Squadron, both operating from North Weald. No incidents took place, and all returned safely at 4.45 p.m. Many of the pilots, excited about their first taste of the occupied countries, argued considerably after having landed about the positions of each specific section. Jens Müller silenced the argument when he got out a drawing of the positions of each section.

Date: 10.05.1942
Spitfire: Vb, FN-O AR328
Built: Westland
Length: Unknown
Where: North Weald

Lundsten listed this sortie as a convoy patrol in his logbook, but he is not listed among the pilots flying convoy patrols this day in the ORB. On this rather cold day in May (according to the ORB), Anton Hagerup and Ottar Malm did a convoy patrol at 9.55 a.m., while Jens Müller and Tarald Weisteen made another convoy patrol at 1.45 p.m. with no incidents. During the day there was a scramble with no incident.

Date: 17.05.1942
Spitfire: Vb, FN-N AR298
Built: Westland

Length: Unknown
Where: North Weald–Boulogne–Hawkinge–North Weald

Norway's national day of independence—a very symbolic day for all. The squadron paraded at 8 a.m., and Lundsten flew AR298 on a sortie at 10.30 a.m. escorting Boston bombers to Boulogne docks with fifteen other fighter squadrons, including North Weald residents 222 and 121. The ORB stated that the flak over Boulogne was 'fantastic'. Lundsten landed at Hawkinge to refuel together with Kristian Nyerrød. Rolf Arne Berg and Svein Heglund pancaked at Manston, also for a refuel. There was much anxiety at North Weald until they knew all four of the 'refuelers' were safe. Lundsten went to Manston later on to pick up Rolf Arne Berg. The Bostons returned safely to home base, but as many as twelve of the escorting Spitfires from other squadrons got shot down—there were eight pilots lost. No. 331 had been lucky to escape with no fatalities or aircraft losses.

As for AR298, it would play its own part in history to come. It was flown by Jens Müller when he was shot down by Fw 190s on 19 June 1942, a month and two days after Lundsten flew AR298 on this sortie. Müller got out of the Spitfire and spent sixty-six hours afloat in his dingy before making land. He was captured by the Germans. Müller, together with fellow Norwegian Per Bergsland, would be one out of only three pilots of the Great Escape to avoid capture. After escaping through the tunnel in Stallag Luft III, they made their way to Stettin in Germany (now Poland), from where they caught a ship to neutral Sweden, becoming two of just three who successfully escaped from occupied Europe.

Date: 19.05.1942
Spitfire: Vb, FN-V BL821
Built: Castle Bromwich
Length: 0:50
Where: North Weald

A sector reconnaissance in BL821; almost an hour's flying time.

Date: 20.05.1942
Spitfire: Vb, FN-V BL821
Built: Castle Bromwich
Length: 0:35
Where: North Weald

A cannon-firing test in BL821. Due to thunder and heavy showers there were few operations.

Date: 21.05.1942
Spitfire: Vb, FN-O AR328
Built: Westland
Length: Unknown
Where: North Weald–Channel–North Weald

Another convoy patrol in AR328 according to his logbook, but the sortie was not listed in the ORB.

Date: 27.05.1942
Spitfire: Vb, FN-O AR328
Built: Westland
Length: 1:45, 1:35
Where: North Weald–Channel–North Weald

Two convoy patrols in AR328. First, a dawn patrol at 5.15 a.m. together with Karl Jacobsen, and then another one at 11 a.m. with the same wingman. The weather was bright with heavy storm clouds, which made for dramatic summer conditions.

Jacobsen's career as a Spitfire pilot would sadly be short-lived. On 19 June 1942, he would be the first Norwegian to be killed in dogfights with German fighters.

Date: 29.05.1942
Spitfire: Vb, FN-O AR328
Built: Westland
Length: 1:10, 1:50
Where: North Weald–St Omer–Cap Gris Nez–North Weald; North Weald–Neufchâtel-Hardelot–Le Touquet–Boulogne–North Weald

There was plenty of action for Leif Lundsten on 29 May, with persistently unsettling weather—rain at times, in addition to strong winds. First up was a Rodeo at 11 a.m., led by Wing Commander Scott-Malden. The squadron swept over the French coast to St Omer coming out at Cap Gris Nez. There was nothing to be seen, and no Germans around in the skies. Lundsten and 331 landed back at North Weald at 12.15 p.m. For Lundsten, he had a few hours breather before another Rodeo at 6.50 p.m. This one was led by Helge Mehre, they crossed the French coast at Neufchâtel-Hardelot, turned south and came out by Le Touquet, and then crossed the coast again between Boulogne and Cap Gris Nez. No German fighters seen, but plenty of flak. With Lundsten landing AR328 back at North Weald 8 p.m., it would conclude his operations for May.

11

Spitfire Summer: June 1942, 331 Squadron, North Weald, Essex

Date: 01.06.1942
Spitfire: Vb, FN-O AR328
Built: Westland
Length: 1:35
Where: North Weald–Dunkirk–Calais–North Weald

Lundsten listed his sortie on 1 June as a Roadsted, while ORB listed it as a Rodeo. The squadron took off at 10.35 a.m. There was nothing to be seen of the Germans while the squadron swept in over the French coast by Dunkirk and came out over Calais. Lundsten and the rest of the squadron were back at North Weald by 11.45 a.m.

Date: 03.06.1942
Spitfire: Vb, FN-O AR328
Built: Westland
Length: 0:40
Where: North Weald–Le Touquet–Cap Gris Nez–North Weald

Circus 184 to France. Twelve Spitfires took off from North Weald, including Lundsten in FN-O. The squadron did a sweep down the Channel towards Le Touquet, they then turned starboard and went back just off Gris Nez. No. 331 Squadron operated at 28,000 feet. No action from the Luftwaffe.

Date: 04.06.1942
Spitfire: Vb, FN-O AR328
Built: Westland
Length: 1:40, 1:30
Where: North Weald–Calais–North Weald; North Weald–Dunkirk–North Weald

A clear and hot day at North Weald. Wing Commander Scott-Malden led 331 for a Rodeo at 1.45 p.m. They met with the Debden Wing over Clacton, and picked up 121 Squadron over Bradwell. Lundsten puts (correctly) down Calais in his logbook as their area of operations during this Rodeo—there were no incidents. No. 331 was back at North Weald by 3.15 p.m. Another sortie was scheduled for the evening, and Lundsten was yet again on the roster of pilots to participate. Wing Commander Scott-Malden led eleven Spitfires from 331 Squadron, taking off at 7.11 p.m. for Circus 186. No. 331 would serve as escort for six Boston bombers to Dunkirk flying at 13,000 feet—again, there were no incidents.

Date: 05.06.1942
Spitfire: Vb, FN-O AR328
Built: Westland
Length: 1:20
Where: North Weald–Calais–Dunkirk–North Weald

Lundsten wrote 'Rodeo–Calais–Dunkirk' in his logbook. The weather was still fine and hot when 331 Squadron took off at 9.10 a.m. together with 222 Squadron. No. 121 Squadron was noted to not rendezvous as planned. A quick sweep inland was done, crossing the French coast just east of Calais (as Lundsten put down in his logbook) and came out again west of Dunkirk. No German fighters were seen. An unlucky Fredrik Fearnley undershot during landing and broke the undercarriage of his Spitfire BL987. He was reprimanded by Group Captain Pike, who wrote a note in his logbook. Everyone was back at 10.20 a.m.

Date: 09.06.1942
Spitfire: Vb, FN-T EN786
Built: Castle Bromwich
Length: 0:20
Where: North Weald

A local cine-gun test in EN786 was flown, a Spitfire often used by Kaj Birksted, in the summer of 1942. EN786 would have a short life; it was shot down over the Channel by Jagdgeschwader 26 on 31 October 1942. At this time, EN786 had already been transferred to 453 Squadron. On the day of EN786s loss, Pilot Officer J. Barrien and Flying Officer G. G. Galway noticed ten Fw 190s somewhere over Canterbury and the surrounding area, and climbed to engage the fighters—Galway flew EN786. Then the Australians spotted another thirty German fighters in separate formations. JG26 was indeed participating in an attack on Canterbury, and the two

Australians had ended up in the middle of the raid. In the ensuing combat, Galway's Spitfire (EN786) was hit and the Australian had to bale out. He spent the night in his dinghy before being rescued the following morning. Barrien made it back to base—EN786 was lost in the depths of the sea.

Date: 10.06.1942
Spitfire: Vb, FN-O AR328
Built: Westland
Length: 1:10
Where: North Weald

Lundsten took AR328 up for interception practice. In his logbook, he wrote: 'Practis nightfighterinterseption'.

For the Norwegians, it was not always easy to get the English language correct when writing or talking. Many Norwegians spoke very good English, and the British were generally very pleased with their language skills compared to the Poles, French, and the Czechs, for example. However, there were always exceptions. Some of the ground crew hardly knew any English at all upon arrival in Canada or Britain. The first 331 Squadron leader, Odd Bull (a rather interesting name in the English language), spoke poor or perhaps strange English with a strong Norwegian accent. In 1943, 331 Squadron leader Arne Austeen had a reputation of speaking 'odd' English as well. John Nordmo wrote Casseltown in his logbook (Castletown).

The Norwegians, during their time in Canada, developed a new language simply called *Længvitschen*, a constructed language with Norwegian, English, and American-English mixed together. It was naturally developed as a way of connecting poor English skills with their Norwegian native language. As time progressed, more and more English aviation terms were added. The general idea was to construct Norwegian-type sentences where they adopted English words. This way of writing and talking stayed with the Norwegians during the Second World War, and can be easily spotted in those who kept diaries. After the Second World War, English became more widespread in the media, and English words were adopted into the Norwegian language. This trend has continued and increased in impact as the years have passed; in other words, it is nothing new for English words to be continuously added to the Norwegian vocabulary.

Date: 11.06.1942
Spitfire: Vb, FN-O AR328
Built: Westland
Length: 1:40, 1:30 (short stop at Tangmere)
Where: North Weald—Mardyck—Tangmere; Tangmere—Boulogne—North Weald

No. 331 Squadron went on a sweep; however, the ORB noted it as a 'test'. The squadron flew 10 miles off Mardyck, then down the Channel, 40 miles east of Tangmere. They turned north and landed at Tangmere at 1.55p.m. They stayed at Tangmere for a bit over an hour, taking off again at 3.20 p.m. They seemed to have taken a quick sweep on the way back, just touching Boulogne. They were back at North Weald at 4.50 p.m., and were all released off camp at 6.20 p.m. for some well-deserved rest. Correctly, Lundsten listed both legs of the sweep in his logbook.

Date: 17.06.1942
Spitfire: Vb, FN-O AR328; Vb, FN-P AD509
Built: Westland, Castle Bromwich
Length: 0:30, 0:35, 1:30
Where: North Weald–local area–North Weald; North Weald–Ostend–North Weald

The first sortie of the day was an air-firing test in the local skies above Essex. Then another short half-hour local flight. One may speculate that AR328 had certain technical issues that prevented Lundsten from using it for the shipping reconnaissance—his third flight of the day. He flew AD509 instead during this afternoon. The squadron took off in warm weather, heading for the Dutch coast alongside 222 Squadron. The mission was abandoned after 222 had pulled up to 2,000 feet for top cover just near the coast. The weather was closing in on the two squadrons. They did spot some shipping, but did not attack as the breakaway would have meant they had to go through the Ostend flak. Everyone was back at base by 6.30 p.m. It would be the last sortie for Lundsten for almost a week. On 22 June he gave a lift to what he described as the 'ATC boys' (air traffic controllers) in the Miles Magister. The bus flying took about three hours' time. While Lundsten was off operational flying, 331 lost two pilots. Lieutenant Karl Jacobsen and Jens Müller of later 'Great Escape fame'. Jacobsen was killed in action and left a very young widow back in England, Sonia Irgens. She would later marry Kaj Birksted.

Date: 23.06.1942
Spitfire: Vb, FN-O AR328
Built: Westland
Length: 1:35, 1:25
Where: North Weald–Dunkirk–Nieuport–North Weald; North Weald–Dunkirk–North Weald

This was Lundsten's first operational sortie with 331's sister squadron, 332 Squadron who had just arrived from Catterick, in Yorkshire. It was reported to be a fine day with some low mist and haze early on. At 5.05 a.m., Lundsten took off in FN-O for a Rodeo alongside 332 Squadron. They joined up with 121 Squadron over North Foreland. They climbed to 19,000 feet, and kept flying as far as Nieuport before heading back home, with nothing to be seen from the Luftwaffe.

Lundsten's next sortie for the day would be a Ramrod, supporting twelve Bostons to Dunkirk according to his logbook. Over Dunkirk, they were flying at 24,000 feet where heavy flak was encountered. Enemy fighters were also reported to be in the area, but there were no engagements. No. 331 was back home at 4.10 p.m.

Date: 25.06.1942
Spitfire: Vb, FN-O AR328
Built: Westland
Length: 1:40
Where: North Weald–Channel–North Weald

Channel duties together with Kristian Nyerrød in BL987.

Date: 26.06.1942
Spitfire: Vb, FN-U P8707
Built: Castle Bromwich
Length: 1:30
Where: North Weald–Le Touquet–North Weald

Leif wrote in his logbook: 'Rodeo south of Le Touquet', which was fairly accurate. ORB stated the squadrons, led by Wing Commander Scott-Malden, took off at 2.45 p.m. and made their way to Beachy Head. The wing was then ordered to fly to Somme. Halfway there, they made a wide left turn and followed the French coast up to Gris Nez. They returned to North Weald at 6.45 p.m. Before their sortie, a flight sergeant from Fighter Command had given the Norwegians an interesting talk on his escape from Germany.

As for P8707, Squadron Leader A. P. Burton test flew P8707 with cannons installed eleven months earlier. He wrote, 'cannon firing, nearly hit a boat load of fishermen!!' This happened on 8 July 1941 according to Dilip Sarkar's *Spitfire Ace of Aces: the True Wartime Story of Johnnie Johnson*.

Fredrik Fearnley also belly landed the aircraft at Manston on 29 June 1942. Their target had been marshalling yards at Hazebrouck. The Spitfire was repaired and eventually transferred to the Royal Navy in 1944.

Date: 29.06.1942
Spitfire: Vb, FN-O AR328
Built: Westland
Length: 1:30
Where: North Weald–Le Touquet–St Omer–North Weald

Circus 295, escorting six Bostons to Hazebrouck. The squadrons crossed the French coast just north of Boulogne, then flew onwards to St Omer where the wing split up and 331 headed north. Helge Mehre and Martin Gran claimed two Fw 190s damaged. As previously noted (26.09.1942), Fearnley got into a bit of trouble and received several cannon shots in his Spitfire, one of them exploding behind his seat armour and damaging his selector gear so he could not lower his wheels and flaps.

Date: 29.06.1942
Spitfire: Vb, FN-O AR328
Built: Westland
Length: 0:25
Where: North Weald–Manston

The squadron, including Leif Lundsten, moved to Manston for a couple of days. It was a quick flight down to the coast from North Weald.

Date: 29.06.1942
Spitfire: Vb, FN-O AR328
Built: Westland
Length: 0:25
Where: Manston

A scramble at 6.35 p.m. together with Martin Gran in AR296. They were back safely at 7 p.m., with no incidents. In fact, there would be no more flying from Manston for Lundsten. However, he stayed with the squadron until 7 July. There would be very few operations from the squadron due to bad weather. It turned out to be more of a holiday than anything else. The Norwegians spent their time playing snooker, sunbathing, swimming in the sea, and exploring local pubs.

12

Four Pilots Lost:
July 1942, 331 Squadron,
North Weald, Essex

Date: 07.07.1942
Spitfire: Vb, FN-O AR328
Built: Westland
Length: 0:25
Where: Manston–North Weald

This was a return flight from Manston to North Weald.

Date: 08.07.1942
Spitfire: Vb, FN-O AR328
Built: Westland
Length: 0:40
Where: North Weald

An interesting day for everyone at North Weald. Ole Reistad, commander of Little Norway in Canada, visited the Norwegians at North Weald. For this occasion, the squadron would do formation flying in honour of his visit. Reistad also met with Wing Commander Scott-Malden, who told him directly that he (Scott-Malden) looked at 331 to be up there with the best English squadrons and it would not take long until 332 was up there as well.

Date: 11.07.1942
Spitfire: Vb, FN-O AR328
Built: Westland
Length: 0:50
Where: North Weald

An air-firing exercise in AR328.

Date: 12.07.1942
Spitfire: Vb, FN-O AR328
Built: Westland
Length: 0:45, 0:20, 1:35, 1:40
Where: North Weald local; North Weald–Le Touquet–Boulogne–North Weald; North Weald–Le Touquet–Calais–North Weald

Lundsten wrote this one down as 'cameragunpractice' in his logbook. There was another test flight later on in the day, this time it was a radio test. Then things were about to get busy, Scott-Malden led the wing on a Rodeo operation over Northern France. German aircraft were reported to be around the Abbeville area, but in the end there were no fighters nor any flak observed. Yet another sortie later on in the afternoon, this one Circus 198. Nothing out of the ordinary happened, and Lundsten was safely back at North Weald at 8.15 p.m.

Date: 13.07.1942
Spitfire: Vb, FN-O AR328
Built: Westland
Length: 1:45
Where: North Weald–Flushing–North Weald

A Roadsted operation to the Flushing area. It turned out to be another sortie with little action and the Norwegians, according to their diary, started to wonder where the Germans had gone to.

Date: 17.07.1942
Spitfire: Vb, FN-O AR328
Built: Westland
Length: 1:40
Where: North Weald–Channel–North Weald

This day featured several convoy patrols. Four Spitfires most likely led by Kaj Birksted took off at 9.30 a.m. Together with Birksted in EN786 was Lundsten in his regular Spitfire, alongside Yves de Castro Henrichsen in BL987, and Knut Bache in AR298. All were safely back at 11.10 a.m.

Date: 27.07.1942
Spitfire: Vb, FN-O AR328
Built: Westland
Length: 2:55
Where: North Weald–Ostend–Flushing–North Weald

A shipping recce was the primary agenda of the day. The squadron took off at 6.35 p.m. from North Weald led by Wing Commander Scott-Malden. It turned out to be a very long sortie, stretching the Spitfires limited fuel capacity to the max. Although there was a very low cloud base over England, nothing out of the ordinary happened. There's nothing in the ORB to explain Lundsten's ten-day absence from flying. Most likely he enjoyed some well-deserved rest.

Date: 28.07.1942
Spitfire: Vb, FN-O AR328
Built: Westland
Length: 1:45, 1:45
Where: North Weald–Ostend–Walcheren–North Weald; North Weald–local–North Weald

Two sorties on 28 July. First, a Roadsted at 1.55 p.m. and then a scramble from North Weald at 5.25 p.m. with Finn Normann Bordal in BL891—both were uneventful.

Date: 29.07.1942
Spitfire: Vb, FN-O AR328
Built: Westland
Length: 3:35
Where: Unknown

Another Circus took place on 29 July. Lundsten took off from North Weald at 12.45 p.m. Only six Spitfires took part, and it was most likely led by Kaj Birksted in EN786. They were not back before 5.20 p.m., which might indicate a stopover somewhere (for fuel), but there is nothing in the ORB about this. Lundsten did not list this sortie in his logbook (it is listed in the ORB). It could perhaps be a mix-up of dates.

Date: 30.07.1942
Spitfire: Vb, FN-O AR328; Vb, FN-X AR296
Built: Westland
Length: 2:25, 1:45
Where: North Weald–Le Touquet–Berck–North Weald; North Weald–St. Omer–North Weald

Circus 200 to Le Touquet–Berck area. Lundsten wrote 'Blue 1' in his logbook, which means he was leading Blue Section. The unit was acting as top cover for six Boston bombers attacking Abbeville. The Germans finally showed up, and attacked the Norwegians from above; twisting and turning around the skies over Berck, 332 Squadron's hot young talent, nineteen-year-old Marius Eriksen, shot down the squadron's first German fighter.

For the second sortie on this warm and sunny day, Lundsten jumped into FN-X, AR296, for a Circus to St Omer. It turned out to be uneventful. All were back safely at 7.20 p.m. Lundsten had not previously flown this Spitfire. AR296 stayed with the Norwegians until 453 Squadron received the Spitfire on 12 October 1942. The Spitfire was struck off charge 17 June 1944, at the time serving with 234 Squadron.

Date: 31.07.1942
Spitfire: Vb, FN-X AR296
Built: Westland
Length: 1:00, 1:45, 1:45
Where: North Weald–local–North Weald; North Weald–Le Crotoy–North Weald; North Weald–French coast–North Weald

This day in July would be a day that Lundsten would most likely remember for a good while. He seldom added information out of the ordinary to his logbook, but made an exception after the day was over. Four pilots from 332 Squadron would be lost on the same sortie. Their trade for the day, Circus 201, would take the wing to Le Crotoy, Cayeux area, just west of Abbeville. No. 332 Squadron was attacked in force by the Luftwaffe. Olaf Tandberg, Svein Nygaard, Erik Hagen, and Kjell Hansen were all shot down. Hagen and Hansen both survived, becoming POWs. Tandberg and Nygaard both got killed in action with the Focke-Wulf 190s. For Lundsten and 331, they returned with no losses. Only Heglund and Jørstad made claims. In his logbook, Lundsten wrote all four of their names down—adding missing after their names.

His last sortie on this day was a direct result of the day's sad happenings. It's a search for the four Norwegians lost, led by Kaj Birksted. None of them were found, and thus concluded Leif Lundsten's operations in the very hectic month of 1942.

13

Battle over Dieppe: August 1942, 331 Squadron, North Weald, Essex

Date: 01.08.1942
Spitfire: Vb, FN-O AR238
Built: Westland
Length: 00:20, 1:00
Where: North Weald–Sawbridgeworth–North Weald; North Weald–Manston–North Weald

According to Lundsten's logbook, this was a quick flight to RAF Sawbridgeworth. However, this is not the whole story. At this airfield, North American P-51 Mustang fighters were operating. Kaj Birksted brought four pilots, including Leif Lundsten, to test fly these new aircraft. Lundsten does not mention this little but interesting fact. He did not list flying P-51s in his logbook, was he just observing them?

The second sortie of the day brought Lundsten and the Norwegians to Manston. Not for dangerous operations over the Channel or France, but for physical training and swimming. Lundsten listed it as a picnic instead—though, one can say it's in the eyes of the beholder. Three hours were spent swimming in the ocean, drinking tea, and sunbathing; however, on their return to North Weald, an incident occurred that several pilots of 331 Squadron would remember long after the war. For once, it was not due to loss of lives or near-death experiences, but due to a practical joke and one angry Dane.

Svein Heglund wrote in his autobiography *Høk over Høk* (1997) that Scott-Malden ordered the squadron to fly line astern on its way back to North Weald. Kaj Birksted, perhaps thinking of things other than formation flying, started to drift off course. Heglund told how Scott-Malden came on the radio giving Birksted a proper verbal lecture in formation flying. The interesting part was that it wasn't Scott-Malden doing the talking. According to Martin Gran, fifth in line in the formation, it was someone else—Rolf

Arne Berg and Leif Lundsten. One of them (Lundsten or Berg) went on the radio first, pretending to be Scott-Malden, saying, 'Number three from the front [Birksted], you are not flying line astern!'

The second one followed up with, 'Number three from the front, for Christ's sake, can't you fly formation?' Back at North Weald, Birksted was furious and took it out on poor Knut Bache. Although he played an innocent part in the little prank, Bache was pulled off operational flying for a week (*Spitfire Saga II*, 2009). Although this story is little more than detail, it is one of the few stories about Leif Lundsten told in print by his fellow pilots after the war.

Date: 03.08.1942
Spitfire: Vb, FN-O AR238
Built: Westland
Length: 1:40
Where: North Weald–Manston–North Weald

This was a convoy patrol with Kristian Nyerrød, flying BL987 in changing weather conditions.

Date: 11.08.1942
Spitfire: Vb, FN-O AR238
Built: Westland
Length: 0:50
Where: North Weald local

Simply noted as a test. No further information about this, other than it was close to an hour's flight.

Date: 12.08.1942
Spitfire: Vb, FN-O AR238
Built: Westland
Length: 1:15
Where: North Weald–Clacton–Frinton–North Weald

A practice Rhubarb by 331 Squadron Spitfires. They attacked several ground targets around the coastal district near Clacton and Frinton.

Date: 13.08.1942
Spitfire: Vb, FN-O AR238
Built: Westland
Length: 1:50
Where: North Weald–Berck-sur-Mer–Dieppe–Fécamp–North Weald

The entire wing participated in this sortie, which was a Roadsted operation—242, 331, 332, and 121 Squadrons all flew together. Enemy fighters was reported somewhere above land, and two Fw 190s were observed at long distance, but there were no engagements from either side. Lundsten landed back at North Weald at 7 p.m.

Before this operation took place, the Norwegians were told that they would be moving to Manston the next morning. Lots of rumours went around about the reason for this move, though they would soon know—the now infamous Dieppe raid was about to take place.

Date: 14.08.1942
Spitfire: Vb, FN-O AR238
Built: Westland
Length: 0:40
Where: North Weald–Manston

Eighteen Spitfires from 331 Squadron would be on their way to Manston for the upcoming Dieppe landings. Nos 331 and 332 were placed side by side at the airfield. The place was packed with aircraft, and the Norwegians quickly started to wonder what would happen if German bombers came over with all those fat targets on the ground.

Date: 17.08.1942
Spitfire: Vb, FN-O AR238
Built: Westland
Length: 1:55 and 1:45
Where: Manston–Gravelines–Dunkirk–St Omer–Calais–Manston; Manston–Dunkirk–Nieuport–Manston

A Rodeo was led by Wing Commander David Scott-Malden. No enemy fighters were seen during this sortie over several of the regular hot spots of enemy activity.

The next sortie of the day was Circus 204, a diversion sortie where they would meet up with Defiant fighters and three B-17 bombers. The Defiants showed up, but the bombers did not. The wing continued inland in a large left turn and then headed back to Manston and all arrived safely at 6.25 p.m.

Date: 18.08.1942
Spitfire: Vb, FN-O AR238
Built: Westland
Length: 1:25
Where: Manston–Flushing–Walcheren–Haamstede–Manston

This mission was a Rodeo over Walcheren, during which no incidents took place and all arrived back safely to North Weald. It was noted in the ORB that many felt tired due to lack of sleep. No. 331 Squadron had been up since 4 a.m. Lundsten's sortie this day would be his last before the big day.

Date: 19.08.1942
Spitfire: Vb, FN-O AR238
Built: Westland
Length: 1:50 and 1:45
Where: Manston–Dieppe–Manston; Manston–Dieppe–Manston

The Norwegians got up (again) as early as 4 a.m., ground crew and pilots alike—331 for the fourth morning in a row. Bad coffee and sandwiches were served according to 332 pilot Bjørn Ræder. There was wonderful weather outside, but the atmosphere inside was reported to be tense. Some of the pilots were adding finishing touches on their wills, and asked others to sign them. Others were tossing a coin for fun, to see if they return back safely or not.

Leif Lundsten participated in two of the four missions during the Dieppe raid—the first and the third sortie. The first sortie of the day, was scheduled for take-off at 6.10 a.m. from Manston. No. 331 Squadron arrived over Dieppe at 6.50 a.m. at 5,000 to 8,000 feet. They were attacked by twenty enemy aircraft and several dogfights took place. Helge Mehre and Kaj Birksted both claimed 190s destroyed. Frederik Fearnley, Stein Sem, and Guy Peter Lockwood Owren claimed a 190 between them as probably destroyed. Rolf Arne Berg and Helner Grundt-Spang also claimed a 190 damaged. Lundsten made no claims. Johannes Greiner of 331 was shot down, but was picked up by a motor launch ten minutes after he landed in the sea.

The third sortie happened between 2.15 p.m. and 4 p.m. No. 332 shot down a Hawker Typhoon by mistake and 331 got into a dogfight once more with 190s. Heglund once again claimed a 190 as destroyed. Rolf Arne Berg was shot down after being jumped by eight 190s. He was picked up by a rescue vessel and survived. Once again, Lundsten made no claims. Frederik Fearnley flew AR238 on the other two sorties of the day. From Lundsten logbook: 'Cover commando raid on Dieppe. 331 got 7 destroyed and nobody lost. 332 Squadron 6 destroyed and lost Staubo and Bergsland'. The day had been an eventful one.

Date: 20.08.1942
Spitfire: Vb, FN-O AR238
Built: Westland
Length: 1:30
Where: Manston–St Omer–North Weald

There was no time to rest after the events of the previous day for Lundsten and 331. A diversionary sweep for Circus 206 was on the agenda. The squadron was fully operative the day after the Dieppe landings, which was quite an achievement. No. 331 and Lundsten rendezvoused at Beachy Head with nine Defiants after take-off at 4.10 p.m., then set course for Neufchâtel-Hardelot climbing to 28,000 feet. The Defiants were left behind before crossing the French coast, but the squadron continued making a wide left turn towards St Omer, crossing over the French coast by Calais. The attack force itself were attacked by Jagdgeschwader 2, and a Spitfire from 91 Squadron got shot down. With no incidents, the squadron returned directly to North Weald.

Date: 21.08.1942
Spitfire: Vb, FN-O AR238
Built: Westland
Length: 0:15
Where: North Weald–Channel–North Weald

Rear support to Rotterdam, supporting B-17s bombing the city—at least that was the plan. The bombers were late, and the wing was recalled. Lundsten once again flew as Blue 1.

Date: 26.08.1942
Spitfire: Vb, FN-O AR238
Built: Westland
Length: 0:20
Where: North Weald local

Local cloud flying over the Essex countryside.

Date: 27.08.1942
Spitfire: Vb, FN-O AR238
Built: Westland
Length: 0:20 and 1:35
Where: North Weald–St Omer–North Weald; North Weald–Rotterdam–North Weald

This day was exceptionally hot—one of the hottest of the year. At 11.40 a.m., the wing took off for a Roadsted operation, with Helge Mehre leading the Wing to St Omer, supporting twelve B-17 Flying Fortresses. No. 332 Squadron pilot Haldor Espelid was hit by flak and had to make a forced landing.

Wing Commander Scott-Malden had left the Norwegians on 26 August, to the great sadness of everyone at North Weald. He had been a fantastic leader and mentor during these first months of operations for 331 and 332 in the south.

Lundsten was back at North Weald by 1.15 p.m., just in time to greet Major General Wilhelm von Tangen Hansteen, Commander-in-Chief of the Norwegian forces. He was accompanied by Rear Admiral Riiser-Larsen, Chief of Norwegian Air Forces, and by Lieutenant Colonel Bjarne Øen, Colonel Odd Bull, and Captain Brun. Several photographs taken that day show Leif Lundsten talking to the visitors, still wearing his Mae West from the sortie he had flown just two hours earlier.

At 4.50 p.m., the squadron took off once again, leaving the top brass behind at North Weald—they set course for Rotterdam, to support, yet again, twelve B-17s (according to Lundsten's logbook). They orbited about 18 miles off the Dutch coast, near Rotterdam, and then escorted the Fortresses back to Orfordness. No enemy aircraft had been observed during this mission and everyone had returned by 6.35 p.m. It turned out to be quite a hectic day, with two sorties and several important visitors to take care of in the midst of all their duties.

Date: 28.08.1942
Spitfire: Vb, FN-S BL891
Built: Castle Bromwich
Length: 1:45
Where: North Weald–Dunkirk–Caen–North Weald

The mission for this day was Circus 210, a diversionary sweep to Caen— Lundsten flew this sortie in BL891. They rendezvoused with nine Defiants over Naze, and the squadron climbed to 22,000 feet while the Defiants lost height. All participants landed safely back at North Weald at 1.05 p.m.

Date: 29.08.1942
Spitfire: Vb, FN-T EN786
Built: Castle Bromwich
Length: 1:05
Where: North Weald–Dunkirk–North Weald (aborted sortie due to oxygen trouble)

During this mission, Leif Lundsten and Finn N. Bordal were forced to return early due to oxygen trouble. The rest of the squadron got into a fight with several Fw 190s, claiming four 190s damaged and one probable.

A big dinner party took place during the evening, with Birksted and Mohr celebrating their newly received DFCs. No. 332 Squadron pilots, previously with 331 (Thorsager, From, Mollestad, and Christie), also joined in on the fun. ORB stated that it had been a very successful party, almost too successful in some ways (no further details).

Date: 30.08.1942
Spitfire: Vb, FN-O AR238
Built: Westland
Length: 1:35
Where: North Weald–Channel–North Weald

The day's mission was a convoy patrol in the hot weather; AR328 was back in the air in the hands of Lundsten, but it was an uneventful day.

From 1 September, Dane Kai Birksted led 331 Squadron, after Helge Mehre left for a well-deserved rest period at the Royal Norwegian Air Force headquarters in London.

14

'Heavy Flak, Damn Close!'
September 1942, 331 Squadron,
North Weald, Essex

Date: 02.09.1942
Spitfire: Vb, FN-O AR238
Built: Westland
Length: 1:30
Where: North Weald–Channel–North Weald

There was a midday convoy patrol over the English Channel, with take-off at 12.15 p.m.—it was an uneventful patrol. Weather was overcast and misty, but cleared up later on. Wing Commander Wilfrid Duncan-Smith, having replaced Wing Commander Scott-Malden, gave a talk in the afternoon about various training sessions to be held during the coming winter period.

Date: 04.09.1942
Spitfire: Vb, FN-O AR238
Built: Westland
Length: 1:30
Where: North Weald area

Over an hour's worth of practice interception in AR238.

Date: 05.09.1942
Spitfire: Vb, FN-O AR238
Built: Westland
Length: 1:55
Where: North Weald–St Aubin–North Weald

A morning Ramrod to France and back, led by Wing Commander Duncan-Smith. Nothing was seen, and everyone was back safely at 11.20 a.m.

King Haakon, Crown Prince Olav, and Crown Princess Martha visited the squadron on this day, and His Majesty spoke a few words and thanked the squadrons for the good work they had done. Many photographs were taken by enthusiastic pilots and ground crew. The day was a bit hampered by very strong winds.

Date: 06.09.1942
Spitfire: Vb, FN-O AR238
Built: Westland
Length: 1:45
Where: North Weald–Ostend–Dunkirk–North Weald

The mission was Circus 215, a diversionary sweep led by Major Birksted. Nos 332 and 121 Squadron also participated together, with nine Defiants. The wing climbed to 21,000 feet and made landfall by Ostend, where they turned right and followed the coast south to Dunkirk. There was enemy activity all around them, and heavy flak over Nieuport. Major Birksted's radio malfunctioned, so Rolf Arne Berg led the wing instead of the Dane. Everyone was back at North Weald at 5.40 p.m.

Date: 07.09.1942
Spitfire: Vb, FN-O AR238
Built: Westland
Length: 1:35
Where: North Weald–Ostend–North Weald

Another Circus was flown this day, this one was numbered 217. While flying at 22,000 feet over Ostend, the Norwegians (together with 121 Squadron) spotted ten Focke-Wulf 190s below them. The Germans had no interest in taking up the fight, and set course for home. The action taken by the Germans was exactly what the wing wanted in order to let the bombers be free of interference. Everyone was back at 10.40 a.m.

> Heavy flak, damn close!
>
> Reidar Haave Olsen, logbook.

Date: 07.09.1942
Spitfire: Vb, FN-O AR238
Built: Westland
Length: 1:00
Where: North Weald–Martlesham Heath

After the events over Ostend, Leif Lundsten flew to Martlesham Heath, together with fifteen other Norwegian Spitfires, for a week of air-firing practice.

Date: 08.09.1942–13.09.1942
Spitfires: 08.09.42–11.09.42: Vb, FN-O AR238
11.09.42: Vb, FN-Z BL897
11.09.42: Vb, FN-T EN786
13.09.42: Vb, FN-Y AD509
Built: Westland, Castle Bromwich
Length: 0:15, 0:50, 0:35, 0:10, 0:20, 0:25
Where: Martlesham Heath area

The mentioned dates have been added into one section as they were all air-firing practice at Martlesham Heath.

BL897 was eventually struck off charge on 23 June 1945. Before arriving with the Norwegians, it had been flown in combat by Canadian Flying Officer Duncan Marshall Grant, DFC. He claimed a Fw 190 damaged while flying BL897 in April 1942. On 29 July, he claimed a Fw 190 destroyed 10 miles south of Brighton flying the same Spitfire. Marshall was killed in action flying a Mustang on 27 September 1942, only twenty-four days after Lundsten flew his former Spitfire at Martlesham Heath.

AD509 was previously given the squadron letters FN-P. At Martlesham Heath, Lundsten listed it as FN-Y.

Date: 20.09.1942
Spitfire: Vb, FN-O AR238
Built: Westland
Length: 1:20
Where: North Weald–Channel–North Weald

Back at North Weald, after several days of no flying, Lundsten flew a convoy patrol together with Martin Gran flying AR296 in the afternoon.

Date: 21.09.1942
Spitfire: Vb, FN-O AR238
Built: Westland
Length: 1:25
Where: North Weald–Channel–North Weald

Another convoy patrol; although, this time, it was in rainy, misty weather. Once again, it was flown together with Martin Gran.

Date: 22.09.1942
Spitfire: Vb, FN-O AR238
Built: Westland
Length: 0:45
Where: North Weald–Channel–North Weald

Together with Knut Bache, flying in BL403, they flew an afternoon convoy patrol—there was heavy rain at times.

Date: 23.09.1942
Spitfire: Vb, FN-O AR238
Built: Westland
Length: 1:40
Where: North Weald–Channel–North Weald

There were some quiet days for Lundsten and the Norwegians at North Weald, with yet again convoy patrols on the agenda. Once again, low-pressure systems covered most of their area of England.

Date: 24.09.1942
Spitfire: Vb, FN-O AR238
Built: Westland
Length: Unknown
Where: North Weald–Channel–North Weald?

Lundsten listed this sortie as a convoy patrol, but no flying has been registered in the ORB. Instead, there was air-firing practice, aerobatics, and practice homing going on at North Weald. This concluded Lundsten's operations for September 1942, a quiet month with a great deal of bad weather according to the ORB. The last part of September, in particular, had little action.

15

Nuts to Nazis: October 1942, Squadron, North Weald, Essex

Date: 02.10.1942
Spitfire: Vb, FN-O AR238
Built: Westland
Length: 0:25
Where: North Weald–Manston

No. 331 lost two pilots in dogfights during Circus no. 221 on 2 October—Roald Sørensen and Frithjof Cleve. Lundsten did not participate in this sortie. At 6.25 p.m., 331 flew down to Manston, with Lundsten in AR238. The pilots wondered if there was another type of Dieppe-raid getting planned out.

Date: 03.10.1942
Spitfire: Vb, FN-O AR238
Built: Westland
Length: 0:30
Where: Manston–Channel–Manston

The squadron searched for Roald Sørensen, who was lost the previous day. He had reported that his engine was smoking, but was alright himself. No. 331 took off at 5.20 p.m. to look for the missing Sørensen, but did not find anything. They naturally also looked for the other pilot, Cleve, but did not find him either. They could only conclude that both pilots, shot down on 2 October, had been killed.

Date: 04.10.1942
Spitfire: Vb, FN-O AR238
Built: Westland
Length: 1:00
Where: Manston–Channel–Manston

This day featured a convoy patrol with Fredrik Fearnley, in AD474, with no incidents. Instead of another Dieppe, the Norwegians threw a party during the evening.

Date: 06.10.1942
Spitfire: Vb, FN-K unknown serial. IX FN-K BS445
Built: Castle Bromwich
Length: 0:25
Where: North Weald–Manston

Lundsten listed the Spitfire as FN-K, which was the squadron letter lost with Roald Sørensen on 2 October. There's no FN-K flying with 331 until a month later, when the squadron had converted from V to IX (FN-K being BS445). BS445 first flew on 11 September 1942, and was delivered to 331 Squadron on 29 September 1942. With both squadrons at the time going to Manston a few days later, there's a small possibility that Lundsten went back to North Weald to pick up the brand-new Spitfire IX as a replacement for the lost Spitfire V. On 7 October, the ORB stated that those pilots left at North Weald (while the rest were at Manston) had been practising flights with the new IX. Eighteen of them had arrived at North Weald on 5 October. This transport flight could very well be Lundsten's first flight in a Spitfire IX. What speaks against such a scenario is that Lundsten, on 9 October, wrote 'practice on type' and specifically added 'IX' to his logbook. He does not do so on the 6th. Why he wrote 'K', when the Spitfire was lost just days before, remains a mystery.

BS445 was more than likely nicknamed *Nuts to Nazis*, and was flown by Norwegian-American Reidar Haave Olsen (nicknamed Pilot-Olsen due to his very keen attitude to fighting the Germans) in 331 Squadron. The Spitfire was struck of charge 27 November 1947. It also served a period with 332 Squadron in 1943.

Date: 09.10.1942
Spitfire: IX FN-M BS466
Built: Eastleigh
Length: 0:35
Where: North Weald area

Leif Lundsten's first official flight in a Spitfire IX. Spitfire mark IX BS466 was built at Eastleigh, and Knut Bache flew it on 17 May 1943 when 331 Squadron was attacked by Focke-Wulf 190s during a mission to escort B-17s bombing Lorient, in France. The day was extra special as it was Norway's national day. Later, serving with 229 Squadron, BS466 overshot during a landing attempt, struck obstacles, and nosed over at Detling on 28 May 1944. This happened just over a year after Bache's previous encounter with 190s over France.

Date: 11.10.1942
Spitfire: Vb, FN-M BM295; IX FN-R BS467
Built: Castle Bromwich and Eastleigh
Length: 1:50
Where: North Weald–St Omer–North Weald; North Weald area

Leif Lundsten was temporarily back to flying the mark V on a Rodeo to St Omer on this day. It was a fine, cold day with scattered clouds. The Norwegians rendezvoused over Bradwell with the Hornchurch and Debden wings. The course was set for the Belgian coast, which was crossed just west of Nieuport. They turned right, and came out just west of Dunkirk at 25,000 feet. Enemy aircraft were observed, but there were no engagements.

BM295 had earlier been with 313 (Czechoslovak) Squadron and had seen action. On 23 June 1942, it was flown by Josef Prihoda, DFC, a highly skilled and respected Czech pilot. On this day, he shot down his fifth enemy aircraft over Morlais, making him an ace. Prihoda was killed only seven months later flying Spitfire Vb BP862 during an escort mission to Brest—he was twenty-nine years old.

Back home at North Weald, there was more practise with the IX, and Lundsten would fly his first flight in what would become his personal Spitfire IX. Gone was AR238, he would now be acquainted with BS467, a brand-new mark IX. His first flight in BS467 was cloud flying and formation practice.

BS467 had its first flight on 25 September 1942. It had a flying accident on 24 March 1943 with category 'B' damage—which meant it was beyond repair on site, but repairable at a maintenance unit or at a contractor's works. Lundsten flew the fighter on 14 March, and another Spitfire on the 23rd. It is unclear who flew BS467 on the day of the incident, but it wasn't back in Leif's hands until 13 April the same year. On 14 September 1943, basically a year after it first saw service with 331, it was transferred to 47 Maintenance Unit before being sent to Casablanca, Morocco, on 23 September. It arrived in Casablanca on 10 October 1943, joining the Northwest African Air Service command. NAASC was a sub-command of the Northwest Air Forces, itself being a sub-command of the Mediterranean Air Command. These Allied organisations were created at the Casablanca conference in January 1943, to promote cooperation between the RAF and the USAAF and their ground and naval forces in the North African and Mediterranean theatres of operations. In December 1943, two months after BS467 arrived at the theatre, NAASC was disbanded and reorganised in the newly established Mediterranean Allied Air Forces. BS467 was then transferred to the Middle East on 5 April 1945. At one point, if the photograph is indeed BS467, it seems the fighter had clipped wings during its time there.

The fighter was struck off charge as late as 5 February 1948.

Date: 13.10.1942
Spitfire: IX FN-R BS467
Built: Eastleigh
Length: 1:00
Where: North Weald area

A simple formation and cannon test.

Date: 15.10.1942
Spitfire: IX, FN-R BS467
Built: Eastleigh
Length: 0:45; 0:45
Where: North Weald–Ford–Le Havre–North Weald

Twelve aircraft from 331 Squadron, together with 332, took off from North Weald at 1.50 p.m. bound for RAF Ford, to refuel before Circus no. 227 took place. Their mission was to escort twelve Boston bombers to the Le Havre docks. The Norwegians rendezvoused with the Hornchurch wing over Littlehampton. They flew on the deck for twelve minutes before climbing steeply to 23,000 feet. Two Spitfires stayed behind at Ford due to radio trouble. Lundsten landed safely at North Weald at 4.15 p.m.

Date: 16.10.1942
Spitfire: IX, FN-X BS470
Built: Eastleigh
Length: 1:15
Where: North Weald area

The day was used to practise squadron formation flying, and Lundsten flew BS470, FN-X. The 'X' letter is usually connected to Kristian Nyerrød, but several pilots flew BS470, including Martin Gran and Fredrik Fearnley.

The once so proud BS470, with considerable action to its name, was sold as scrap in February 1950.

Date: 17.10.1942
Spitfire: IX, FN-X BS470
Built: Eastleigh
Length: 0:45, 0:45
Where: North Weald–Ford–North Weald

An escort mission to Le Havre cancelled; everyone landed back at North Weald at 4.50 p.m. from Ford.

Date: 21.10.1942
Spitfire: IX, FN-R BS467
Built: Eastleigh
Length: 1:30
Where: North Weald–Beachy Head–North Weald

The entire squadron were patrolling Beachy Head and Dungeness all day. Leif Lundsten, in BS467, and Fredrik Fearnley, in BS470, were doing their bit from 9.45 a.m. to 11.20 a.m. Another patrol was done in the afternoon.

Date: 24.10.1942
Spitfire: IX, FN-R BS467
Built: Eastleigh
Length: 1:10
Where: North Weald area

Formation and cloud flying took place this day. Weather was cloudy early on, but cleared in the afternoon.

Date: 27.10.1942
Spitfire: IX, FN-R BS467
Built: Eastleigh
Length: 1:50, 0:40
Where: North Weald–Channel–North Weald

Early morning scramble from North Weald together with Erik Fossum in BS143. Lundsten wrote 'convoy' in his logbook, which might indicate the scramble had something to do with convoys in the Channel. Later on, he did forty minutes of local and stunt flying. There was broken cloud throughout the day, and it was damp and cold.

This concluded his operational flying for October 1942. By the end of October, Leif Lundsten had done a total of 32.50 hours on patrols, 32.00 hours on convoy patrol, and 62.50 hours on sweeps.

16

Heavy Flak over Dunkirk: November 1942, 331 Squadron, North Weald, Essex

Date: 06.11.1942
Spitfire: IX, FN-R BS467
Built: Eastleigh
Length: Unknown
Where: North Weald–Channel–North Weald

Lundsten wrote the sortie down as a shipping reconnaissance, but he is not listed in the ORB for this day.

Date: 08.11.1942
Spitfire: IX, FN-R BS467; IX, FN-D BS137
Built: Eastleigh
Length: 0:40, 1:45
Where: North Weald area; North Weald–Dunkirk–Knocke–Flushing–North Weald

This was an interesting day for Leif Lundsten. Firstly, he took part in a mock attack on a Short Stirling. Then there was an afternoon sweep over Flushing at 16,000 feet, led by Major Kaj Birksted. The wing observed four ships, which led Birksted to head back immediately to report the sighting. He landed at Manston to personally make the report. The rest returned to base and landed safely at 5.40 p.m.

> No enemy aircraft, but flak over Flushing in Holland. Heavy flak over Dunkirk. Spang and Sem hit, but came home. One missed me by a few feet.
>
> Reidar Haave-Olsen, logbook.

Date: 09.11.1942
Spitfire: IX, FN-R BS467
Built: Eastleigh
Length: 0:40, 1:45
Where: North Weald–St Omer–Dunkirk–Cap Gris Nez–North Weald

The mission was a Rodeo no. 109. Four 190s dived on the Norwegians from above. Yellow 3 fired a short burst and Yellow 2 attacked another. He was able to get in a two good bursts and claimed it as a probable. It is unclear who flew in the Yellow Section of 331.

Date: 10.11.1942
Spitfire: IX, FN-R BS467
Built: Eastleigh
Length: 1:45, 1:15
Where: North Weald–London–North Weald and North Weald–Gravelines–North Weald

Formation flying over London during this hazy, but fine October day. Then a few hours later, a Rodeo to Gravelines. Enemy aircraft were reported in the area, so the Norwegians orbited, but nothing more was seen. Blue 1 was hit in the fuselage by what could only be flak, its port wing slightly damaged. All were back safely at 5 p.m. Leif Lundsten often flew as Blue 1, but it is unclear if he was the one being hit.

Date: 11.11.1942
Spitfire: IX, FN-R BS467
Built: Eastleigh
Length: 1:45
Where: North Weald–London–North Weald

The squadron patrolled London in the afternoon. The London patrols were a reaction to German activity over the capital. Lundsten simply calls it 'formation flying', making it sound like it was some form of exercise. However, the patrols were serious enough.

Date: 17.11.1942
Spitfire: IX, FN-V BS469
Built: Eastleigh
Length: 1:15
Where: North Weald–London–North Weald

A fine, cold day, with lots of practice flying and another patrol over London. Lundsten flew BS469, the Spitfire his B-flight leader, Stein Sem, would fly when he lost his life over the Channel on 12 December 1942, north of Dieppe. Sem reported trouble with this engine while participating on Circus 242. He turned for home together with Ottar Malm—Malm had reported trouble with his oxygen. Just as they passed the French coast, they were attacked by a Fw 190. Sem was hit and pulled sharply up to the left. He sent out a mayday signal, which was picked up in England, and a rescue boat, alongside Spitfires from Tangmere and Biggin Hill, was sent to look for him; he was not found.

Date: 18.11.1942
Spitfire: IX, FN-Z BS388
Built: Chattis Hill
Length: 1:30
Where: North Weald–Channel–North Weald

The squadron rendezvoused with 124 at Bradwell and set course for Schowen at sea level for a shipping recce. However, the weather deteriorated rapidly, and the Norwegians turned for home just as they could spot the coast.

   BS388 first flew 26 June 1942, and arrived at North Weald on 27 September 1942. It was used for Air Service Training in March 1943. According to the production list, it was damaged in combat with Fw 190s in April 1943 while escorting Venturas to Caen. In August 1945, a tyre burst on landing and BS388 tipped up on its nose. Regarding the first incident, Fredrik Eitzen flew BS388 on 14 April 1943, but no such event has been reported in the ORB.

Date: 20.11.1942
Spitfire: IX, FN-R BS467
Built: Eastleigh
Length: 0:50, 1:30
Where: North Weald area and North Weald–Southend–North Weald

Dogfighting practice was the first task of the day, followed by twelve Spitfires going to Southend for air-firing practice. A bit of low flying and homing practice then followed. Everyone was glad to see David Scott-Malden as he stopped by the Norwegians at North Weald after returning from his recent overseas trip to America.

Date: 24.11.1942
Spitfire: IX, FN-X BS470; FN-T BS471
Built: Eastleigh
Length: 1:05 and 1:00
Where: North Weald area and North Weald–Channel–North Weald

Formation flying in the morning, followed by a convoy patrol with Kristian Nyerrød flying BS388 in the afternoon. The weather was overcast, with considerable haze. A symphony concert was held in the evening, at which a number of pieces by Edvard Grieg were played.

BS471 was lost 2 May 1943 over Noordzee, 10 km west of Vlissingen, in Holland. The pilot flying the Spitfire was Fredrik Eitzen of 331 Squadron. No. 331 Squadron got involved in dogfights over the western tip of Walcheren. The wing was about to turn for home when Yellow Section, in 331, called for help. Fredrik Eitzen and Rolf Engelsen, both in Blue Section, were seen straggling behind the rest of Blue Section and were attacked by 190s.

Nos 331 and 332 were the only two squadrons operating over France, Belgium, and southern Holland, so the Luftwaffe was able to put up a strong fight. The Norwegians lost four pilots during the sortie—two from 331 and two from 332. Nils Jørgen Fuglesang and Marius Eriksen (both 332) survived—Eriksen jumped out, Fuglesang force-landed. Eitzen was killed in the engagement.

Date: 27.11.1942
Spitfire: IX, FN-R BS467
Built: Eastleigh
Length: 0:25
Where: North Weald area

Local flying was done on this day. The weather was reported to be overcast with slight drizzle.

Date: 28.11.1942
Spitfire: IX, FN-R BS467
Built: Eastleigh
Length: 0:55, 0:55
Where: North Weald area

This day focused on low flying, homing exercises. The squadron was released off camp from 1 p.m.; however, practice flying continued until 4.15 p.m. This was due to the weather playing in their favour, and the squadron took advantage of it. Lundsten flew two sorties at 12.55 a.m.

17

B-Flight Leader:
December 1942, 331 Squadron,
North Weald, Essex

Date: 01.12.1942
Spitfire: IX, FN-R BS467
Built: Eastleigh
Length: 1:50
Where: North Weald–Sawbridgeworth–North Weald

Lundsten and five other pilots went to Sawbridgeworth, carrying out Army co-operation exercises, returning at 1.50 p.m.

Date: 04.12.1942
Spitfire: IX, FN-R BS467
Built: Eastleigh
Length: 0:50
Where: North Weald area

Lundsten took BS467 up for a test flight; it was reported to be a fine, hazy day.

Date: 06.12.1942
Spitfire: IX, FN-R BS467
Built: Eastleigh
Length: 1:45
Where: North Weald–Lille–North Weald

The Norwegians provided an escort to the Flying Fortresses that were bombing Lille. Two enemy aircraft were spotted over Ostend, but they were well below the bombers. After the Fortresses had released their load, two Focke-Wulf 190s dived from above, head on, almost vertically through the wing and down inland. Blue Section from 331 turned on them, but little action took place. Everyone was safely back at the airfield at 1.10 p.m.

Date: 07.12.1942
Spitfire: IX, FN-R BS467
Built: Eastleigh
Length: 1:15
Where: North Weald area

Low flying over the local area, with overcast skies and strong winds.

Date: 09.12.1942
Spitfire: IX, FN-R BS467
Built: Eastleigh
Length: 1:15, 1:20
Where: North Weald area and North Weald–Calais–Dunkirk–North Weald

Over one hour of aerobatics followed by a Rodeo sortie over France led by Kaj Birksted. The Norwegians left the English coast over south Foreland, and climbed all the way up to 29,000 feet. The French coast was crossed just south of Calais. Some sections of the wing were slightly inland. No flak, no ships, nothing of interest spotted, and all landed safely at 4 p.m.

Date: 11.12.1942
Spitfire: IX, FN-R BS467
Built: Eastleigh
Length: 1:15, 1:20
Where: North Weald area

Practice interception and aerobatics. Wing Commander Patrick Jameson, having replaced Duncan-Smith on 8 December, came over to 331 and flew together with the squadron.

Date: 12.12.1942
Spitfire: IX, FN-R BS467
Built: Eastleigh
Length: 1:35
Where: North Weald–Ford–South of Dieppe–North Weald

Circus no. 242. Both squadrons, having refuelled at Ford, set course for the deadly French coast. They would provide an escort for seventy-eight B-17 Flying Fortresses going all the way to Romilly-sur-Seine. This was one of the longest missions yet undertaken by the Americans, and covered a greater distance than the Spitfires could escort them. Also in the air were the Biggin Hill and Kenley wings. Knut Bache force-landed in a field near Ford due to engine trouble. As previously mentioned, Stein Sem was shot down after being attacked by 190s on the homebound journey. Ottar Malm, also attacked by 190s, jumped out. He survived, but with a nasty cut over his right eye—the sortie would be his last on operations. Five out of twelve pilots in 331 suffered technical difficulties. Lundsten landed back at North Weald 12.30 p.m., with other pilots arriving back at North Weald between 12.30 p.m. and 1.30 p.m. Lundsten landed alone, followed by Helner Grundt-Spang five minutes later. The last to arrive back at the base were Kai Birksted (1.30 p.m.), Rolf Arne Berg (1.30 p.m.), and Reidar Haave Olsen (1.35 p.m.). The mission was aborted due to poor weather over the target, with no bombing taking place. Lundsten was possibly one of the five with problems, or perhaps one of the men following Grundt-Spang back home.

Due to the loss of Stein Sem, Leif Lundsten moved up to become CO of B-flight. B-flight was stationed on the east side of North Weald. Today, a considerable amount of RC model fliers use the grounds, as well as the Gnats display team.

Date: 13.12.1942
Spitfire: IX, FN-R BS467
Built: Eastleigh
Length: 2:20
Where: North Weald–French coast–North Weald

A search was carried out to find missing Stein Sem. The Norwegians stayed in the air for as long as possible, with the limited fuel capacity of the Spitfire always giving them challenges. Nothing was found, and the Norwegians had to return to North Weald empty handed. The loss of Sem, a popular character, was hard to take.

Date: 14.12.1942
Spitfire: IX, FN-R BS467
Built: Eastleigh
Length: 1:20
Where: North Weald–Ypres–Ostend–North Weald

Twelve 331 Spitfires took off at 2.45 p.m. for Rodeo no. 133. They flew as far as Ypres before turning back home, crossing the coast at Ostend. No flak and no enemy fighters were observed. Lundsten was back at 4.05 p.m. The weather was reported to be fine with fair wind.

Date: 16.12.1942
Spitfire: IX, FN-R BS467
Built: Eastleigh
Length: 1:30, 1:40
Where: North Weald–Channel–North Weald

Two convoy patrols—one at 9.45 a.m. and one at 11.45 a.m. Lundsten's partner for the first convoy, Johannes Greiner (ER982), had engine problems and came back at 10 a.m.—Rolf Engelsen took his place (BS466). The weather was unsettled, with occasional rain.

Date: 21.12.1942
Spitfire: IX, FN-R BS467
Built: Eastleigh
Length: 0:55
Where: North Weald area

Formation flying. No operational sorties.

Date: 22.12.1942
Spitfire: IX, FN-R BS467
Built: Eastleigh
Length: 1:40
Where: North Weald–unknown

There was a scramble at 3.30 p.m., flying alongside Martin Gran (BS470). Nothing was reported from the scramble—it was completely uneventful. Back on the ground, the Norwegians prepared for traditional Christmas celebrations.

Date: 27.12.1942
Spitfire: IX, FN-R BS467
Built: Eastleigh
Length: 0:35
Where: North Weald–Channel–North Weald

Convoy patrol with Kristian Nyerrød flying BS388.

Date: 30.12.1942
Spitfire: IX, FN-R BS467
Built: Eastleigh
Length: 1:20
Where: North Weald–Mardyck–North Weald

Twelve Spitfires from 331 took off with 332 Squadron at 3.15 p.m. They crossed the English coast over Bradwall, and then crossed the coast over Mardyck at 26,000 feet. All were back safely at 4.35 p.m.

Date: 31.12.1942
Spitfire: IX, FN-R BS467
Built: Eastleigh
Length: 1:05
Where: North Weald–Gravelines–Cap Gris Nez–North Weald

On the last day of the year, the weather was fine and sunny, but about an inch of snow fell over North Weald during the night—perhaps a welcoming sight to Norwegians, with the snow reminding them of home. Some were up as early as 4 a.m., clearing snow in front of the parked Spitfires. Others stayed in bed and slept peacefully. The North Weald Wing did one sortie during the day. The wing rendezvoused with the Biggin Hill wing over Manston, climbing all the way, and crossing the French coast by Gravelines. They then turned right going over St Omer, and then came out over Cap Gris Nez.

As the day came to an end, Kaj Birksted wrote the following in the ORB:

As the old year goes out we remember the busy times and the battles we have had—they are fresh in our memory, and ever to remain, so are those good fellows we have lost. Some we know will not return, we have hope that others may be alive. Jens Müller and Espelid we know to be prisoners of war. We believe that the New Year will require more of us than ever, it is bound to do so, but these memories are part of our inspiration—there are also many other things and wishes that inspires us to go on.

Signed, K. Birksted, Major
Officer Commanding 331 Squadron

18

Leading 331 Squadron: January 1943, 331 Squadron, North Weald, Essex

Date: 02.01.1943
Spitfire: IX, FN-Z BS388
Built: Chattis Hill
Length: 1:25
Where: North Weald–Gravelines–Lille–North Weald

The year was only two days old when Lundsten was back in the air. Rodeo no. 243 was scheduled to take place, a diversionary sweep in support of Circus no. 243. Twelve Bostons would attack the Cherbourg-area. No. 331 took off with ten Spitfires at 11.55 a.m., led by Kaj Birksted. Leading 332 was Wilhelm Mohr—no. 332 were also leading the wing. Climbing all the way, they crossed the French coast over Gravelines, then swept right reaching as far as Lille. There were thick clouds over France, and it was reported after the sortie it had been hard to see anything. Enemy activity was observed in the murky conditions, but the Luftwaffe did not engage the wing. The wind was very heavy at the squadrons designated height as well. Lundsten flew BS388, FN-Z, during the sortie.

Jerries up, but the dull fellows wouldn't fight.

Reidar Haave Olsen, logbook.

Date: 03.01.1943
Spitfire: IX, FN-Z BS388
Built: Chattis Hill
Length: 0:15
Where: North Weald–aborted sortie–North Weald

The weather on this day was fine and clear, but very cold. The wing would do another diversionary sweep. Boston bombers would release their load over Cherbourg, while the Americans would bomb St Nazaire. Leif Lundsten turned back to North Weald after just fifteen minutes due to problems with his drop tank. Erik Fossum (BR954) and Eyolf Berg-Olsen (BS4459) also had to return due to the same issue. Lundsten simply wrote 'I returned' in his logbook. Lundsten rarely aborted sorties, this was one of very few occasions.

Date: 05.01.1943
Spitfire: IX, FN-R BS467
Built: Eastleigh
Length: 1:05
Where: North Weald area

It was clear and cold weather over Essex this January day. The squadron was kept busy doing low flying and pinpointing exercises.

Date: 08.01.1943
Spitfire: IX, FN-R BS467
Built: Eastleigh
Length: 0:30, 1:45, 1:35
Where: North Weald

Another aborted sortie for Lundsten, again due to drop tank problems, an issue that haunted the Norwegians for a considerable amount of time at the start of 1943. The rest of the squadron went to Dunkirk or Gravelines, but nothing was seen.

Later, during the afternoon, two patrols were carried out over Canterbury. All of 331 Squadron were busy doing these patrols, including Lundsten.

Date: 09.01.1943
Spitfire: IX, FN-R BS467
Built: Eastleigh
Length: 0:45
Where: North Weald area

Squadron formation practice. Snow had fallen during the night, and the cold weather had also resulted in hard frost on the ground.

Date: 17.01.1943
Spitfire: IX, FN-M BS466; IX, FN-T BS471
Built: Eastleigh
Length: 2:05, 1:05
Where: North Weald–Ostend–Walcheren–North Weald; North Weald local

The day was set for Rodeo no. 150, with take-off at 11.45 a.m. There was cloudy weather over Europe. No. 332 Squadron was bounced by two 190s. Peder Mollestad and Torstein Strand (332) shot one of them down. Robert Hassel Hauge (also 332) damaged the second one. All were back safely at 1.50 p.m.

Back home after his previous sortie to Walcheren (notice Lundsten flew BS466), Lundsten took Spitfire BS471 up for an hour of local flying. Interestingly, Kaj Birksted had flown BS471 on the sortie to Walcheren.

Date: 18.01.1943
Spitfire: IX, FN-R BS467
Built: Eastleigh
Length: 0:45
Where: North Weald–Ford–North Weald

A return trip to Ford. This show was cancelled before they got underway.

Date: 20.01.1943
Spitfire: IX, FN-R BS467
Built: Eastleigh
Length: 0:45
Where: North Weald–Manston area–North Weald. North Weald area

Twelve Spitfires were scrambled from North Weald at 12.35 p.m. to meet a mass German raid against the south coast and London. The first wave of German bombers reached their target. The second wave was turned back by the RAF. A third wave consisted of fighters only. One or several bombs hit Sandhurst Road School, in Greenwich. Thirty-eight children and two adults were killed. There were no engagements from 331 during these raids. No. 332 got into dogfights with 190s, which resulted in squadron veteran Peder Mollestad lost south of Calais. The Norwegians had chased the Germans back over the channel. Mollestad managed to land his stricken Spitfire in France, but died in an ambulance due to loss of blood. He was twenty-four years old.

Later on, Lundsten was up flying squadron formation practice. A very busy, but sad day for the British civilian population, as well as the North Weald Wing.

Date: 21.01.1943
Spitfire: IX, FN-R BS467
Built: Eastleigh
Length: 1:00, 1:45, 1:15
Where: North Weald–Ford–Caen–North Weald; North Weald–Mardyck–Calais–North Weald

A very busy day for Leif Lundsten and his fellow countrymen. First up, Circus no. 252 with take-off set for 10.20 a.m. After refuelling at Ford, they took off again at 11.45 a.m. to provide target support for twelve Venturas bombing Caen airfield. Bombs were reported to hit the airfield. On the way out, 332 was attacked by two 190s. No. 331 also got into the fray, but no results observed. Everyone landed back at 1.35 p.m. for a well-deserved lunch.

Next up was a very special occasion for Leif Lundsten. He would for the first time lead the squadron. This would take place during Rodeo no. 156 over the Mardyck–Calais area. Nils Jørstad returned early with the (almost) everlasting squadron problem of not being able to release the drop tank. The rest landed back at North Weald between 4.15 p.m. and 4.40 p.m., Lundsten was the first to land at 4.15 p.m., Reidar Haave Olsen (BS530) the last alongside Tarald Weisteen (BS534) and Svein Heglund (BS299) all 4.40 p.m.

One would perhaps think this was a sortie worth making a special note of in the logbook, but nothing is written from Lundsten's point of view. Another interesting fact is that he flew BS467 for over three hours this day–a considerable amount of flying.

Date: 22.01.1943
Spitfire: IX, FN-R BS467
Built: Eastleigh
Length: 1:30
Where: North Weald–St Omer–North Weald

Circus no. 253 to St Omer in support of twelve Bostons. Take-off was at 2.10 pm. Lundsten and 331 never spotted the bombers on their way to France. Svein Heglund's Spitfire (BS144) had an engine fire, but managed to nurse his Spitfire back to England. Helner Grundt-Spang broke formation and claimed to have shot down two Messerschmitt 109s over Westhhoofd, in Holland. According to author Cato Guhnfeldt (*Spitfire Saga III*, p. 207), it is more likely he lied about the claims in order to avoid trouble for breaking formation without asking for permission, but nothing is certain. Lundsten landed back safely at 3.50 p.m.

Date: 23.01.1943
Spitfire: IX, FN-R BS467; IX, FN-V BR594
Built: Eastleigh
Length: 0:30, 0:50, 1:00
Where: North Weald area

Cannon tests were the focus of the day. There was overcast weather over Essex. The two first flights were flown in his regular BS467. Then a third in BR594. The latter was Rolf Engelsen's Spitfire when he was shot down on 2 May 1943 (see report from 24.11.1942).

Date: 25.01.1943
Spitfire: IX, FN-R BS467
Built: Eastleigh
Length: 0:40, 0:50
Where: North Weald area

Two squadron formation practice sessions, both in BS467. Thin layer of clouds at 6,000 feet.

Date: 26.01.1943
Spitfire: IX, FN-R BS467
Built: Eastleigh
Length: 1:55
Where: North Weald–Dunkirk–Calais–Vlissingen–North Weald

Circus no. 246 to the marshalling yards at Bruges, Belgium, supporting Ventura bombers. The usual fog was blowing in from the estuary at take-off time (11.45 p.m.). The squadron flew on the deck (nearly zero altitude) until 10 miles north-east of Dunkirk, when they climbed sharply to 5,000 feet. Here, they turned right and went along the coast as far as Calais, then they turned around and followed the coast eastwards. The squadron never saw the Venturas. The squadron, with Leif Lundsten in BS467, was back at 1.30 p.m. This day turned out to be a very sad day; Emil Samuelsen, from 332 Squadron, failed to pull out of a power dive and went straight in at Matching Green, Essex. Some 332 Squadron pilots were ordered to dig for pieces of the pilot. The engine was buried so far down that they simply gave up trying to find it. The speed on impact was considered to have been 'like nothing they had seen before'. No. 331 Squadron pilot Helner Grundt-Spang referred to a situation like this in his book from 1971 (*Den hemmelige kampen*, pp. 58–59). He does not mention any names, and it could be another similar scenario, but it was clear it made a big impact on them to dig for remains of their friends.

Date: 28.01.1943
Spitfire: IX, FN-R BS467
Built: Eastleigh
Length: Unknown
Where: North Weald–Ostend–Flushing–North Weald

Shipping reconnaissance at 11.05 a.m. in the morning, with thick haze, damp conditions—this was poor weather with low visibility. Lundsten and the Norwegians from 331 flew at sea level all the way, making landfall southwest of Ostend. Then they continued along the coast to the Flushing estuary. Two unidentified aircraft were spotted just below cloud over the Westhoofd, but there were no engagements.

Date: 29.01.1943
Spitfire: IX, FN-R BS467
Built: Eastleigh
Length: 0:35, 1:45
Where: North Weald–Flushing–North Weald

Fine, but variable weather. Lundsten took BS467 for a test flight during the day to check the Spitfires radio transmitter. It was deemed to be alright, as he followed 331 on a sortie to Flushing at 3.05 p.m. In an attempt to get the Luftwaffe up in the air for a fight, Lundsten and his B-flight stayed on the deck with 332 Squadron. The move did not make the Germans react, and they turned for home, returning at 5.10 p.m.

Date: 30.01.1943
Spitfire: IX, FN-R BS467
Built: Eastleigh
Length: Unknown
Where: North Weald area

Overcast skies, with rain in the air. Six pilots flew to Debden to take a closer look at the American P-47 Thunderbolt. Lundsten remained back at North Weald, doing a bit of low flying, thus ending his flying for January of 1943. It had been a busy month for the Norwegians, with several losses. This day would see another casualty; Johan Nicolay Eyde from 332 Squadron died when his Spitfire was struck by lightning over Cambridge.

19

'I Got One!'
February 1943, 331 Squadron, North Weald, Essex

Date: 01.02.1943
Spitfire: IX, FN-R BS467
Built: Eastleigh
Length: 1:15
Where: North Weald area

There were strong winds at North Weald on this day. Nonetheless, Lundsten did over an hour of low flying. Nine pilots went to Debden once again to look at the American P-47 Thunderbolt.

Date: 02.02.1943
Spitfire: IX, FN-R BS467
Built: Eastleigh
Length: 1:20
Where: North Weald–St Omer–North Weald

Circus no. 257 to St Omer. Eleven Spitfires, led by Captain Rolf Arne Berg, took off at 9.35 a.m. to be target support for twelve Venturas bombing St Omer aerodrome. Yellow Section in 331 Squadron shot down a Messerschmitt 109 over Ypres. Helner Grundt-Spang, Svein Heglund, and Eyolf Berg-Olsen all taking part in the action. Heglund and Grundt-Spang claimed their pray as a shared kill. Lundsten and the rest of the squadron were all back safely at 1.15 p.m. In the afternoon a convoy patrol took place, but nothing has been written in the ORB about this patrol.

Date: 03.02.1943
Spitfire: IX, FN-R BS467
Built: Eastleigh

Length: 0:15
Where: North Weald–Courtrai–North Weald

A fine and clear day. The task of the day was Circus no. 247 too Courtrai, target support for Ventura bombers. The squadron climbed for altitude straight out of North Weald. However, Lundsten was listed as returning to base only fifteen minutes after take-off, together with Erik Fossum in BR594. The rest of the squadron returned exactly an hour later. Could this have been another case of the drop-tank issue? The squadron took off again for a similar sortie in the afternoon, but without Lundsten among them, which might indicate there had been a technical issue with BS467 on Lundsten's aborted sortie.

> Bloody cold flying at 22,000 feet. No Jerries attacked. No business. No fun. Brassed off!

> Reidar Haave-Olsen, logbook.

Date: 04.02.1943
Spitfire: IX, FN-R BS467
Built: Eastleigh
Length: 1:35
Where: North Weald–St Omer–Ypres–North Weald

Rodeo no. 162 to St Omer–Ypres area. There had been good weather for the past few days, which put the Norwegians in good spirits.

Take-off was at 11.45 a.m. Having arrived over the St Omer area, several large formations of Focke-Wulf 190s and Messerschmitt 109s were observed. The number could have been as high as sixty German fighters both above and below the Norwegians height. Rolf Arne Berg and Nils Jørstad broke away from formation and attacked two 190s, both making claims. Berg claimed his as destroyed. No. 332 Squadron also took part in the fighting. Leif Lundsten made no claims during the encounter, but being in the middle of such melee of dogfights must have been quite nerve-wrecking and exciting at the same time. The squadron had claimed several German fighters in the past days, which gave everyone a considerable burst of energy.

> Enemy aircraft all over. Dogfights issued. Up to 37,000 feet. Cold, but good fun.

> Reidar Haave-Olsen, logbook.

Date: 06.02.1943
Spitfire: IX, FN-R BS467
Built: Eastleigh
Length: 0:35
Where: North Weald area

After the intensity on 4 February, Lundsten had a well-deserved day of rest on 5 February. He was back in the air the next day. Strong winds and rain over Essex did not prevent Lundsten from taking BS467 up for some local test flying.

Date: 07.02.1943
Spitfire: IX, FN-X BS470; IX, FN-M BS466
Built: Eastleigh
Length: 1:30, 0:55
Where: North Weald area

Air-firing practice in the morning, then formation flying by seven Spitfires after tea-time. One Spitfire made mock attacks on the formation. Lundsten flew BS470 and BS466 during the day.

Date: 10.02.1943
Spitfire: IX, FN-R BS467
Built: Eastleigh
Length: 0:30, 0:55
Where: North Weald area

Test flight in BS467 in the morning, which explained the absence of Lundsten's personal Spitfire on 7 February. It had most likely been in for a regular service, or due to other technical aspects.

The day started out fine and cold, with wisps of cloud. As the day progressed, it became overcast with thick haze. Kaj Birksted led 331 Squadron on Rodeo no. 167 together with 332 Squadron. Visibility was down to 400 yards when they took off at 11.25 a.m. The squadrons became separated shortly after take-off due to the poor weather. Birksted requested a return to base due to the weather closing in further while they were over the Channel. Four Spitfires from 331 stayed on as top cover for 332 Squadron as they had not heard the order to return for home. Lundsten was back home with the first batch at 12.20 p.m. No. 332 Squadron pilot Reidar Watne Kluge jumped out mid-Channel due to engine trouble, and he drowned before rescue came for him. The incident was vividly remembered by Finn Thorsager of 332 Squadron in the years to come after the war had ended.

Date: 14.02.1943
Spitfire: IX, FN-R BS467
Built: Eastleigh
Length: 2:00
Where: North Weald–Ostend–Flushing–North Weald

Afternoon Ramrod to the Ostend–Flushing area. As on 10 February, the weather deteriorated as the day went on. At Ostend the Norwegians turned 180 degrees as they met a wall of fog. The Norwegians followed the coast down to Cap Gris Nez before they turned for home. The day was uneventful.

Date: 15.02.1943
Spitfire: IX, FN-R BS467
Built: Eastleigh
Length: 1:15, 1:35
Where: North Weald–Dunkirk–St Omer–Le Touquet–North Weald; North Weald–Dunkirk–North Weald

I got one!

Leif Lundsten, logbook

The 15 February 1943 turned out to be a day to remember for Leif Lundsten. Two sorties were done on this day, both to Dunkirk.

For the next few days, the Norwegians would focus their energy towards a specific ship located in the harbour of Dunkirk—the *Coronel*. It would turn out to require a lot of effort from the North Weald Wing due to poor weather conditions and German engagements. However, there were fine periods of weather with sporadic showers and fine wind from the west on this day.

Twelve Spitfires from 331 took off with their sister squadron, 332, at 12.10 p.m. for Circus no. 265. Captain Leif Lundsten flew as deputy wing commander to Patrick Jameson during this first sortie—a first for Lundsten. The Norwegians were to be target support for twelve Bostons bombing an armed merchant ship in Dunkirk harbour. The wing crossed in just east of Dunkirk at 12,000 feet, but a bank of cloud obscured Dunkirk from view. The wing swept west of St Omer and 10 miles east of Le Touquet. Then they turned back along the same route, and left the enemy coast over Nieuport. They never saw the bombers, nor did they see the Biggin Hill wing, which was supposed to be in the area. One Spitfire landed at Manston with engine trouble. Lundsten was safely back at North Weald at 1.25 p.m., a whole twenty minutes before the rest. Bjørn Stenstad in BR982 was with him. Most likely, either Lundsten or Bjørnstad had drop tank trouble (once again), which explained their early return.

After a quick lunch the pilots were called to briefing in the Station Intelligence Office in connection with Circus no. 267. At 3.05 p.m., 331 Squadron left North Weald behind, led by Kaj Birksted. Their task for this second sortie of the day was to provide rear support of twelve Liberators bombing the Dunkirk harbour. No. 331 flew as top cover to 332. By the time they reached the French coast, five Fw 190s were spotted flying line abreast at 20,000 feet. Wing Commander Jameson led a section from 332 Squadron towards the Germans. John Bernard Gilhuus from 332 Squadron claimed to have shot one of them down, and Jameson another. Another batch of 190s appeared, and Jameson engaged them with his section from 332 for a second time. Jameson claimed a second destroyed, Marius Eriksen also claimed one shot down.

Leif Lundsten and 331 Squadron were still busy escorting the Liberators back to England from having bombed the Dunkirk harbour successfully. Over the Channel, about five Focke-Wulf 190s were spotted diving towards France. No. 331 concluded the bombers were almost back at Manston by his point in time, and headed after the Germans. Blue Section, led by Leif Lundsten, took chase and dived down after them. They turned 180 degrees in the process. Yellow Section also joined in. Red Section stayed on as top cover for the other two sections. Gaining on the 190s, Lundsten opened fire at long range. He spotted his number three (Helner Grundt-Spang in BS470) and number four (Knut Bache in BR594) passing, above and to the left to him. He was about to disengage when one of the 190s pulled up 100 yards in front of him, trying to attack Grundt-Spang. Leif Lundsten was now close enough to get in a good burst, and fired at the 190. It went over on its back, and dived down. Lundsten followed him down and observed him go straight into the sea. Another splash appeared in front of him, which he concluded was the 190 later claimed by Grundt-Spang.

Combat report in Lundsten's own words:

I was flying at Blue 1 and when about 20 miles South-East of North Foreland escorting bombers back home, I saw five FW 190s diving back towards France, and at about 12,000-15,000 feet, I made a sharp turn to the left and started to fire. I gave one short burst at long range, then I saw my Nos. 3 and 4 passing above and to the left. I was on the point of breaking off, being unable to get nearer when a FW 190 pulled up 100 yards in front of me trying to attack my No. 3. I have the E/A few seconds burst and it went over on its back, diving steeply. I followed him down and saw him go straight into the sea. As I pulled up

I saw another splash about 1,000 yards in front, which I think must be the one claimed by No. 3.

Ammunition:　　　　　Cannon

　　　　　　　　　　　　　　　　　　　　　　　　　　Capt. Lundsten

In his logbook he wrote: 'I got one!'

The problem was, according to journalist and author Cato Guhnfeldt, the Norwegians claimed too many destroyed enemy aircraft compared to the actual losses of the Luftwaffe that day (four destroyed compared to two actual 190s lost). Based on his research, he credited only Lundsten and Marius Eriksen for actual kills (*Spitfire Saga III*, p. 244).

In the evening, having had such success in the air, the Norwegians threw a party in the mess.

Date: 16.02.1943
Spitfire: IX, FN-R BS467
Built: Eastleigh
Length: 1:50
Where: North Weald–Dunkirk–North Weald

An afternoon sortie was on the agenda for this day. More specifically, Rodeo no. 170 to the Dunkirk area. No. 331 Squadron was led by Leif Lundsten and Tarald Weisteen. The wing was once again led by Patrick Jameson. There was nothing to report from the Norwegians side of things, and they all landed back at North Weald at 5.55 p.m.

Date: 17.02.1943
Spitfire: IX, FN-R BS467
Built: Eastleigh
Length: 2:05
Where: North Weald–Dunkirk–North Weald

Overcast and hazy weather over North Weald. For a third time, Leif Lundsten would lead the squadron (according to *Spitfire Saga III*, p. 249, the sortie was led by both Weisteen and Lundsten, the ORB stated Lundsten led the Norwegians). The squadron went through thick cloud on their way up to 10,000 feet. Due to cloud and poor weather, the bombers they escorted aborted their mission. The Norwegians turned port along coast to Ostend, then returned to the Calais area, then once again flying back to Ostend before a return to Calais—there were no incidents. Nos 331 and 332 arrived back at home at 11.40 a.m. No. 124 Squadron, also based at North Weald, were involved in dogfights with the Luftwaffe. Being far outnumbered, they tragically lost four pilots.

Flying low over sea along coast of France. No business. No Flak. 124 Squadron had 4 missing.

Reidar Haave-Olsen, logbook.

Date: 18.02.1943
Spitfire: IX, FN-R BS467
Built: Eastleigh
Length: 1:15
Where: North Weald–Dunkirk–North Weald

Yet another sortie to Dunkirk in support of bombers attacking the *Coronel*. This sortie did not take place until well into the afternoon. The wing was led by Wing Commander Jameson. Due to the thick cloud cover, the bomber sortie was cancelled. The North Weald Wing turned for home somewhere over Northern France. This would be the Norwegians last sortie for a while, as the weather would close in and it would not clear up until 26 February. Lundsten would not be back in the air for six days.

Flying at 22,000 feet. No business. A waste of petrol.

Reidar Haave-Olsen, logbook.

Date: 24.02.1943
Spitfire: IX, FN-R BS467
Built: Eastleigh
Length: 1:10
Where: North Weald area

The weather finally broke up after several days of poor weather. North Weald had, for the most part, been under a thick carpet of fog. On 24 February, however, Lundsten took BS467 for formation flying and dusk landings.

Date: 25.02.1943
Spitfire: IX, FN-R BS467
Built: Eastleigh
Length: 1:05 Where: North Weald area

The 'everlasting fog' cleared after lunch, which gave Lundsten and 331 a chance to do some formation flying.

Date: 26.02.1943
Spitfire: IX, FN-R BS467
Built: Eastleigh
Length: 1:35, 1:40
Where: North Weald–St Omer–North Weald; North Weald–St Omer–North Weald

With the weather finally back to suitable conditions for operational flying, Kaj Birksted led 331 on Circus no. 274. Patrick Jameson led the wing. Jameson ran into problems with his Spitfire, and Finn Thorsager from 332 Squadron took over the wing in his absence. There was thick cloud during the entire sortie. Enemy aircraft were reported, but none were seen. Everyone arrived back at North Weald at 12.15 p.m.

The afternoon sortie, a repeat from the sortie done in the morning, would turn out to be very different. Circus no. 274 repeat was led by Leif Lundsten, his third sortie in command of the squadron. The wing set course for St Omer, climbing all the way over the Channel. Enemy aircraft were reported south of St Omer, and Lundsten led the Norwegians eastwards. They spotted nothing, and turned north again flying as high as 34,000 feet. On this northern course, the Norwegians spotted several German fighters flying in pairs. No. 331 Squadron spotted about twenty-five Focke-Wulf 190s below them. Lundsten ordered the squadron to dive on the Germans in an attempt to surprise the enemy fighters. In the fighting that followed, several pilots in 331 made claims, including Leif Lundsten, Bjørn Bjørnstad, and Helge Sognnæs.

Lundsten got behind one 190, which was flying straight and level. He opened fire at 700 yards, and closed in to 100 yards—his thumb never left the firing button. He saw a big piece fly off from the cockpit area. His Spitfire reached high speeds and he broke off the attack and pulled up. From Lundsten's point of view, the 190 seemed to be out of control and went straight down inverted.

Whether or not Lundsten shot down the German remains unknown. Guhnfeldt's research on this day in 1943 points to one German fighter being shot down (*Spitfire Saga III*, p. 252). This was not a 190, but a 109, which makes the connection to the Norwegian engagement more unclear. It could indicate that the 190 Lundsten attacked made it back to base.

Lundsten's own report from the fighting over St Omer:

I was flying as Red 1, leading 331 (N) Sqdn. We were vectored onto the Huns, and climbed to 32,000 feet. Over St Omer I first sighted two

FWs and called up the bottom Sqdn, but they did not see them. A few seconds later I saw about 20/30 FWs approximately 8,000 ft. below us. I called up the Wingco, and told him I was going with all of 331 Sqdn. I got head on to one FW, which was flying straight and level. I opened up and at about 700 yds.—and closed in to about 100 yds.—firing all the time. I saw a big piece fly off the cockpit. This piece hit my No. 2 in the left wing and damaged it slightly. I had by then a quite high speed, and pulled up again. The last I saw of the E/A was that he was diving down very steeply on his back, and appeared to be out of control.

Ammunition: 56/20 mm
                       60/.303

Capt. Lundsten

This engagement on 26 February, ended the squadrons, and Leif Lundsten's, sorties for February 1943. A very busy month indeed.

20

It Exploded and Went Into the Sea: March 1943, 331 Squadron, North Weald, Essex

Date: 02.03.1943
Spitfire: IX, FN-R BS467
Built: Eastleigh
Length: 0:20, 0:10
Where: North Weald–St Omer–North Weald

There was overcast weather over North Weald. Twelve Spitfires from 331 Squadron sprung to life at 12.10 p.m. Major Birksted led the wing. They were recalled almost as soon as they were airborne. Later on, five Spitfires, including Leif Lundsten in BS467, were scrambled at 1.30 p.m., but they were only in the air for about ten minutes. Totalling two sorties cancelled in one day.

Date: 03.03.1943
Spitfire: IX, FN-R BS467
Built: Eastleigh
Length: 1:05, 1:00
Where: North Weald area and London

Another quiet day. Still overcast over North Weald with strong easterly winds. In the morning, the squadron did formation and cine-gun practice. In the afternoon, several Spitfires beat up a gun post somewhere in London as part of a training exercise. Fifty German bombers attacked London at night, most of them dropping their load on the countryside. Suffolk, Essex, and Cambridgeshire were all hit, but fortunately the casualties were not high.

Date: 04.03.1943
Spitfire: IX, FN-R BS467

Built: Eastleigh
Length: 0:35
Where: North Weald area; North Weald–Ypres area–North Weald

While the pilots were eating their breakfast in the morning, they received orders to scramble. Thirteen Spitfires took off, including Leif Lundsten. It was feared that the Germans would do another bombing run like the one they had done during the night, potentially aiming for North Weald itself. Everyone was therefore on high alert. The Luftwaffe turned back before reaching the English coast, and no engagements took place.

Back to a more usual sort of trade in the afternoon. It was time for Rodeo no. 174 to the Ypres area. The wing crossed the English coast over Southend at 3,000 feet and climbed to 20,000 feet before they crossed the coast over Dunkirk. They swept right over Ypres, Merville, and St Omer and left the French coast. They crossed the English coast over Sandgate. Tarald Weisteen (BS531) had to make a forced landing at Manston due to engine failure over the Channel.

Date: 07.03.1943
Spitfire: IX, FN-R BS467
Built: Eastleigh
Length: 1:00
Where: North Weald–Clacton–North Weald

Six Spitfires from 331 Squadron were scrambled at 1.20 p.m. to intercept enemy aircraft in the Clacton area. Knut Bache and Kaj Birksted claimed one aircraft each. Lundsten arrived back with the other five Spitfires at 2.20 p.m., with much excitement over their success.

Date: 08.03.1943
Spitfire: IX, FN-R BS467
Built: Eastleigh
Length: 0:50, 2:50
Where: North Weald–Tangmere; Tangmere–Rennes–North Weald

A very long day for Lundsten and the Norwegians from North Weald. The wing flew down to Tangmere to refuel their Spitfires. After lunch, they took off from Tangmere at 2.10 p.m. to be second fighter support in Ramrod no. 40. American B-17 Flying Fortresses would bomb Rennes. Three Spitfires had technical issues after take-off from Tangmere, and returned to base. The rest met up with the bombers over St Lô and escorted them back to the English coast. One bomber went into the sea, having been watched carefully by Yellow Section from 331. A Walrus was scrambled to find the Americans. Sadly, there were no sign of life when the Walrus arrived, and the bodies were too deep into the sea to be brought back. Lundsten was back at North Weald at 5 p.m.

The lost B-17 bomber was B-17 41-24588 named *Carter and his Little Pills*. The aircraft sustained battle damage from anti-aircraft fire and enemy fighter attacks. It ditched in the Channel 10 miles off Selsey Bill, while Yellow Section from 331 Squadron could only look helplessly at the doomed bomber going in.

At 5.55 p.m., just an hour after Lundsten was back from escorting the Fortresses, sections of two were scrambled from North Weald. Lundsten took off with Kristian Nyerrød in BS470 at 5.55 p.m. to patrol Barrow Deep. Helge Sognnæs, in AB457, and Ingar Knudsen, in BS299, had already been scrambled at this time. Lundsten and Nyerrød did not spot anything out of the ordinary, and came back at 7 p.m.

Date: 09.03.1943
Spitfire: IX, FN-R BS467
Built: Eastleigh
Length: 1:20
Where: North Weald–St Omer–North Weald

Ten Spitfires from 331 Squadron, led by Kaj Birksted, took off for Rodeo no. 178 to the St Omer area. No. 332 Squadron was led by Finn Thorsager. Reidar Haave-Olsen damaged a 109 near St Omer. Lundsten arrived back home safely at 4.55 p.m.

Date: 10.03.1943
Spitfire: IX, FN-T BS471
Built: Eastleigh
Length: 1:40, 1:20
Where: North Weald–Flushing–North Weald; North Weald–Canterbury–North Weald

BS467 stayed behind at North Weald when Leif Lundsten led 331 Squadron to Walcheren flying in BS471. They flew alongside 332 Squadron and Wing Commander Jameson. Rodeo no. 179 was on the agenda on this fine, hazy spring day. Marius Eriksen, from 332, joined 331 Squadron on this occasion. While the Norwegians would be over the Flushing area, a squadron of Thunderbolts would make a sweep over Walcheren. For some reason, the Americans had arrived already, instead of coming in over Walcheren behind the Norwegians—as was originally planned. When Lundsten and the Norwegians arrived, the Luftwaffe were therefore up in force. Two groups of about ten to thirty-two enemy fighters were encountered when the wing turned out from Knocke, and a massive dogfight took place. No. 332 Squadron got into the thick of things, and claimed five damaged and two probable. 331 Squadron claimed one damaged. According to Guhnfeldt (*Spitfire Saga IV*, p. 275) there were no losses on the German side this day. However, plenty of the Germans went home with damages from their encounter with the North Weald Wing this day—Lundsten wrote the claims down in his logbook.

In the late afternoon, Lundsten, together with Fredrik Eitzen in BR595, did a patrol over Canterbury, which was uneventful. They turned for home when their time was up, and landed at 7 p.m. It had been another eventful day.

Date: 12.03.1943
Spitfire: IX, FN-X BS470
Built: Eastleigh
Length: 1:05, 2:05, 1:40
Where: North Weald–Bradwell area–North Weald; North Weald–Rouen–North Weald; North Weald–Neiuport–Ypres–North Weald

On this fine spring day, most pilots were out of bed by 6 a.m., with some able to snatch an early breakfast, others were more tired than hungry and hoped to get it later. Briefing for the day was finished about 7.05 a.m. No. 331 Squadron pilots had barely arrived at dispersal when the whole squadron was scrambled. Enemy fighters had been reported approaching Bradwell. With the sun just having appeared over the horizon, with a dull, red glow through the haze, the Norwegians took off from North Weald to meet the foe. According to a much-impressed writer of the ORB, it was the best looking take-off he had ever seen. It was a quick getaway, to the tune of eleven thunderous roars of Rolls-Royce Merlin engines. To be taking off under such (almost) romantic setting, it is tempting to say the day could only have one outcome—a successful one.

Leif Lundsten would lead Blue Section during the encounter, which consisted of himself and Fredrik Eitzen in BS388. Note that Lundsten did not fly his regular BS467, but rather Kristian Nyerrød's often-used BS470.

No. 331 Squadron caught up with the 190s between Bradwell and the French coast and attacked them. Leif Lundsten chased down a group of 190s located just a few miles off the French coast. He was about 600–700 yards away from a formation of ten German fighters when they seemed to throttle down—he felt that he had closed in very quickly. He opened fire at one of them from 100 yards. After a few seconds, the 190 exploded and went into the sea. He then fired at another 190, which had been flying abreast with the first. He gave this one a short burst and saw strikes on the fuselage, followed by clouds of black smoke. The German fighter then pulled up sharply, which forced Lundsten to break away as the remaining 190s were about to attack him.

In his own words:

I was leading Blue Section and was detailed off to attack the 'Hornchurch 190s'. I chased these e/a flying out within a few miles of the French coast and was about 6–700 yds. behind a formation of about 10. They seemed to throttle back because I closed in very quickly and fired at one of them from about 100 yds and after a few seconds burst it exploded and went into the sea. I then fired at another FW190 which had been flying line abreast with the first. I gave him a short burst and saw strikes on the fuselage followed by clouds of black smoke. He pulled up sharply and I had to break away because the remaining e/a were preparing to make attacks on me. I consider the second e/a would have been destroyed but was unable to see its finish.

Ammunition: 72 cannon
                            195 M/G

Everyone returned safely to North Weald at 8.35 a.m. No. 331 claimed six 190s shot down and four damaged, which were impressive numbers. The newspapers get hold of the fighting and reported 'Norwegians bag seven Huns before breakfast', and locals offered free pints of beer in all the pubs in the afternoon as well. However, Cato Guhnfeldt has looked into the numbers of German losses (*Spitfire Saga IV*, p. 279), and raises the question as to how accurate they were. Leif Lundsten reported seeing his prey explode and fall into the sea. Others reported a parachute and several other 190s going straight in. The statistics from the German side speak of a whole different matter. They report two losses (one apparently credited to a Typhoon squadron from the RAF), and one other 190 went down over Belgium during this day. The conclusion from Guhnfeldt is that there is no explanation for the Norwegian's high claims—they simply do not add up.

From researching Lundsten's logbook, and his particular way of reporting dogfights, he appears to have been careful to not make a claim unless absolutely certain it had been accomplished. Not even over Dieppe, in 1942, where the Norwegians were quite liberal with claims, did he make any (even if he only flew two sorties that day).

The following scenarios are most likely to explain Lundsten's encounters on this day in March 1943 (although they are only speculative):

1. There is a chance that Lundsten misunderstood what he saw (the 190 explosion and the subsequent crash into the sea).

2. Lundsten, being in good spirits after such bravado, got carried away by other pilots' claims and stories and claimed one himself.

3. Another possibility is that the German losses and reports were wrong, perhaps to cover up an embarrassing amount of losses and a mission gone horribly wrong.

4. The Typhoon Squadron's claim of a 190 shot down thirty minutes after the Norwegians dogfight was, in fact, Lundsten's kill.

The key to the mismatch of claims and German losses could have come from Lundsten's number two, Fredrik Eitzen. However, his report was short and gave little information:

I was Blue 2 and followed Blue 1 against the 'Hornchurch 190s' going flat out at zero ft. I overtook a straggler and attacked from astern and slightly above. My first burst hit the water behind it, so I fired again and hit the e/a in the cockpit. It pulled up with clouds of black smoke pouring from it, made a few slight turns and went straight into the sea.

Comparing the two reports, it may seem Eitzen was referring to the second 190, as they both spoke of an enemy fighter pulling upwards. If Eitzen followed Lundsten as he said during the whole encounter, it is odd why he did not mention the explosion from Lundsten's first claim. They landed with only five minutes between them (Lundsten first at 8.30 a.m. and Eitzen at 8.35 a.m.), without this giving much answer to the question.

One can only come to the conclusion (like Guhnfeldt) that there is no good explanation for the huge claims compared to the official German losses. But, speaking of Lundsten's character and sense for details and professionalism, it seems odd he would imagine things or suddenly start to blatantly lie about claims.

After a well-deserved breakfast, Kaj Birksted led 331 Squadron on Ramrod no. 42 to Rouen marshalling yards, providing escort to sixty Flying Fortresses (according to Leif Lundsten's logbook). They rendezvoused with the Americans over Beachy Head. All went as planned as far as 331 were concerned. No. 332 claimed one destroyed and one damaged 190 during the escort mission, and all returned safely at 1.45 p.m.

As if that was not enough during this very hectic day, Leif Lundsten (Red 1) led nine Spitfires from 331 Squadron on Rodeo no. 183. No. 331 provided top cover for 332 Squadron, which stayed further below them. Lundsten led the squadron to 19,000 feet over Neiuport, then swept starboard and continued the climb to 31,000 feet over Ypres. They left France over Ambleteuse. Enemy aircraft were reported when the wing was over the English Channel. The Norwegians did a wide orbit, but nothing further was seen. All landed safely back at base at 5.20 p.m. Readiness continued till dusk, about 7.38 p.m.—almost fourteen hours of readiness on this day, with three big shows. It is to no surprise that it was mentioned specifically in the ORB that many pilots were tired after such hectic day. Lundsten flew BS470 on all three sorties throughout this very long day.

Date: 13.03.1943
Spitfire: IX, FN-R BS467
Built: Eastleigh
Length: 1:45
Where: North Weald–Amiens–North Weald

The English weather provided the Norwegians with scattered clouds, haze, and fair wind on 13 March. Just after lunch, Lundsten and 331 were called for briefing in connection to yet another escort sortie. This time it was for Ramrod no. 43. Eighty American Flying Fortress bombers from 91, 303, 305, and 306th Bomb Group were to attack several targets in Northern France, with their main target set as Amiens. Ten Spitfires from 331 took off at 2.05 p.m., led by Wing Commander Jameson, and 332 were led by Finn Thorsager.

The wing rendezvoused with the bombers over Beachy Head a few minutes after schedule. The French coast was crossed over Dieppe where heavy flak met them. The bombers had already gone off course, perhaps due to heavy cloud. Wing Commander Jameson was told by Sector Controller to recall the bombers due to this problem, but they did not seem to notice. The Americans continued off course, and the Spitfires from North Weald were told to head for home independently from the bombers.

It would seem heavy flak and bombers off course wasn't enough action for one day, as the Luftwaffe sent large forces of fighters to meet with the formation. On their way back, while over the Somme Estuary, Yellow Section from 331 Squadron spotted four Me 109s above them, flying towards the bombers. Yellow 1, squadron veteran Helge Sognnæs from Bergen (AB457), pulled up towards the Germans alongside his number two, Tore Larssen (Yellow 2). Larssen was able to attack one of them, and claimed it as damaged. Sognnæs claimed a 190 damaged near Dungeness when he spotted two 190s who came out of clouds, turned port, and attacked one of them. Even with all the German fighters up, none of the bombers were shot down and all returned safely to their bases in England.

Date: 14.03.1943
Spitfire: IX, FN-R BS467
Built: Eastleigh
Length: 1:25, 1:45
Where: North Weald–Barrow Deep–North Weald; North Weald–Walcheren–North Weald

On this day, an early morning patrol was flown over Barrow Deep at 2,000 feet. Take-off was at 8.25 a.m. alongside five other Spitfires from 331 Squadron. Lundsten was back safely after an hour in the air. However, the day would not end with this. Rodeo no. 187 took place at 1.30 p.m., and 331 flew as top squadron, with 332 on the bottom. It was originally thought to be a sweep around the north of Walcheren, but cloud conditions prevented them from doing so. The Norwegians went down to sea level instead and flew about 3 miles off shore along the coast as far as Gravelines to intercept enemy aircraft reported to be in the area—they were thought to be on their way back home after raiding Clacton. However, nothing was seen, and everyone was back home at 3.15 p.m.

Date: 17.03.1943
Spitfire: IX, FN-R BS467
Built: Eastleigh
Length: 1:15
Where: North Weald area

The reason for the decrease in flying was yet again due to the poor weather. Fog caused severe problems for daily operations. However, there was a decent period of weather during 17 March, which was spent practising formation flying. The following days would stay mostly the same regarding the weather. After a very hectic period for Lundsten and the squadrons at North Weald, perhaps this was a welcome rest.

The 17 March was also the last sortie Leif Lundsten did with BS467.

I take a shower and dress up, but I do not have the will to walk down to the others at the bar. I lie down in my bed, in the same room that I have shared with Karsten* for so long. I am so terribly tired. I have at this point over hundred sorties behind me, and lately I've felt a strong unwillingness to take to the air. Some days it is so bad that I have to fight it hour by hour, and more than often I want to stay in bed, just sleep it all away.

Helner Grundt-Spang, *Den hemmelige kampen*, 1971, p. 51

*Karsten is a fictional name, most likely a reference to his friend Helge Sognnæs who perished 22 June 1943 in combat with FW 190s.

Date: 22.03.1943
Spitfire: IX, FN-Z BS388
Built: Chattis Hill
Length: 0:35
Where: North Weald area

Aircraft test in BS388, then formation practice later on during the day. All flying was most likely done after lunch, as thick haze covered North Weald in the morning. Twelve Spitfires took part in the formation flying.

Date: 23.03.1943
Spitfire: IX, FN-M BS466
Built: Eastleigh
Length: 1:15
Where: North Weald area

Despite the murky conditions surrounding North Weald, Lundsten took BS466 up for formation flying. It was foggy and cold in the morning, but it cleared up in the afternoon. The formation flying took place at 2 p.m.

Date: 25.03.1943
Spitfire: IX, FN-M BS466
Built: Eastleigh
Length: 1:40
Where: North Weald–St Omer–Calais–North Weald

Rodeo no. 193 took place on this day, with take-off at 3.05 p.m. Weather was still shabby, with overcast skies and slight rain. From Maidstone, the wing climbed rapidly upwards and crossed the French coast at Neufchâtel-Hardelot. Then they turned north and followed the coast 15-miles inland, making a clockwise orbit over St Omer. Two ships were spotted in Boulogne harbour. However, the mission was uneventful. Lundsten flew BS466 as he had done the day before.

Date: 28.03.1943
Spitfire: IX, FN-O BR982; IX, FN-M BS466
Built: Eastleigh
Length: 1:00, 0:40
Where: North Weald–French coast–North Weald; North Weald–Clacton–North Weald

On Sunday, 28 March 1943, Major Birksted led the wing on Ramrod no. 48. Over 100 American Liberators and Fortresses were planned to bomb Rouen and its railway system. The Norwegians intended to rendezvous with the Americans over Beachy Head, but the bombers did not turn up. The show had been cancelled due to poor weather over France. Most of the bombers did not receive the message and flew to Rouen anyway to bomb the target as planned. The Norwegians also flew to France, at 30,000 feet, but returned with nothing to report.

On this Ramrod, Lundsten flew a Spitfire he had not before taken to the skies, BR982. The Spitfire first flew 30 June 1942 and was transferred to 72 Squadron in July 1942. It had a brief spell with 401 Squadron, with the squadron letters YO-I, before being transferred yet again in December 1942 to 331 Squadron at North Weald. On 14 July 1944, it was transferred to 611 Squadron, Royal Canadian Air Force. It stayed with this squadron until Canadian J. B Story crash-landed the Spitfire near Utrecht on 5 September 1944 during a ground attack sortie. Story was taken prisoner, and the Spitfire was a write-off.

> Flying at 30,000 ft, cold as hell. No huns and no flak and no fun. Landed and refuelled at Manston.
>
> Reidar Haave-Olsen, logbook

With the weather finally having cleared, the Norwegians enjoyed a day with fair winds and clear skies. Lundsten's second take-off during this fine day in March was at 5.15 p.m., when ten Spitfires were scrambled to Clacton—he was now flying in BS466.

Date: 29.03.1943
Spitfire: IX, FN-M BS466
Built: Eastleigh
Length: 1:20
Where: North Weald–Abbeville–North Weald

Eleven Spitfires took off at 1 p.m. for Circus no. 277. No. 331 Squadron was led by Kaj Birksted. Major Helge Mehre, having returned to North Weald a few days earlier, also joined in on the sortie. The Norwegians flew as first fighter echelon to cover the retreat for Ventura bombers going to Abbeville. The wing left France south of Cayeux, and all landed safely at 2.20 p.m.

Date: 30.03.1943
Spitfire: IX, FN-T BS471
Built: Eastleigh
Length: 1:25
Where: North Weald–Clacton–Ashford–North Weald

Early morning patrol over Clacton and Ashford, with no reported incidents. Lundsten flew BS471 in the overcast weather, with very strong winds coming in from the west. Most likely the sort of weather no present day Spitfire pilots would like to risk their valuable birds in.

With this sortie, Lundsten's operational career for March 1943 ended. With still several months to go before his rest period, there would be plenty of action still to come.

21

Blue Section Attack: April 1943, 331 Squadron, North Weald, Essex

Date: 03.04.1943
Spitfire: IX, FN-T BS471
Built: Eastleigh
Length: 1:15
Where: North Weald–Beachy Head–Dungeness–North Weald

The first flight in April turned out to be a scramble. The squadron took off between 2.45 p.m. and 3 p.m. The enemy turned out to be friendlies after the squadron had orbited Beachy Head and Dungeness for about an hour. The poor weather in March had given way to fine weather, scattered clouds, and just slight haze.

Date: 04.04.1943
Spitfire: IX, FN-X BS470
Built: Eastleigh
Length: 2:00
Where: North Weald–Rouen–North Weald

April was only four days old when the Norwegians engaged the Luftwaffe again, and Leif Lundsten led 331 Squadron during the action. The wing was led by Helge Mehre. The sortie for the day was to act as withdrawal support for American bombers going to Paris to bomb the Renault factory. In more official terms, it was Ramrod no. 51. Lundsten led the squadron to their designated meeting point over Rouen, and then started their escort back home. When they reached the French coast, twenty-five German fighters were spotted below them. Lundsten gave the word to dive on four of them and attack. In return, the Germans were focusing their efforts on the American bombers, attacking them. Several dogfights took place when the Norwegians jumped the German fighters. Bjørn Bjørnstad, in BS468, claimed one destroyed, and Haave-Olsen, in AB511, claimed one probably destroyed and one damaged. Several pilots in 332 also made claims during the fierce encounter with the enemy.

Date: 05.04.1943
Spitfire: IX, FN-X BS470
Built: Eastleigh
Length: 1:55
Where: North Weald–Antwerp–North Weald

Weather was still fine, with scattered, thin cloud and fair wind—the wind then increased in the afternoon. Helge Mehre led twelve Spitfires from 331 alongside 332 to take part in Ramrod no. 52. They were to provide withdrawal cover for Liberators bombing Ford motor works at Antwerp. They rendezvoused as planned over Tholen at 3.40 p.m. at 28,000 feet. When they approached Hampstead, they get reports of about fifty enemy fighters coming in from the Dunkirk area. Just as they got this message, five German fighters approached from the ten o'clock position. Then several more Germans came in from the opposite side. No. 332 got the brunt of the fighting and made several claims. Sverre N. Larssen from 332, on his first sortie, was killed during the battle. Four pilots from 332 Squadron made claims; however, 331 made no claims, but got involved in the dogfights as well. The Norwegians escorted the Americans back to Bradwell and then went back to North Weald. No 331 Squadron pilots were lost, but it was yet another sad day for the North Weald Wing.

> I drink until I'm escorted back to my hotel room. That's the custom. Sleep takes over almost before I lie down, with my uniform still on.
>
> Helner Grundt-Spang, *Den hemmelige kampen*, p. 61

Date: 08.04.1943
Spitfire: IX, FN-R BS125
Built: Eastleigh
Length: 1:40
Where: North Weald–Dieppe–North Weald

Lundsten was back with his usual letter 'R' aircraft, but it was with a brand-new Spitfire. BS125 had its first flight on 23 July 1942. It had had a spell with 611 Squadron before it arrived with the Norwegians just four days before Lundsten took it up for its first flight, with him behind the controls on this day.

The Spitfire stayed with the Norwegians until late summer of 1943. While serving later with 313 Squadron, it was repaired on site on 5 September 1944. It also had spells with 611 Squadron (October 1944) and 312 Squadron (March 1945). With 312 Squadron (Czech), it suffered a landing accident at Manston after having departed from Maldegem in Belgium. The pilot was Jindrich Zarecky. Its undercarriage suffered minor damage, and Zarecky got away with no injuries. BS125 then went to South Africa as late as April 1948, still flying.

Lundsten's first sortie in BS125 would bring him to Dieppe on Circus no. 280. The wing made a wide orbit to port, then went up as high as 32,000 feet. Four Fw 190s were spotted 6,000 feet below them, and Red Section dived on them, followed by Yellow Section. Blue Section (most likely with Lundsten) stayed up to cover them. Surprisingly, going at enormous speed downwards, 331 did not close in on the 190s. The Norwegians concluded the Germans had started to dive as well. Torstein Strand from 332 was shot down by 190s during this encounter. He jumped out, badly injured, lost half his teeth, and his left eye was later taken out by a German doctor. He was repatriated in 1944. Everyone except Strand was back home at 7.45 p.m.

Date: 09.04.1943
Spitfire: IX, FN-R BS125
Built: Eastleigh
Length: 1:40
Where: North Weald–Walcheren–North Weald

This day featured an uneventful Rodeo to Holland. No. 331 Squadron was led by Kaj Birksted. No. 332 Squadron kept one section as low as 2,000 feet, but the Germans did not take the bait. All were back at 5.20 p.m. to 5.25 p.m. The weather throughout the day was overcast and dull.

Date: 11.04.1943
Spitfire: Vb, FN-Y/P EP769/BM408
Built: Castle Bromwich
Length: 1:45
Where: North Weald–Channel–North Weald

On this day, convoy patrols were flown from early noon until 5.15 p.m. Lundsten took his turn, together with Ingar Knutsen, with Knutsen flying AR343. The convoy patrol was uneventful, but the squadron's choice of equipment of the day was a very different matter. The older and slower V was back on the scene; in this case, there is confusion as to which Spitfire V Lundsten took to the air. The ORB listed EP796, but Lundsten listed

BM408—however, both were still in Norwegians hands in 1943. Some of these Vs were kept at North Weald for station defence, the training of new pilots, convoy patrols, and for several more purposes. It might be the case that the Norwegians did not receive new Spitfire IXs fast enough to replace the ones lost. Some of the Vs even had clipped wings.

EP769 had had an extremely long career in the air during the war. Before 331 got its hands on the Spitfire, it had been with Phillips and Powis, South Marston, and a shadow factory at Woodley, near Reading. It arrived there a month or so after it had been with 9 Maintenance Unit. Its first squadron was in fact 331 Squadron, where it arrived just nine days before Lundsten flew it on the convoy patrol. It stayed at North Weald performing the aforementioned tasks for the V version before being transferred to 310 Squadron on 14 August 1943. A month later, it was transferred to 504 Squadron. In January 1944, it was given to 67 Group United States Army Air Force. Shortly after D-Day, it was transferred to 277 Squadron before it was finally struck off charge 25 April 1946.

BM408 had a similar career, having spells with 315 Squadron before it arrived with 331. With 315 Squadron, it suffered a flying accident. Following repairs, it had a brief spell with the USAAF before arriving at North Weald. It was transferred from North Weald to 349 Squadron in August 1943. It had a period with 57 OTU before being struck off charge in June 1945.

Date: 13.04.1943
Spitfire: IX, FN-R BS125
Built: Eastleigh
Length: 1:45, 1:50
Where: North Weald–Flushing–North Weald; North Weald–Caen–North Weald

The day (13 April) ended in disaster for two pilots from 331 Squadron, following an extremely hectic mission day—Leif Lundsten participated in both of these two sorties this day.

First up was a Ramrod to Flushing, escorting twenty Venturas. The sortie turned out to be uneventful, and the squadron was back home at 1.30 p.m. It would be the sortie to Caen that would cause a serious blow to the Norwegians, and especially 331.

At 3.25 p.m., Lundsten pushed the throttle open on his Spitfire, and took off from North Weald. Together with 331 Squadron, he made his way to Selsey Bill where one orbit was made before the Ventura bombers arrived. According to Lundsten, there were twenty of them in the air. The bombers' target was Caen, France. Lundsten climbed together with the squadron, starting their climb halfway across the English Channel. They reached 17,000 feet before they levelled out. Enemy fighters were quickly reported first to the east of them, then to the west, but at an unknown height. At this point, one can assume most of the Norwegians had a slightly quicker heartbeat.

Just when they were south-west of Caen, the Germans made their presence visually known. Eight Focke-Wulf 190s dived on the closest escort of the Ventura bombers. Yellow Section, from 331, went after them, and Helge Sognnæs, Yellow 3, quickly shot one down. Then Red Section, led by Helge Mehre, was attacked by a further four 190s coming out of the sun—it caught them off-guard. Fredrik Eitzen, flying BS388 and part of Red Section (Red 3), barely made it to Ford after having been attacked and hit several times during the attack. Red 2 and Red 4 (Birk Leif Gilje, in BS468, and Eyolf Johannes Berg Olsen, in BS299, respectively) decided to break out of formation and chase after the Germans, but it turned out to be a trap. Several other enemy fighters came down on the two Norwegians and shot them both down. It was a hard blow to take, as both the pilots had had a reputation of being keen and considerably skilled pilots. Berg-Olsen had actually been in reserve for the sortie, and took Rolf Engelsen's place when he returned to North Weald with engine trouble.

It is not known in what section Lundsten flew and how he played his part. If he led Blue Section, which is very likely, he was north of the attack. Perhaps feeling a bit vulnerable, he climbed higher (to 22,000 feet) where he reported seeing more enemy fighters diving down after the Germans had spotted the Blue Section fliers, and Lundsten quickly came upwards towards them. Lundsten landed at Manston with several other pilots. He refuelled and eventually came back to North Weald at 8 p.m.

Revenge for their losses (if one can call it that) came three days later, and Leif Lundsten was the one to provide it.

Date: 14.04.1943
Spitfire: IX, FN-R BS125
Built: Eastleigh
Length: 1:45
Where: North Weald–Flushing–North Weald

As mentioned, revenge for their losses on 13 April would come, but not until two more sorties were flown. The 14th was a fine day, with a bit of haze and scattered clouds. Their sortie of the day was a repeat from the one done the day before (the first one). Ten Spitfires from 331 Squadron were led by Wing Commander Jameson. Together with 332, they flew to Walcheren. Enemy fighters were reported over Ostend, so the Norwegians set course towards them. Nothing was seen, and they were all back home safely at 5.30 p.m. Dane Kaj Birksted, 331 Squadron Leader, left the Norwegians this day for a well-deserved rest period. Birksted had, overall, been a hugely popular leader with the Norwegians.

Date: 15.04.1943
Spitfire: IX, FN-R BS125
Built: Eastleigh
Length: 1:00
Where: North Weald–St Omer–Neufchâtel-Hardelot–North Weald

Helge Mehre led nine Spitfires from 331 Squadron to the St Omer area. However, it was a rather late take-off—they didn't get airborne until 5.15 p.m. Five Spitfires returned early, so only four Spitfires were left of the original nine. Enemy aircraft were yet again reported, but these turned out to be friendly. Two Spitfires landed at West Malling, and Lundsten arrived back at North Weald at 6.15 p.m.

Date: 16.04.1943
Spitfire: IX, FN-R BS125
Built: Eastleigh
Length: 1:30
Where: North Weald–Flushing–Ostend–North Weald

Summer arrived in Essex on this day in April 1943. It was clear and warm with a slight haze. Under such weather, Lundsten and 331 Squadron would certainly be flying somewhere, although nothing was noted in his logbook, the sortie would be special for Lundsten—it was his 100th with 331.

It would be another sortie to Walcheren (an area some pilots called 'their graveyard' due to their heavy losses in the area). Wing Commander Jameson led the Norwegians on Circus no. 283, which provided plenty of action. Thirteen Ventura bombers targeted a chemical factory in the Ostend area. Spitfires from Northolt would provide close escort, while the Kenley, Biggin Hill, and North Weald Wings would make sure to keep the Germans a good distance from the Venturas. Jameson led the Norwegians over Walcheren at 20,000 feet, and a wide orbit to starboard was made. Just north-east of Flushing, four or five Focke-Wulf 190s were spotted. While Yellow Section and Helge Sognnæs had been at the front of the attack on 13 April, and Lundsten and his Blue Section had kept distance, this day would be different. The 190s were 8,000 feet below the Norwegians, and going westwards. Blue Section, led by Leif Lundsten, broke formation and dived on the enemy fighters, and Yellow Section and Red Section provided cover for the attack.

Going down towards the Germans, they caught up with them at 12,000 feet. Lundsten had three German fighters in front of him, and decided to go for the middle one. Fredrik Eitzen, Blue 2, went for the right one, and Helmer Grundt-Spang, flying as Blue 3, went for the left one. Lundsten opened fire at 800 yards, and closed in to 400 yards. Something then exploded in the 190 ahead of Lundsten. It caught fire and went straight down. Lundsten then saw three big splashes in the sea just off Walcheren—Grundt-Spang and Eitzen also saw the splashes. In Lundsten's own words:

I was flying as Blue 1 when over Walcheren Island, Red 3 reported some Huns at 3 o' clock below us. I saw them, and the whole of Blue section went down to attack them. We saw 3 FW 190s flying in line abreast, the port one a little below. This was at 12.000 feet. I attacked the middle one. I started firing at about 800 yards, closing in to about 400 yards when the FW 190 had an explosion and started burning. He went straight down. I saw afterwards three big splashes in the sea just off Walcheren Island. Blue 2 & 3 saw these splashes.

Ammo used: 126/20 mm
                                  70/303

Capt. Lundsten

According to *Spitfire Saga* (p. 323), these three 190s had very experienced pilots behind the controls. One of them was the commander of II. Gruppe/ Jagdgeschwader I, Gruppenkommandeur Major Herber Kijewski, the other Oberleutnant Hans Mohr. Both Kijewski and Mohr were shot down and killed in the attack. The third one, though, seems to be a bit more uncertain and might have gotten away.

However, Lundsten and his Blue Section's success did not come without a price. Gustav Koren, Blue 4, was last seen diving down towards a convoy in the Channel shortly after the encounter with the 190s. Lundsten went on the radio and ordered Koren to return to his place in Blue Section. Lundsten did this twice, but there were no reply from Koren. It was the last they saw of the young and inexperienced Norwegian pilot. With one man short, they all landed back at North Weald safely in the afternoon. Revenge had somewhat come, but they paid for it with the life of a young pilot.

Date: 17.04.1943
Spitfire: IX, FN-R BS125
Built: Eastleigh
Length: 1:50
Where: North Weald–Foulness–Ypres–Hazebrouck–Béthune–Lens–Lille–Gravelines–North Weald

Spitfire Glory

Another fine, warm, and hazy day. Helge Mehre led eight Spitfires from 331, together with 332, on Rodeo no. 206. Lundsten and the Norwegians climbed straight away from North Weald up to 25,000 feet. They flew past several French hot spots for German fighters. Enemy aircraft were reported by Appledore control, but none were seen by the fighters. What made the day rather special was their stop at West Malling to look at Focke-Wulf 190s that had landed there during the night. The squadron returned home at 2.40 p.m.

Date: 17.04.1943
Spitfire: IX, FN-R BS125
Built: Eastleigh
Length: 0:35
Where: North Weald–Clacton–North Weald

A scramble took place at 4.20 p.m., and Lundsten led three Spitfires to Clacton, but nothing out of the ordinary was seen. After another hectic start to the month, he would now get a rest of two days.

Date: 20.04.1943
Spitfire: IX, FN-R BS125
Built: Eastleigh
Length: 1:35
Where: North Weald–Zeebrugge–North Weald

The squadron was called to readiness at 1.45 p.m. and told to be off the ground at 2.35 p.m.; however, they were not airborne until 2.55 p.m.—it would be another Lundsten-led sortie. This time he led Circus no. 289— Lundsten and his company of Spitfires would provide target support to twelve Venturas bombing Zeebrugge. No enemy fighters were seen, and there was no flak, making the sortie very uneventful. Everyone was back home in one piece.

Marius Eriksen, from 332 Squadron, shot down a Junkers 88 over Clacton on this day.

Date: 21.04.1943
Spitfire: IX, FN-R BS125
Built: Eastleigh
Length: 1:20
Where: North Weald–Abbeville–North Weald

The day started out with sunshine and fine weather, but deteriorated throughout the day ending with rain and wet conditions. However, it did not stop Lundsten from leading nine Spitfires from 331 Squadron to Abbeville together with 332—Patrick Jameson led the wing. They swept inland towards Abbeville, and spotted some friendly bombers with escort coming out behind them. The North Weald Wing then went to Gris Nez and made a wide starboard orbit. Throughout the mission, the Luftwaffe did not show up.

Date: 25.04.1943
Spitfire: V, FN-N BM295
Built: Castle Bromwich
Length: 1:20
Where: North Weald–Channel–North Weald

The mission of the day was a convoy patrol with the old Mk Vs, which were still kept at North Weald. Lundsten had flown BM295 several times before, but with the squadron letter 'M' instead of 'N'. The weather was variable, and there was a strong wind over Essex.

Date: 28.04.1943
Spitfire: V, FN-N BM295
Built: Castle Bromwich
Length: 0:40
Where: North Weald–Martlesham Heath–North Weald

Lundsten took BM295 to Martlesham Heath and then returned the same day. The Norwegians performed cine-gun practice and squadron formations during the day. This could be connected to his flight to Martlesham Heath.

Date: 29.04.1943
Spitfire: V, FN-T BS471
Built: Eastleigh
Length: 1:20
Where: North Weald–Abbeville–St Omer–North Weald; North Weald–Flushing–North Weald

With the weather clearing up, Lundsten joined 331 Squadron on Ramrod no. 66 to Abbeville. The Norwegians provided cover for Westland Whirlwinds bombing railway lines in the area. They swept in over Berck-sur-Mer at 19,000 feet. By the time they were over Gravelines they had reached 26,000 feet. Enemy fighters were reported to the south of them, but none were seen by the Norwegians. There was reported to be a wind speed of over 100 miles per hour at 20,000 feet, coming in from the north. All participating pilots landed safely at 1.10 p.m.

They had time for a quick bite to eat and perhaps a cup of coffee before Lundsten and his fellow pilots took off once again. This time for a diversionary sweep in the Flushing area. The wing refuelled at Manston and took off from there at 5.25 p.m. Helge Mehre led the Norwegians on the deck for the first ten minutes of the sortie, and then climbed up to 25,000 feet. They continued to make a wide right-hand orbit over Walcheren. Over Flushing and Ostend, they were met with very heavy flak, but no one got hit.

Another month done with several friends gone, but the Norwegians had once again stood their ground against the opposition. Leif Lundsten had survived for over 100 operational sorties, and could add another destroyed German fighter to his name during this busy month in 1943.

22

Junkers Ju 88 Shot Down: May 1943, 331 Squadron, North Weald, Essex

Date: 01.05.1943
Spitfire: IX, FN-T BS471
Built: Eastleigh
Length: 2:00
Where: North Weald–Caen–North Weald

The first day of May started out cloudy, with occasional, typical-English showers. Lundsten and 331 Squadron were up fairly early, and were briefed for Circus no. 293, which was planned for 10.10 a.m. Their task for the day was to fly as forward support for twelve Bostons bombing the Caen marshalling yards. Due to thick cloud cover, the wing became split up over the French coast. Lundsten and his fellow colleagues orbited off Le Havre, and then set off for home. They were back exactly two hours after take-off.

It is to worth mentioning that Leif Lundsten did not participate on the disastrous sortie on 2 May 1943, where four Norwegian pilots were shot down over Walcheren, including what was largely accepted as 332 Squadrons most talented pilot, Marius Eriksen. Lundsten lost a pilot who often flew with him in Blue Section, and had stuck with him during the fights of 12 March 1943—this was Fredrik Eitzen. Rolf Engelsen, flying with Blue Section from time to time, was also lost. Engelsen and Eriksen survived the war as POWs. Eitzen was killed during the fight, and Nils Jørgen Fuglesang was murdered after he participated in the 'Great Escape'. While the Norwegians got into serious trouble over Holland, Leif Lundsten was busy flying the Tiger Moth to Biggin Hill with a passenger.

Date: 03.05.1943
Spitfire: IX, FN-O BR982
Built: Eastleigh
Length: 0:55
Where: North Weald–Walcheren–Dunkirk–North Weald

The weather was clear, but cold during the day. There was no action until late in the afternoon when Leif Lundsten got the task of leading 331 Squadron on Rodeo no. 212. The squadron took off at 5.05 p.m., with 332 Squadron and Wing Commander Jameson (who flew with 332). Over Walcheren, they saw plenty of American P-47 Thunderbolts. They left the enemy coast over Dunkirk and came home without any incidents.

Date: 04.05.1943
Spitfire: IX, FN-O BR982 or FN-X BS470
Built: Eastleigh
Length: 1:30
Where: North Weald–Le Tréport–Abbeville–Le Crotoy–North Weald

Leif Lundsten listed BR982 as his Spitfire for this sortie; however, the ORB listed BS470 as his Spitfire of the day and Helner Grundt-Spang was flying BR982. Lundsten had also written down that he had damaged a 190 in combat on 3 May, which was incorrect. Instead, he had damaged the aircraft on 4 May. So with that in mind, he may have mixed up his dates and the Spitfires that he was flying during these first days of May. He also added 'X' on his reference to his cine-gun, which more than indicates his logbook is wrong on this occasion.

The squadron took off as late as 7 p.m. for Circus no. 294 to France, with Wing Commander Jameson leading. No. 332 Squadron also came along with nine Spitfires. They left the English coast over Rye at 5,000 feet, and continued to climb to 31,000 feet over the Abbeville area. Someone, or several pilots in 331 Squadron, then spotted two boxes of enemy fighters about 2,000 feet below and slightly behind. No. 331 turned sharply and dived down on the Germans while 332 stayed up as cover—it was a perfect bounce. Lundsten, who was leading Blue Section, damaged a 190. The Norwegians claimed three 109s destroyed and three damaged.

> I was Blue 1. Blue 3 dived on the first lot of e/a and I tried to take the second lot. When I was about 1,000 yds behind the last one, the Me 109s must have seen me as they started to dive. I followed and closed to about 4–500 yds and fired a short burst seeing strikes on the port wing and a piece fall off. I then had to break away. I claim the e/a as damaged.

Ammunition: Cannon 18
                     MG: 50

Cine-gun carried and exposed. Ref. 331/4/5/X.

Date: 07.05.1943
Spitfire: IX, FN-R BS125
Built: Eastleigh
Length: 1:30
Where: North Weald–St Omer–North Weald

The Norwegians quickly adopted English traditions, such as tea time. This was even mentioned in the squadrons ORB from time to time—as it was on this day. No. 331 Squadron left North Weald behind after tea at 6.10 p.m. There were ten Spitfires from 331 Squadron involved, and Lundsten led Blue Section as normal, while Helge Mehre led the whole of 331. No. 332 Squadron stayed below 331. They started their climb over Maidstone, and crossed the enemy coast over Berck-sur-Mer. They then headed for St Omer and gradually climbed upwards. Four Me 109s were spotted over St Omer, heading south. A section from 332 broke away to attack them, with two pilots making claims (damaged) in the encounter that followed.

Date: 08.05.1943
Spitfire: IX, FN-R BS125
Built: Eastleigh
Length: 0:50
Where: North Weald–local–North Weald

This historic day provided both Lundsten and several onlookers on the ground plenty of action. Interestingly, it would also be Lundsten's last sortie in BS125, and his last using the 'R' squadron letter. It would turn out to be a memorable last sortie.

During the early morning, Luftwaffe had sent eight Junkers 88 over Britain to cause trouble. They used the cloud cover as protection while over England. The weather had deteriorated, and strong winds had also set in. This was of little trouble to Leif Lundsten and Knut Bache—they were at readiness in the early morning, ready to fly if needed.

Most people at North Weald were still asleep when the alarm went off. A Junkers 88 had just flown straight across North Weald Airfield. From their position at B-flight, Knut Bache and Leif Lundsten ran to their Spitfires and took off to hunt down the intruder. Airborne in short time, they were told to patrol the base, which they did for thirty minutes. They were then informed by the flight controller that a bandit was flying towards London at 4,000 feet. Lundsten and Bache, having stayed below cloud cover until now, asked to go up above the clouds, which they were given permission to do. They quickly spotted an unknown aircraft, which one of them (or both) identified as a de Havilland Mosquito flying south. Controller gave them a new course, which they followed. It was at that minute that they spotted a Junkers 88 at three o'clock going in the same direction as the two Norwegians. Lundsten decided to climb higher before attacking the German, and took his Spitfire up to 6,000 feet, Bache was following behind. Gaining on the Junkers, Lundsten dived down and opened fire from dead astern—he did not miss. The port engine caught fire and the Junkers dived downwards. Lundsten then broke away, and let Knut Bache finish the German off. Down at 3,000 feet, Bache opened fire at the stricken Junkers 88. Several hits were observed, including in the cockpit area, and the German then flicked over, broke into three large pieces, and crashed into a field just 6 miles south-west of North Weald, at Stapleford Hall Farm. One piece of the enemy aircraft was seen explode when it hit the ground. One of the crew had managed to get out, but his chute did not open properly and he went down fast. Lundsten and Bache turned back and landed at North Weald, under an hour after their take-off.

Very rarely, or at all, had the war come so close to the Norwegian ground crew at North Weald—this was more common back in 1940, during the Battle of Britain. Many of them had heard the Junkers 88 fly over the base before Lundsten and Bache took off. Several others had witnessed the fight from the ground. Many of the pilots had woken up from the sound of shooting, or heard what was going on from wherever they may have been during that morning. Finn Thorsager, CO of 332 Squadron, heard the shooting while he was at the Officers Mess. Bjørn Ræder, also 332 Squadron, woke up to loud, excited voices talking about an enemy aircraft over the base. A lot of these witnesses have spoken about their experiences during this encounter in *Spitfire Saga IV* (pp. 37–38). Here are some of them, translated:

I'm lying down [in bed], snoring away when I wake up to noisy voices outside on the terrace. I understood from them there was a German aircraft very close by the base.

Bjørn Ræder.

When Lundsten shot down the German this morning before breakfast, it is possible he only managed to shoot with one of his cannons. He went to high school at Gjøvik while I was in middle school at Raufoss. He was a quiet but very likable guy.

Paul Kjølseth, ground crew.

I heard shooting while I was in the Officers Mess, which was unusual and went outside. I was soon told that a Junkers 88 was shot down.

I jumped into a car and drove to where the wreck was located. The aircraft was on fire, and everyone onboard was killed.

Finn Thorsager

On the day of the shooting down of the Junkers 88, I was farming at Hammonds Farm, Stapleford Tawney. I heard ack-ack fire to the west and I went outside to see what was happening. The ack-ack fire had stopped. There was a bank of cloud to the west stretching from north to south and a plane came out of the cloud. The Spitfires dived on the Junkers with cannon fire. The plane was losing height and the Spitfires were coming in from both sides firing cannons. The noise was terrible and pieces were flying off the Junkers including the upper gun turret which fell in the field not more than 150 yards away [however, the Junkers did not have a gun turret like this]. The Spitfires continued firing and the Junker was getting lower and lower, and was on fire as it passed over St Mary's church at Stapleford Abbots. I was in the Home Guard and found one of the crew who had landed in a small meadow beside the church. His parachute had been cut off his back—I imagine by the tail plane. The Junkers crashed in flames just north of Stapleford Hall, not far from the church. I think the rest of the crew were killed. I collected the gun turret and machine gun and handed it in.

John Mugleston, Home Guard.

I was one of those who buried the four Germans that was shot down the other day, they got a pretty good ceremony. Six men from each of the squadrons [Nos 331, 332, and 124 Squadrons] were picked out to join the ceremony and from S.H.Q plus 24 men from the RAF regiment at the airfield. Their caskets covered with the swastika flag and flowers from officers and privates from the airfield.

Ragnvald Myhre, ground crew.

1 Ju. 88 destroyed six miles from base by Lundsten & myself. Crew of four were killed.

Knut Bache, logbook.

The names of the Junkers 88 who met their fate over Essex this morning in May 1943 were Oberfeldwebel F. Kiesel, Unteroffizier P. Shonwalder, Obergefreiter Alfred Kloske, and Gefreiter H. Bosse. Three of them are

found in the main wreck, and a fourth are found with the tail section
four hundred yards away

Spitfire Saga IV, p. 37

After the war, Ragnvald Myhre—a member of the ground crew at North
Weald—recalled how he often thought about how crazy war seemed to
be. They had just buried four young Germans in British soil, and back in
Germany their families did not even know they were gone.

The tail section from the Junkers was later put on display in Epping, with
a sign that read 'Shot down by Norwegians'. A part of the Junkers 88 was
later hung up on the wall in 331 Squadron's dispersal, A-flight. Both Bache
and Lundsten were reportedly offered souvenirs from the Junkers 88 for
their own personal collections.

The intelligence combat report from this day:

Blue section of 331 Squadron was scrambled at 0710 hours and
ordered to patrol base below cloud at 2,000 feet which they continued
to do for thirty minutes. They were then informed by sector controller
(Flight Lieutenant Cook) of a Bandit, believed to be a Ju 88, flying
towards London at 4,000 feet southwest of base. The section received
permission to go above cloud and climbed to 5,000 feet into the sun.
Turning, they sighed a Mosquito heading south, which they followed
for about one minute when a vector of 210 degrees were received while
they were just over base. This course had just been set when they Ju
88 was sighted at 3' clock, 1,500 yards away, travelling in the same
direction. Blue section climbed to about 6,000 feet and then dived on
the enemy aircraft from dead astern. Blue 1—Captain Lundsten—
opened fire at 400 yards and closed to 200 yards. He saw hits on the
tail united and port engine and set the starboard engine on fire. Blue
1 then broke away and the enemy aircraft went into a steep, diving
turn to starboard, flattening out at about 3,000 feet. Blue 2—Second
Lieutenant Bache—then went in to attack, firing a long burst from
200 yards and seeing hits on the cockpit and port engine. The enemy
aircraft flicked over out of control, broke into three large pieces and
crashed into a field six miles southwest of base at Stapleford Hall Farm.
One piece of the enemy aircraft exploded on the ground.

Blue 2 saw a parachute at 2,000 feet, but this was either on fire or
did not open properly and went down very fast.

The bodies of three of the crew were found in the burnt out wreckage,
while the tail unit of the enemy aircraft and the other body were about 400
yards from the main wreck. Throughout the combat no return fire was

received and the enemy aircraft took no evasive action whatever, flying straight and level and being perfectly silhouetted against a background of white clouds. Most of the combat was witnessed by personnel at North Weald, including the writer who also visited the wreckage of the aircraft. It was coloured greenish gray with very dirty black crosses and lettering hardly visible. The underneath of the aircraft was black.

Sector Intelligence Officer, RAF Station North Weald

Lundsten, Captain, K. Bache, Second Lieutenant

The words of Lundsten and Baches combat quickly reached the civilian population. There was a never-ending flow of free pints of beer to all Norwegians during the evening.

Date: 11.05.1943
Spitfire: IX, FN-T BS471; V, FN-P BM408
Built: Eastleigh, Castle Bromwich
Length: 0:25, 1:25
Where: North Weald–local–North Weald; North Weald–Channel–North Weald

Lundsten was back to his usual routine at North Weald after the Junkers 88 had been shot down a few days earlier. It was a clear and sunny day at North Weald, although rather cool.

Lundsten took off in BS471 for Circus no. 295. Newcomer Gregers W. Gram flew Lundsten's (up until now) personal Spitfire BS125. While still gaining height over North Weald, they received orders that the operation was cancelled, and the squadron landed again.

Helner Grundt-Spang and Bjørn Bjørnstad left 331 Squadron for a rest period. Svein Heglund and Martin Gran came back for a new tour of operations. It was only a matter of days now until Lundsten too would get his rest period. Heglund subsequently took over B-flight once Leif Lundsten left.

The cancelled show was followed by an evening convoy patrol with Gregers W. Gram. Both flew the older mark Vs on this occasion. It was said about Gram that he did not have to swallow when he drank beer.

Date: 12.05.1943
Spitfire: IX, FN-T BS471
Built: Eastleigh
Length: 0:40
Where: North Weald–Coltishall–North Weald

The day featured a round trip to Coltishall. Lundsten was one of eleven Spitfire pilots who went and returned in the afternoon. There are no details about the trip or why they went to Coltishall.

Date: 15.05.1943
Spitfire: IX, FN-S MA225
Built: Castle Bromwich
Length: 1:40
Where: North Weald–Abbeville–Amiens–North Weald

It was a nice, warm summer day on 15 May 1943. In the afternoon, the Norwegians provided an escort for B-25 Mitchell bombers going to Caen airfield. Fifteen minutes later, Hawker Typhoons would come in and attack the same airfield. The North Weald Wing provided a fighter echelon for the bombers, led by Helge Mehre (now Wing Commander, having replaced Patrick Jameson). Just north of Amiens, 331 Squadron bounced two groups of 190s, and Mehre claimed one destroyed. The wing then reformed over the Somme Estuary, and flew home towards North Weald.

Lundsten flew his first sortie in MA225 on this day. It had arrived only four days earlier—factory fresh—and it stayed with 331 Squadron for nearly a year. It participated in Operation Starkey and had red, white, and blue cannon fairings painted on. From 19 June 1944, it served with 229 Squadron. On 15 September 1944, Flight Sergeant J. Manley and Flight Sergeant O'Reilly took off at 9.10 a.m. on a Jim Crow to patrol areas of Holland. The weather was poor and became worse as they crossed the channel. They made landfall an hour later, approximately north of Limuiden. They turned north and crossed out again at 200 feet where they were met with intense flak from the coastal area. Manley, in MA225, was hit. They then set course 280 degrees for base, and climbed to 3,000 feet as Manley knew he would most likely need to bale out. O'Reilly formatted on him, and saw how Manley's rudder was shot away. When about 30 miles west of Limuiden, Manley was seen by O'Reilly to prepare to bale out. Flames and white smoke came out of MA225s exhaust and the Spitfire went into a spiral. Manley managed to jump out, and the chute was seen to open at 500 feet. It remained in the water for about five minutes, but Manley was not seen. O'Reilly climbed up to 3,500 feet and set course for home as there was nothing more he could do for his colleague. Manley was killed and Lundsten's former Spitfire disappeared in the Channel.

Date: 17.05.1943
Spitfire: IX, FN-S MA225
Built: Castle Bromwich
Length: 1:10, 1:40, 1:05
Where: North Weald–RAF Bolt Head, Devon–Lorient–Warmwell–North Weald

The 17th was Norway's national day of independence, and there were several arrangements organised to celebrate the special day. Sports competition and a dance at the station seemed to have been of the highest interest. However, although it was national day, it did not mean Lundsten and the Norwegians got the day off. They were airborne as early as 7.30 a.m., acting as second withdrawal cover for American Fortresses on their way back from bombing the submarine base at Lorient. No. 331 had to land at RAF Bolt Head, Devon, to refuel. The airfield was nothing more than a strip of grass. It was noted by somewhat spoiled Norwegians, used to a pre-war airfield like North Weald, that the RAF Bolt Head strip was only 1,000 metres long. On their way back, while escorting the last box of Fortresses, they detected fifteen 190s. Martin Gran, just back from his rest period, flew in Lundsten's section as Blue 3, and Knut Bache was Blue 4. Gran took special notice of one 190 at 20,000 feet. He called up and simply said, 'going down!'—he took Bache with him, and they both claimed one 190 destroyed. The dogfight was observed by Lundsten and he confirmed that he had seen splashes in the sea. Martin Gran's encounter with the 190s was vividly told in a Norwegian aviation magazine called *Vi Flyr* (translated: 'We are flying') in the 1965 May edition. It was a special edition about Norway's Air Force during the Second World War.

The squadron landed at Warmwell before they went home to North Weald, where they arrived back at 4.30 p.m. Celebrations for 17 May could finally begin. It remains unclear just how hungover the pilots were the day after, when they went to Abbeville.

Date: 18.05.1943
Spitfire: IX, FN-S MA225
Built: Castle Bromwich
Length: 0:10
Where: North Weald–Abbeville–North Weald

Rolf Arne Berg led 331 Squadron on Circus no. 300. They took off at 2.20 p.m., but Lundsten turned back after only ten minutes. It is unknown what kind of difficulty made him turn MA225 back to North Weald so early.

Date: 19.05.1943
Spitfire: IX, FN-S MA225
Built: Castle Bromwich
Length: 1:30, 0:30
Where: North Weald–Béthune–North Weald; North Weald–Channel–North Weald

Two sorties were flown by Lundsten on this clear and warm spring day. Ten Spitfires, led by Rolf Arne Berg, swept as far as Béthune at 29,000 feet before they turned for home. The Luftwaffe did not come up to fight.

In the evening, Lundsten did a patrol between 7.10 p.m. and 7.40 p.m. without incident.

Date: 20.05.1943
Spitfire: IX, FN-S MA225
Built: Castle Bromwich
Length: 1:20
Where: North Weald–Ypres–Neufchâtel-Hardelot–North Weald

The day was described as a hot summer's day. Lundsten flew with 331 as usual. No. 332 Squadron was led by Wing Commander Mehre. Their task was Rodeo no. 222 over France. All aircraft and pilots returned safely.

Date: 21.05.1943
Spitfire: IX, FN-S MA225
Length: 0:45
Where: North Weald–Channel–North Weald

Another cancelled event, this time as Lundsten was halfway across the channel. B-25 Mitchell bombers were supposed to bomb Abbeville, but the weather quickly deteriorated, and the sortie was cancelled (according to *Spitfire Saga IV*, p. 67). In the squadrons ORB, it states that the wing was recalled due to trouble with jettisoning their extra fuel tanks.

Date: 22.05.1943
Spitfire: IX, FN-T LZ920
Built: Castle Bromwich
Length: 0:50
Where: North Weald–Channel–North Weald

Lundsten flew an air test in a brand-new Spitfire—LZ920—on this day. Some sources stated the Spitfire did not arrive until the day after, but Lundsten did indeed test the Spitfire on 22 May. It stayed with the Norwegians until 26 September 1944 when it went to 611 Squadron. On 2 May 1945, Miroslav Kratochvil from 310 Squadron had an engine failure while flying LZ920. He force-landed the Spitfire near Tangmere, but hit a tree in the process. It was therefore struck off charge and did not fly again. Kratochvil was injured, but fortunately he survived.

Date: 23.05.1943
Spitfire: IX, FN-T LZ920
Built: Castle Bromwich
Length: 1:15
Where: North Weald–Zeebrugge–North Weald

The popular (and now legendary) man from Orkanger, Norway, Rolf Arne Berg led 331 Squadron on Circus no. 302. Wing Commander Mehre flew with 332 Squadron. They acted as withdrawal cover for Ventura bombers leaving the Belgian coast near Zeebrugge. However, it was an uneventful sortie. The weather closed in during the night, which would prevent any flying the next day except for the following convoy patrol.

Date: 24.05.1943
Spitfire: V, FN-J BL862
Built: Castle Bromwich
Length: 1:20
Where: North Weald–Channel–North Weald.

A convoy patrol was flown in one of the remaining mark Vs at the base. This was BL862, and it was Lundsten's first flight in this specific Spitfire. The weather was horrible with heavy rain, but the convoy patrol was done regardless.

Built at Castle Bromwich, BL862 had a long career. At 340 Squadron, in March 1942, it was given the squadron letter GW-H. It flew as GW-H over Dieppe during the raid in August the same year. It had a spell with the US Air Force the same year before it arrived at 602 Squadron in January 1943. No. 331 Squadron received the Mk V on 13 April 1943. It continued onwards to 504 Squadron in September 1943. With 3 OTU, it had a flying accident on 5 October 1944. It had its last accident at Hibaldstow on 29 March 1945. It taxied into obstacles on the ground and was category 'C' damaged, but it was repaired on site. What happened next to BL862 remains unclear.

Date: 25.05.1943
Spitfire: IX, FN-T LZ920
Built: Castle Bromwich
Length: 1:20, 1:05
Where: North Weald–Neufchâtel-Hardelot–Hesdin–North Weald; North Weald–Le Touquet–North Weald

With the weather having cleared up, Circus no. 304 took place at 10.20 a.m., and the North Weald Wing flew to Neufchâtel-Hardelot and Hesdin at 28,000 feet. While the Norwegians did their bit, B-25 Mitchells bombed Abbeville airfield. It was yet another uneventful sortie, and they were all back safely at 11.45 a.m.—just in time for lunch.

A Rodeo was planned in the evening, and Lundsten was yet again on the roster to participate in the sortie. They made a wide orbit over the Channel close by Le Touquet at 18,000 feet, but the weather was bad and it was decided to return to base.

These two sorties would be the last operational flying for Leif Lundsten until 29 May. The Norwegians continued their operations in his absence.

Date: 29.05.1943
Spitfire: IX, FN-T LZ920
Built: Castle Bromwich
Length: 0:50, 0:10, 0:35
Where: North Weald–Ibsley; Ibsley–Channel–Ibsley; Ibsley–North Weald

The Norwegians left North Weald for Ibsley, just north of Bournemouth. They were to provide withdrawal cover for a large formation of Flying Fortresses bombing St Nazaire and the submarine docks. Leif Lundsten joined the squadron, taking off from Ibsley at 3.40 p.m., but had to return only ten minutes later as he had problems with his drop tank. He was not the only one, and four other Spitfires joined him on his return. He landed back at Ibsley most likely a bit frustrated to see the rest of the squadron head for the Brittany area; however, the rest of the Norwegians did not see anything of the bombers. Back at Ibsley, they were told the bombers passed over the aerodrome just five minutes before they landed.

Date: 30.05.1943
Spitfire: IX, FN-T LZ920
Built: Castle Bromwich
Length: Unknown
Where: North Weald area

Above: Bilitt train station in 1902, shortly after its opening. The station was operational until 1988, when it was demolished in order to expand Rv244 (the road going to Skreia). (*Author's Collection*)

Below: The village of Bilitt, Østre Toten, photographed in the 1950s. Since then, the large building to the left, Espelien gården, has been demolished. The liquour distillery is also long gone, now replaced by an industrial complex. (*Author's Collection*)

Above left: The three Lundsten children visiting the photographer, most likely in the town of Gjøvik in the early 1920s. (*Morten Lundsten's Collection*)

Above right: A school photo of Leif Lundsten. (*Morten Lundsten's Collection*)

Below left: A picture of Leif Lundsten during his Kjeller days—1938–1939. (*Morten Lundsten's Collection*)

Below right: Lundsten at his parents' home (most likely after the family moved to Rånåsfossen). Leif had already obtained his wings, as you can see on his right shoulder. (*Morten Lundsten's Collection*)

Above: Leif Lundsten with his family. It's understandable why Olav Gundersen said Leif 'looked like a Lundsten' by looking at his father (to Leif's right). (*Morten Lundsten's Collection*)

Below: Leif Lundsten (right) at Bilitt, in front of the demolished Espelien gården. The photo was most likely taken in the winter before Leif left for Kjeller. By the amount of snow on the ground, it could be late February or March. (*Morten Lundsten's Collection*)

Leif's Kjeller classmates. Several became legendary pilots within the RAF (and RNAF).
First row: Jan Christie and Stein Sem.
Second row: Rolf Arne Berg, Tycho Moe, Kristian Fredrik Schye, and Tarald Weisteen.
Third row: Anton Chr. Hagerup and Erik Hagen.
Fourth row: Per Adolph Thorén, Leif Lundsten, Øyvind Ofstad, and Werner Christie.
  Schye was involved in a dogfight with a Messerschmitt 110 on 9 April 1940, and he was flying a Gloster Gladiator. Stein Sem became the B-Flight Leader for 331, before he was killed in December 1942. Erik Hagen flew Spitfires with 332 Squadron. Werner Christie became Squadron Leader for 332 and later Wing Commander for the Hunsdon Wing—he survived the war. Rolf Arne Berg was the Wing Commander for 132 Wing, before he was killed in action in February 1945. Anton Chr. Hagerup lost his life in June 1943 when his Mosquito crashed in Stavenes, Norway. Flying with 139 Squadron, Tycho Moe lost his life in a Mosquito in February 1943. Per Adolph Thorén lost his life in August 1943, flying Mosquitos with 85 Squadron. Tarald Weisteen became A-Flight Leader in 331 Squadron before moving to 85 Squadron—he also survived the war. (*Kristian Fredrik Schye's Collection*)

Four graduated pilots from Kjeller, 1938–1939, who all lost their lives during the Second World War. Left to right: Leif Lundsten, Rolf Arne Berg, Per Svanøe Endresen, and Stein Sem. (*Jonas W. Endresen's Collection*)

The entire class of Kjeller 1938–1939. Leif Lundsten is second from the left, on the back row. (*Morten Lundsten's Collection*)

Photograph taken during the official opening party of 'Little Norway' in 1941. Leif Lundsten is on the far left, closest to the camera, with his date by his side. Sixth from the left is Stein Sem. (*Cecilie Waaler's Collection*)

Leif Lundsten, Arnt Hvinden, and Morten Ree in Britain, shortly after arriving from occupied Norway. (*Erik Hagen's Collection*)

A detailed look into just how little was left of the Hurricane's rudder and elevator after Lundsten's mid-air crash with Jens Müller. (*Helge Mehre*)

The collision with a 124 Squadron Spitfire. (*Morten Lundsten's Collection*)

Spitfire IIa P8729 at Skeabrea with the Norwegians. The pilots are Ulf Wormdahl and Morten Ree. Leif Lundsten flew this Spitfire on 19 December 1942. (*Forsvarsmuseet*)

Tarald Weisteen, Leif Lundsten, and Erik Fossum at Skeabrea. Lundsten is seen here smoking a cigarette. (*Svein Heglund's Collection*)

Above left: A photograph of legendary 74 Squadron pilot John Freeborn, who shot down a Dornier 215 in 1940 while flying P7366. (*Author's Collection*)

Above right: Leif Lundsten in front of a Spitfire at North Weald. If the Spitfire is his personal aircraft, it could very well be BS467 or BS125. He flew BS125 for the first time 8 April 1943. (*Forsvarsmuseet*)

Something has caught their attention—possibly a Spitfire coming in for a landing. Lundsten is still with his cigarette. Considering the lack of winter clothes, this could have been taken in the spring of 1942. (*Svein Heglund's Collection*).

On 23 February 1942, Lundsten used Spitfire IIa P7357 on a special convoy patrol. They later received great praise from the admiral of the fleet. (*Forsvarsmuseet*)

Spitfire Vb BL891 (third from left) was flown by Ottar Malm from Catterick to North Weald on 4 May 1942. It ended its days following a crash into a barbed-wire fence in 1944; at the time of this incident, it was under the control of Squadron Leader J. E. Jones. (*Finn Thorsager*)

Spitfire Vb AR328, which would become Lundsten's personal Spitfire, is photographed here at Skeabrea, with Kristian Nyerrød in the cockpit. From left to right (excluding Nyerrød): Erik Fossum, Anton Chr. Hagerup, and Jens Müller. (*Kristian Nyerrød*)

Spitfire Vb AR296, used by Leif Lundsten for a Circus to St Omer on 30 July 1942. In the summer of 1942, it was usually flown by Martin Gran. The Spitfire is shown here at Skeabrea, with Kristian Nyerrød in the foreground. On 31 July 1942, Lundsten also used AR296 on Circus no. 201 to Le Crotoy, in addition to the subsequent search for their mission comrades. (*Kristian Nyerrød's Collection*)

Before the battle over Dieppe on 19 August 1942, fifteen 331 Squadron pilots were photgraphed at North Weald.

Front row, left to right: Reidar Haave-Olsen, Kristian Nyerrød, Fredrik Fearnley and Varg, Kaj Birksted, and Tarald Weisteen.

Middle row, left to right: Helge Sognnæs, Leif Lundsten, Stein Sem, Knut Bache, Anton C. Hagerup, Rolf Arne Berg, Intelligence Officer Philip Yatman, Rolf Engelsen, and Svein Heglund.

Back row, left to right: Johannes Greiner and Martin Gran.

Seven of them survived the war—Nyerrød, Birksted, Weisteen, Engelsen, Heglund, Greiner, and Gran (as well as Intelligence Officer Yatman). (*Ole Friele Backer*)

Back from the sortie over St Omer, Leif Lundsten and Martin Gran listen to General Wilhelm von Tangen Hansteen (left) talking to Helge Mehre (right). In the background is Einar Sem-Olsen. These photogaphs were taken between 1.15 p.m. and 4.50 p.m., before the sortie to France. (*Ole Friele Backer*)

Another photogaph taken by Ole Friele Backer, showing von Tangen Hansteen talking to Leif Lundsten and Martin Gran outside 331 Squadron's dispersal. (*Ole Friele Backer*)

Reidar Haave-Olsen's IX, BS445, *Nuts to Nazis*. While it cannot be concluded that Lundsten flew BS445 on 6 October 1942, it is worth adding the photograph anyway. Reidar Haave-Olsen was a popular character in the Squadron, with an eagerness to take to the air and face the Germans that very few others could match. He lost his life in a flying accident not far from North Weald in February 1944. (*Ole Friele Backer*)

A photo of Leif Lundsten's IX, BS467, the Spitfire he would later fly when he claimed several German fighters shot down in the spring of 1943. In the end, the Spitfire outlived its 'owner' by at least four years. Here photographed in the Middle East. Note the clipped wings. (*Author's Collection*)

Leif Lundsten, Kaj Birksted, Guy Peter Lockwood Owren, and Stein Sem in front of a 331 Squadron Spitfire in November 1943. Lockwood Owren and Sem both lost their lives before the year was over.

Spitfire BS470, FN-X, at North Weald in autumn 1943, with Kristian Nyerrød in the foreground. Lundsten flew the Spitfire on several occasions; the most eventful of these was a sortie on 12 March 1943, when he attacked two Focke-Wulf 190s. (*Kristian Nyerrød*)

Another angle of the opposite image, with more pilots in the frame. From left to right: Reidar Haave-Olsen, Knut Bache, Kristian Nyerrød, Leif Lundsten, Kaj Birksted, Guy Peter Lockwood Owren, and Stein Sem. (*Ole Friele Backer*)

Kaj Birkstead lights Lundsten's cigarette after yet another day of operations at North Weald. Lundsten is seen with a cigarette in his hand in several photographs during the war. (*Ole Friele Backer*)

Drop tanks were a problem that kept haunting the Norwegians at the start of 1943. Leif Lundsten returned prematurely several times due to these issues, as on 8 January 1943. (*Author's Collection*)

An artist's impression of Leif Lundsten's attack on the Junkers 88 on 8 May 1943. There was a rumour that Lundsten only fired one cannon during the attack, but this was widely discredited. (*Antoine Crespin, London: www.facebook.com/AviationArtAntoineCrespin*)

Spitfire VIII JF275, Lundsten's first Mk VIII. Sadly, it was eventually scrapped in Argentina. (*ricardogriffon@ciudad.com.ar*)

Above: MA970 had folded wings and a four-bladed prop. (*Peter Arnold's Collection*)

Below: Spitfire VIII JF880, photogaphed while serving with 417 Squadron in Italy. Lundsten flew the Spitfire on 31 August 1943. (*Author's Collection*)

Seafire III MA970 was an important part of the story behind the aircraft's future development. Lundsten flew the Seafire on several occations during late summer and autumn 1943, the first time being on 24 August 1943. (*Peter Arnold's Collection*)

Aerial view of Chattis Hill shortly after the Second World War ended. (*Author's Collection*)

The impressive Spitfire XII prototype, DP845, first flown by Leif Lundsten on 23 September 1943. (*Crown*)

Spitfire XII MB882, known as 'the last of the XII'. It was picked up at High Post by Leif Lundsten on 24 September 1943 and subsequently test flown. Here it is photographed in October 1943 by Charles Brown; it is being flown by Lundsten's fellow test pilot at the time, Clive Gosling. (*Charles Brown*)

MB882 with 41 Squadron, having been given the squadron letters 'EB-B'. This was perhaps the most photographed Spitfire of the Second World War. (*Author's Collection*)

YEAR 1943		AIRCRAFT		PILOT, OR	2ND PILOT, PUPIL	DUTY					
MONTH	DATE	Type	No.	1ST PILOT	OR PASSENGER	(INCLUDING RESULTS AND REMARKS)					
						TOTALS BROUGHT FORWARD					
September	24	Spit XI	MB937	ŁŁ	O	Production test	29,10				
	24	— " —	"	"	O	— " —	0,05				
	24	Falcon		"	1 pas	G.H.-W.D	0,30				
	24	— " —		"	"	W.D – H.P	0,10				
	24	Spit XII	MB882	"	O	H.P-W.D. She lost spit XII pala	0,15				
	25	" S/F	4M970	"	O	Stabilit.test	0,15				
	25	Falcon		"	1 pas	WD – H.P	0,25				
	25	— " —		"	O	H.P – G.H.	0,15				
	25	— " —		"	1 pas	GH – W.D	0,10				
	26	— " —		"	1 pas	WD – Eastleigh – WD	0,10				
	26	— " —		"	O	— " —	0,20				
	27	— " —		"	O	WD – Hinkwell	1,05				
	27	— " —		"	1 pas	Hinkwell – WD	1,05				
	27	Spit XII	MB882		O	Handling of service load	0,25				
	28	" VIII	36332		O	Production test	0,10				
	28	— " —		"	O	— " —	0,10				
	28	— " —		"	O	— " —	0,10				
	28	Spit XI	MB942	"	O	— " —	0,10				
	28	— " —		"	O	— " —	0,25				
	28	— " —		"	O	— " —	0,10				
	28	Spit XI	MB941	"	O	— " —	0,25				
	28	— " —		"	O	— " —	0,10				
	28	— " —		"	O	— " —					
							36,40				
		GRAND TOTAL [Cols. (1) to (10)]				CARRIED FORWARD					

Solid proof. An entry in Leif Lundsten's logbook, 24 September 1943—MB882 from High Post to Worthy Down. (*Author's Collection*)

Spitfire VIII JG204 was first flown by Leif Lundsten on 5 October 1943. (*Author's Collection*)

Spitfire XI MB945 at Mount Farm in October 1944. It was flown by Leif Lundsten on 7 October 1943. (*Jeffrey L. Ethel Collection/USAAF*)

A German photo of what could possibly be Spitfire MB945—first flown by Leif Lundsten on 5 October 1943. (*Author's Collection*)

Spitfire XI MB948 *Oh Johnny* at Mount Farm in 1944. It was flown by Leif Lundsten on 11 October 1943. (*John S. Blyth, USAAF*)

Screenshot taken from the famous Spitfire short movie *Spitfire 944*. You can see Vernon K. Davidson take Spitfire MB948 to the air during the video. (*Video recorded by Major James R. Savage, USAAF; screenshot provided by William Lorton*)

Spitfire XI MB950 at Mount Farm. (*Jeffrey L. Ethel Collection/USAAF*)

MB950 taking off from Mount Farm. (*Jeffrey L. Ethel Collection/USAAF*)

Antoine Crespin's impression of the rather famous Spitfire XII MB882 parked at North Weald; on 21 October 1943, Leif Lundsten flew the aircraft to North Weald from Hornchurch. (*Antoine Crespin*)

Spitfire XI MB956 *Photogenic Virgin*, flown by Leif Lundsten on 22 October 1943. (*USAAF*)

Spitfire XI PA842 taking off from Mount Farm. It was flown by Leif Lundsten on 30 October 1943. (*USAAF*)

Spitfire XI PA892 was typically flown by Lt Robert Kraft; it was named *My Darling Dorothy*, after his sister. It was the first USAAF Spitfire flown over Berlin. The yellow spinner indicated 'Yellow Flight' and had replaced the previous black spinner. It was first flown by Leif Lundsten on 3 November 1943. (*Jeffrey L. Ethel Collection/USAAF*)

A later shot of PA892. At the end of the war, it was stripped to its natural metal finish with red group markings. (*USAAF*)

Spitfire VIII JG567 *Mary Anne*, flown by Squadron Leader Bob Day, 67 Squadron, in Burma. (*Author's Collection*)

Spring is in the air at North Weald. Squadron veterans Leif Lundsten, Kaj Birksted, and Helge Sognnæs are shown outside dispersal—Lundsten looks deep in thought. (*Forsvarsmuseet*)

Spitfire VIII JG534, flown by Leif Lundsten on 4 December 1943; it is photographed here in 1945, having just been flown by Flight Lieutenant Donald Nicholson. (*Author's Collection*)

Spitfire VIII PA934; the aircraft's name, *Snake,* is clearly visible on the fuselage. (*P. Cairney*)

Spitfire XI MB950 together with MB952 at Mount Farm. (*USAAF*)

Above: A picture of 'Lundsten's Boys'. No. 331 Squadron gathered around their Squadron Leader at Bognor Regis some time in April or May 1944 (before Knut Bache was killed in action on 7 May 1945).
Front, left to right: Kåre Kopperud, Gregers W. Gram and Varg.
Second row, left to right: Bjørn Stenstad, Nils Jørstad, Eivind Tjensvoll, Finn Sørensen, Ole G. Eidsvik, Kjell Tvedt, Leif Lundsten, Olav Ulstein, Odd Knut Roald, and Odd F. Solvang.
On the wing, left to right: Erik Adeler Gundersen, Per Axel Thulin, Kjell Sandvig, Christen Gran, and Paul M. Coucheron.
On top of the engine, left to right: Birger Tidemand-Johannessen and Knut Bache.
Lundsten was often called 'Luden' by his fellow colleagues. (*Forsvarsmuseet*)

Leif Lundsten seated on top of a car with Varg by his side. Lundsten's signature has been added into the photo to exhibit his writing style. (*Forsvarsmuseet*)

Above: A selection of 331 Squadron pilots—with Varg, their mascot—at Bognor Regis in April or early May 1944. From left to right: Knut Bache, Christen Gran, Ragnar Dogger, Kjell Tvedt, Leif Lundsten, and Kjell Sandvig. (*Forsvarsmuseet*)

Below left: Leif Lundsten, back with 331 Squadron. According to several sources, it was a great relief when he took over from Arne Austeen, their former commander. (*Forsvarsmuseet*)

Below right: Leif Lundsten with Varg at Bognor Regis in April or May 1944. Varg had been with the Squadron ever since he was bought by John Nordmo in 1941. (*Forsvarsmuseet*)

Air Marshall Sir Trafford Leigh-Mallory visited Bognor Regis and the Norwegians on 1 June 1944. Right behind him is Helge Mehre, Commander of 132 (N) Wing. Leif Lundsten is about to shake Leigh-Mallory's hand. To the right of Lundsten is Jon Ryg from 332 Squadron and Wing Commander Rolf Arne Berg. (*Forsvarsmuseet*)

Above left: Many pilots had their pictures taken in front of a Spitfire before D-Day. They more than likely expected big losses, and they wanted to make sure their wives and relatives had something to remember them by. Lundsten had his photo taken in front of a Spitfire at Bognor Regis—perhaps this one was FN-Y MK121. (*Forsvarsmuseet*)

Above right: This is thought to be the last photograph taken of Leif Lundsten. He is seen talking to Helge Mehre and Nils Jørstad, among others. The photograph may well have been taken on D-Day. (*Forsvarsmuseet*)

Cine-gun practice somewhere in the North Weald area. It poured down with rain in the morning, but later cleared enough up for flying, but there were no operational sorties.

Date: 31.05.1943
Spitfire: IX, FN-T LZ920
Built: Castle Bromwich
Length: 1:40
Where: North Weald–Flushing–North Weald

Twelve Spitfires, including Wing Commander Mehre flying with 331 Squadron, went to Flushing for Circus no. 309. Even Group Captain Douglas 'Zulu' Morris joined in on the sortie. According to Lundsten, they provided support for twelve B-25 Mitchells doing bombing runs at several targets in the area. Several 331 Squadron pilots observed a Mitchell crashing into the sea, although no German fighters were seen. They pancaked at North Weald at 6.30 p.m.

This sortie concluded Lundsten's flying for May 1943, and he was coming closer and closer to his rest period. He would participate in six more sorties before he was ordered off operational flying.

Date: 01.06.1943
Spitfire: IX, FN-T LZ920
Built: Castle Bromwich
Length: 1:40
Where: North Weald–Hazebrouck–Béthune–Le Touquet–North Weald

June started with plenty of drama and action. It also, sadly, ended with the loss of a Spitfire, however, the pilot survived and became a POW.

The briefing started at 8 a.m. The rising star of the Norwegian Air Force, Svein Heglund, arrived a bit later—he had crashed on his bike. At briefing, Helge Mehre read from a teleprint just received. He spoke to the squadrons while pointing to a large map, while the intelligence officer put pins and ribbons on the map. Rodeo no. 225 was about to get started, and almost fifty Spitfires participated on the sortie. The Kenley Wing provided two squadrons for this Rodeo, and the Norwegians the same. They were told to rendezvous over Ramsgate, and, as Lundsten and many of his fellow pilots had done this trip many times before, further details almost felt unnecessary. There was complete radio silence until they crossed the French coast. Mehre finished his briefing with a few words about not going after any Germans alone, but staying together as a unit. Mehre flew with 332 Squadron during this mission, and Heglund led Yellow Section in 331. Leif Lundsten more than likely led Blue Section as normal.

Over France, two Bf 109-Gs came out of the sun and went for the Kenley boys, however, they had extremely high speed and did not hit anyone. Heglund had his eyes set on them, and eventually brought Yellow Section down to attack them. He shot them both down; however, Heglund's number two, Roy Albert Nielsen, did not return—it was his first time over France, and with no experience he became an easy target. He survived, but remained in captivity for the rest of the war. Lundsten came back to North Weald with his section at 1.05 p.m.

In the very late evening, Lundsten took off with his squadron for Ramrod no. 82, but they were recalled before they reached the crossed the French coast due to poor weather. He was back home as late as 9.25 p.m.

Date: 02.06.1943
Spitfire: V, FN-N BM295
Built: Castle Bromwich
Length: 1:35
Where: North Weald–Channel–North Weald

The mission on 2 June 1943 was a convoy patrol just off Harwich—patrolling about fifteen ships altogether. The weather was horrible throughout the day. Lundsten and Carl Jacob Stousland (EP769) flew the only sortie this day. The patrol was done in the remaining Vs the Norwegians had at their disposal at North Weald.

Date: 04.06.1943
Spitfire: IX, FN-T LZ920
Built: Castle Bromwich
Length: 1:15
Where: North Weald–Le Touquet–North Weald

Eleven Spitfires took off from North Weald at 11.05 a.m. on 4 June, and 331 Squadron was led by Leif Lundsten. When they had crossed the French coast at 15,000 feet, they were ordered to abort their sortie and intercept German fighters returning to France after a raid on Eastbourne. The German bombs had killed six people in Eastbourne.

The story had more to it than just that. According to 332 Squadron pilot Kjeld Rønhof from Denmark, they had more than likely spotted the German fighters flying to Eastbourne to do their damage. The Norwegians had little time to observe the formation, and assumed they were just another formation of Allied fighters going home after a raid. The North Weald Wing did their given task over France and started on their journey home. They met the same formation of fighters once again, now returning to France.

The Norwegians passed the Germans at about 1-km distance, but there were no engagements as no one had any fuel left to do anything. Rønhof wrote: 'Imagine the fight if we had flown straight towards each other!' The Hornchurch Wing made contact with several German fighters and they claimed one shot down and one damaged. Looking at the ORB, one might think they deliberately skipped reporting this rather embarrassing scenario in the official papers.

This sortie was be Lundsten's last in LZ920, and also his last over France for a long time.

Date: 05.06.1943
Spitfire: V, FN-P BM408
Built: Castle Bromwich
Length: 1:15
Where: North Weald–Channel–North Weald

In variable weather, Leif Lundsten flew his last sortie with 331 Squadron in 1943—it was a simple convoy patrol. It was finally time for a long rest.

On the last page of his logbook, written by fellow squadron member Erik Fossum, it is noted in large letters that Lundsten was posted to Vickers-Armstrongs (misspelled with a 'W') on 19 July 1943. It would be a whole different way of life after over year in operational service with a front-line squadron.

23

To Vickers-Supermarine: July 1943, RAF Worthy Down, Hampshire

After a good and relatively lengthy rest, Leif Lundsten reported to RAF Worthy Down, in Hampshire, on 19 July. The airfield was first acquired in August 1917 for use by the Wireless and Observers School, formerly the old Winchester racecourse. A roughly rectangular aerodrome of 480 acres was carved out of the old racecourse, on grassland that sloped markedly down from the old grandstand and gave a maximum run of some 4,800 feet. The main technical buildings consisted (in 1917) of six large aeroplane sheds and a repair and salvage hangar close to the railway line, which formed the eastern boundary.

In August 1940, the airfield was attacked by Junkers 88s. The raiders were part of a large force escorted by Messerschmitt 110s. The force was almost continuously attacked by the RAF on their way to the target. They lost five Ju 88s before they reached Worthy Down, and two Hurricanes were lost. Little damage was done to the airfield, but the station personnel got a nasty fright. Just a month later, on 26 September, there were devastating attacks on the Supermarine factories in Southampton, which caused a crisis in Spitfire production and fears for the rest of the facilities at Eastleigh. Immediate dispersal of the production organisation was ordered, and when two new Bellman hangars became available at Worthy Down, in December 1940, test pilot Jeffrey Quill arrived and took charge of test flying at the airfield. It was under Jeffrey Quill that Leif Lundsten would do his work from July 1943.

The airfield had an infamous hump that resulted in several hairy situations and at least one serious one when Jeffrey Quill collided with a Proctor. It was the result of the hump as he did not see the Proctor until he breasted it—the Proctor was destroyed and the Spitfire badly damaged.

The first Griffon-powered Spitfire was tested at the airfield in 1941, and much of the early Seafire development took place at Worthy Down. Spitfire XIV trials also took place at Worthy Down at the time of Lundsten's time at the airfield. The airfield quickly became very congested, and, as facilities improved at High Post, Supermarine moved their development flying there in March 1944.

On 20 July, just a day after the start of his time as a test pilot, Lundsten went to Eastleigh in a de Havilland DH.90 Dragonfly. He stayed there overnight, and flew back to Worthy Down on 22 July. This day was his first day as a test pilot. His first Spitfire was the Mk VIII version, with serial number JF275.

Lundsten did several flights a day in Spitfires. Due to the drastic change of his career and flying, necessary changes have also been made to the details listed. Naturally, the Spitfires have no squadron codes. Only date, type of mark, serial number, and amount of flights are listed.

Date: 22.07.1943
Spitfire(s): VIII JF275
Built: Eastleigh

Lundsten's first task as a test pilot was a tank-busting trial in Spitfire VIII JF275. JF275 was used for several trials, including very detailed performance analysis now available online. It had its first flight on 21 November 1942. The same year, it had trials with a tropical air intake. In September 1943, it received repairs with a civilian repair unit. It had a spell with the Canadian Forces Staff College in 1945. JF275 was, for example, tested with a Merlin at +25 lbs and climbed at 5,580 feet per minute, and did 409 mph at 14,000 feet.

In 1947, JF275 was bought by a private owner in Argentina. This buyer also purchased an IX (PL194) and an XI (PL972), which can be seen online marked up as LV-NMZ. JF275 was eventually scrapped and only pieces may remain in Argentina to this day. Aviation enthusiasts in Argentina reportedly wanted to maintain or restore the Spitfires, but official administration refused permission.

An undercarriage leg of JF275 remains in the UK.

Date: 23.07.1943
Spitfire(s): VIII JF676; VIII JF836
Built: Chattis Hill

Leif Lundsten took two VIIIs to the air for production tests on 24 July 1943—JF676 and JF836.

Battle of Britain veteran Tim Elkington flew JF676 during his time of service in India. This flight was just twenty five minutes long. He flew the Spitfire between Maidan and Amarda Road, a RAF airfield near

Rasgovindpur village, in Mayurbhanj district of Orissa, India. He noted in his logbook 'very right wing low. As low as I felt'. It was categorised as a write-off on 31 October 1946.

Some aviation enthusiasts have speculated that JF676 could be one of the VIIIs buried in Burma, alongside other Spitfires that enthusiast David Cundall was digging for. The argument is that the Spitfire was repaired in India and then shipped to Burma and eventually crated. This remains to be seen, and no news from the digs have appeared for a long time.

JF836 had its first flight only one day before Lundsten flew it. It was shipped to Casablanca on 1 September 1943 and served in North Africa from November 1943. It was category 'E' damaged (write-off) on 18 October 1945.

Date: 24.07.1943
Spitfire(s): VIII JF707
Built: Eastleigh

Lundsten wrote this one down as 'revs against boost'. He flew JF707 quite a lot at Worthy Down. It underwent tests with an experimental undercarriage, with wheel camber, and toe-in removed to reduce tyre wear. In 1944, it was used to taxi, on take-offs, and landing trials. There was less ground drag and no adverse effects on handling. In June 1945, the Spitfire was transferred to Hong Kong, and then to India a few months later. It was struck off charge on 30 January 1947. Because of its connection to India, JF707 was also be in the lists of rumoured Spitfires in Burma over seventy years later.

During the next couple of days, Lundsten did plenty of flying. On 25 July, he went to Scotland to pick up a passenger in a Dragon Rapide. On 26 July, he went to Cambridge and back. However, there were no Spitfire trials taking place for Lundsten.

24

Spitfires and Seafires: September 1943, RAF Worthy Down, Chattis Hill, and Eastleigh, Hampshire, and High Post, Wiltshire

Date: 04.08.1943
Spitfire(s): VIII JF275
Built: Eastleigh

An hour of tank-busting trials before Lundsten tested JF275 in level speed for another hour during the same day. It was mentioned this was a transfer test.

The following day, on 5 August, Rolf Arne Berg (now commanding 331 Squadron) sent a telegram to Leif Lundsten:

From: Officer Commanding, 331 (N) Squadron, North Weald, Essex.

To: Capt. Lundsten, R.A.F Station, Worthy Down, Hampshire.

Date: 5/8/1943

Ref.: 406/3/P1

Heartiest congratulations on your well-earned D.F.C from all the boys of 331.

Rolf Berg, Major
Officer Commanding
331 (N) Squadron
North Weald, Essex.

Leif Lundsten had been awarded a DFC (Distinguished Flying Cross).

Date: 06.08.1943
Spitfire(s): IX BS118; VII BS299
Built: Eastleigh

His new role as a test pilot did not mean that Lundsten was out of harm's way, and this was proven on 6 August. With the amount of Spitfires he took to the air, he would end up in trouble sooner or later—it turned out to be sooner. Even if the Luftwaffe had not managed to be end of him, technical faults or even poor weather could very well do so. Not since Castletown in 1941, when he had landed a Hurricane with almost all aileron and rudder control gone, had he been involved in a crash-landing. Almost two years since his infamous Hurricane landing, on 6 August, he had another incident.

The day started out with a return trip to Worthy Down from Eastleigh. He had come over the previous day with a passenger, and stayed the night, perhaps due to poor weather or late hours.

Back at Worthy Down, he took Spitfire IX BS188 up for an aileron trim test flight. Then he flew to North Weald in Spitfire VII BS229. Could this be in connection to his DFC? (see also 18 September 1943).

Lundsten listed he flew a VIII to North Weald. However, BS229 was a VII. It was first flown 31 October 1942 and would be used extensively for trials in the coming years. It had been going through trials with rate of roll measurements, with reduced span ailerons and carbon monoxide contamination tests as well as stability tests. In October 1943, it underwent trials with landing flaps used as air brakes. It was scrapped in 1945, after almost three years in service.

The flight back to Worthy Down in BS229 took him forty-five minutes. One can imagine his surprise when the wheels did not come down when he started his preparations to land. He more than likely tried several methods of getting them out, but with no success. His flight to North Weald and back to Worthy Down thus ended in a crash-landing.

Obviously shaken, but unhurt, he flew another test flight later in the day in BS118. This time testing level speeds with a 45-gallon tank attached to the Spitfire. BS229 continued its service after being repaired.

All the pilots who have flown for Supermarine, whether civilians or in the service are inevitably part of the firm's success, and some of them lost their lives in the process.

Jeffrey Quill, *Flight Magazine*, 1953.

Date: 07.08.1943
Spitfire(s): XII MB863
Built: High Post

Lots of flying on 7 August, but only one test flight in a Spitfire, and this one was rather special. It was his first flight in a Griffon-powered Spitfire—the XII version. Before the flight in MB863, Lundsten flew to Harford Bridge and back. Then to Eastleigh and back, as well as a return trip to High Post with a passenger. Lundsten tested ailerons and climb performance in the XII on this day.

MB863 first flew on 7 August 1943. Built at High Post, it went to 41 Squadron in November 1943. With 41 Squadron, based at Friston, it can be last seen in the squadrons ORB on 28 March 1944 in the hands of Pilot Officer P. Cowell. He flew it on a fighter sweep over Évreux. It may very well be that the Spitfire ground-looped at Friston this day due to flaps having malfunctioned. It reportedly ground-looped into a gully and was written-off.

Date: 08.08.1943
Spitfire(s): VIII JF276; IX BS118; VII BS299
Built: High Post, Eastleigh

Another flight in Spitfire BS299, now repaired (the damage could not have been extensive). He flew BS299 to Wittering for what was most likely further trials.

JF276 is another one that was listed as 'BS' in his logbook. He tested its ailerons and then flew the Spitfire to Hamble. From Hamble he flew a Rapide back to Worthy Down. Then he flew BS299 to previously mentioned Wittering, and caught a ride back with Flying Officer Graham. On 9 August, the next day, he did not test any Spitfires, but had stops at Harford Bridge, Chattis Hill, and Boscombe Down.

Date: 10.08.1943
Spitfire(s): VIII JF842; VIII JF841
Built: Chattis Hill

On this day, Lundsten did a production test in JF842. This was the Spitfires first flight. Three days later it went to 6 Maintenance Unit, and had another stop with 222 MU before it went to Malancha in September, and then to India in November. It was finally struck off charge in 1947.

JF841 had quite the same type of career, arriving in India together with JF842 and struck off charge on the same date in 1947 (30 January). Both are loosely rumoured to be buried in Burma.

Date: 10.08.1943
Spitfire(s): VIII JF707
Built: Chattis Hill

The task of the day was to perform a short flight to High Post in JF707. There was no flying on 11 August. The day after (12 August), Lundsten went to Eastleigh and back in a Dragon Rapide before flying Spitfires.

Date: 12.08.1943
Spitfire(s): VIII JF707; VIII JF621
Built: Chattis Hill, High Post

JF707 was picked up again from High Post and flown back to Worthy Down by Lundsten. He then flew a production test flight in JF621. The first flight lasted a mere five minutes time, and after this first flight he flew JF621 six more times throughout the day, ending up on well over two hours flying in this Spitfire. Considerably more than what he did with other Spitfires he tested.

JF621 then went to Australia; the RAAF received about twenty-five Spitfire VIIIs, carrying serials in the JF range. The majority of these were given a serial between JF820 and JF967. Only two, JF620 and JF621, carried lower range serials. JF621 was assigned its RAAF identity, A58-301, on 26 November 1943, and it was struck off charge 15 November 1948.

Date: 13.08.1943
Spitfire(s): XI EN684
Built: Chattis Hill

On 13 August, a production test was flown in Spitfire XI EN684—it was Leif Lundsten's first flight in a Spitfire XI. He flew the fighter three times this day, with the first flight lasting ten minutes, the others twenty minutes. The Spitfire was transferred to 542 Squadron at RAF Benson, a photo reconnaissance squadron. Pilot Officer J. D. Ibbotson later pranged the Spitfire on his return from operations, just after crossing in from the Channel—this due to an engine failure. Fortunately, he was unhurt in this incident. After a spell with 8 OTU in the spring of 1945, EN684 was scrapped in the middle of December 1945. After Lundsten's three flights in EN684, he went to Chattis Hill in an Oxford and returned the same day.

Date: 14.08.1943
Spitfire(s): IX BS118
Built: Eastleigh

Stability test in BS188. Before the flight, he had been to High Post, flying as the passenger of someone with the last name Furlong (the rank was also written, but the handwriting was obscured). This person might have been Frank Furlong. Quill wrote the following about Furlong:

Described as a man of unbounded exuberance and tremendous courage. He had no technical background—he was brought up with horses (he rode the winner of the Grand National in 1935); but he applied a deep-rooted intelligence and enthusiasm to test flying and in the hurly-burly of activity in our war-time experimental flight test department he was the idea chap. He was killed in the prototype Spiteful in 1944.

Jeffrey Quill, *Flight Magazine*, 2 October 1953.

Date: 16.08.1943
Spitfire(s): XII MB875
Built: High Post

On 16 August, a production test was flown in Lundsten's second XII—MB874. This aircraft was later flown by N. Peter Gibbs of 41 Squadron, with squadron letters EB-G. He was responsible for shooting down the squadron's first V-1 bomb, on 20 June 1944. A year later, on 25 August 1944, MB875 had engine trouble on take-off from Lympne. The Spitfire had not taken to the air, but overturned in the breaking process, and was a write-off.

Date: 17.08.1943
Spitfire(s): XII MB875
Built: High Post

This day featured yet another production test in MB875. On 17 August, Lundsten flew to Chattis Hill and back to Worthy Down in a Falcon, together with one unnamed passenger. The same day (17 August), he flew to Oxford and back in—yes—an Oxford. The next day, back at Worthy Down, would be his busiest yet.

Date: 18.08.1943
Spitfire(s): VIII JF846; XI MB889
Built: Chattis Hill

On 18 August, Lundsten had five flights, two Spitfires, and two different marks. In the early morning, he took JF846 to the air for a production test.

JF846 went to the Royal Australian Air Force as A58-309, where it served with 452 Squadron. At Katherine, NT, Australia, it suffered a landing accident in the hands of Pilot Officer M. J. Beaton. It was repaired by 7 Repair & Salvage Unit before it was delivered to 54 Squadron, RAF.

In April 1944, JF846 took off from Gorrie for a delivery flight to Darwin. It was flown by Flight Lieutenant Peter George Fleming Brown.

At 9,000 feet, it suffered an engine failure about 40 miles south of Pine Creek. Brown was told to search for a clearing to force-land, though after gliding down to 1,000 feet he was advised to jump out, due to his inability to locate a proper landing spot. Brown jumped out and the Spitfire went into a dive. It crashed and exploded on impact. Browns parachute opened at approximately 100 feet, but sadly he landed in the burning wreckage and died of his injuries.

After Lundsten's first and very short flight, he flew another flight in JF846 that lasted twenty minutes. Back on the ground, he soon prepared to take a different mark for a test flight—it was another XI, with serial MB889. Not much is known about the career of MB889; it went to India in September 1943 and was struck off charge in June 1945. After a rather busy day in August, Lundsten would not be back in the air for another three days.

Date: 21.08.1943
Spitfire(s): VIII JF872
Built: Chattis Hill

Yet another production test was flown on this day, this time it was flown in JF872. There were two flights, which would be the only Spitfire testing Lundsten did on 21 August.

The Spitfire went to Australia as A58-328. It had an undercarriage collapse during landing on 23 April 1944. It was struck off charge in November 1948. Not much else can be mentioned about JF872, except for one very important factor. It might be one of the very few Spitfires Leif Lundsten flew during the war years that is still in existence today.

In 2009, a new registration popped up at the Civil Aviation Authority. It was quickly deemed to be a provisional ID for the Spitfire. One can read the following on the owner's website:

> The identity here is the one with the highest statistical probability based on the available information. The search was narrowed down to 13 aircraft from a batch of 100—of course someone may come along with new information. We could have chosen a slightly more 'interesting' ID, but there would be nothing solid to base this choice on.

The Spitfire, regardless of the serial, is currently undergoing a major restoration at NWMAS, Hawarden. This involves stripping all existing parts back to component form to check their condition. They stress that all parts have to be airworthy, and, if all goes well, it could be the first surviving Spitfire from Lundsten's long list of Spitfires that will fly again.

Date: 22.08.1943
Spitfire(s): IX BS118; Seafire III LR766; XII MB877
Built: Eastleigh, Westland, High Post

First up on the day's agenda was a stability test at 25,000 feet in Spitfire IX BS188. It would turn out to be one of the busiest day so far this August.

BS118 was used specifically for trials, and it first flew on 15 July 1942, over a year before Lundsten himself flew the Spitfire. Lundsten flew it twice on 22 August 1943, with the flying hours totalling one hour and forty minutes. BS118 is possibly best known as the Spitfire that was used for trial installation of .50 machine guns in the Spitfire wings. The 20-mm Hispano cannon were moved outboard and the .50 Browning heavy machine guns were added to the inner-bay, replacing the outer Browning .303s. The first trials were made in BS118 in November 1943, a few months after Lundsten flew the fighter. The armament later became standard for all Spitfire XIVs used by 2nd TAF fighters (which Lundsten's former squadron, 331, was a part of after his death). BS118 also apparently dived to Mach .89 from 40,000 feet in 1944. Arguably not recognizing its important history, the Spitfire was sold to R. J. Coley (a scrapyard not far from Heathrow) in 1950 where it ended its days.

Seafire LR766 was part of a batch of Seafires built at Westland, and was the second off the production line. It came without the folding wings, due to delays in manufacturing. It arrived at Worthy Down for weighing and contractor flight trials two months before Lundsten's first flight in August. At Worthy Down, the fighter's internal and exterior paint finishes were thoroughly examined, following reports that those applied by the factory were below the required standards and left the airframe open to corrosion. At Worthy Down, LR766 was confirmed as unstable, and a solution had to be found before the type entered operational service. This was likely where Leif Lundsten came into the frame, as he entered 'handling and stability test' in his logbook. At Worthy Down, LR766 was found to be unstable when the centre of gravity was 20-cm aft of the datum. After a considerable amount of work and changes, LR766 was still found to be unstable while the other well-known trial Seafire, MA970, seemed to be on the right track. In 1944, a final effort was to fit a 3.5-lb (1.6-kg) balance weight to the elevator control circuit, which dampened the reaction of the elevators. These trials also concluded with further investigations. Seafire III productions were continuing while these trials took place. Lundsten's flight on 22 August lasted forty minutes.

Last in line during this very busy day was MB877, another XII. This meant Lundsten had flown three different marks of the Spitfires (one being a Seafire), with considerably different handling techniques on the same day.

Lundsten did two fifteen-minute flights in MB877. MB877 subsequently went to 41 Squadron after a lengthy spell with 91 Squadron.

On 17 July 1944, tragedy struck when twenty-one-year-old Roger Lee Short, a flight sergeant, took off from RAF Lympne. Either on his take-off run or shortly after take-off, Short collided with Flight Sergeant Clifford Oddy, flying a de Havilland Tiger Moth. He was also twenty-one years of age, and was a fellow pilot in 41 Squadron. The Tiger Moth crashed near Lympne Castle, and the Spitfire also went down. Both pilots were killed in the accident—Short is buried in Hawkinge, Kent.

The next day had no Spitfire trials, but rather short trips to both Eastleigh and High Post in a Dragon Rapide.

Date: 24.08.1943
Spitfire(s): IX BS188; MA970 (Seafire)
Built: Eastleigh, High Post

Another flight in BS118, this flight was with a focus on reflection shooting. The second flight was done in another important bird, Seafire MA970. MA970 was originally constructed as a IIc, and was used for trials to clear the type for naval service. It first flew from High Post on 28 May 1942 and went to Worthy Down in June for weighing, as the airframe now incorporated twenty Seafire and Spitfire modifications. It was used for numerous of trials in the following months, including adding a tropical filter and a four-bladed prop. It was still at Worthy Down a year later when Lundsten took the well-tested Seafire to the air. When these tasks were done, it was rebuilt as a prototype Seafire III. When Lundsten flew it, it was a Mk III. On this day he flew the Seafire with a raised seat position. The manufacturer kept the Seafire for further testing in the coming months. For example, both LR766 and MA970 were tested loaded with weights. MA970 behaved well, but LR766 was still unstable. MA970, in this case, donated its entire tail section to LR766 for further trials.

Done with MA970 for the day, Lundsten strapped on BS188 once again. During this flight, he tested the Spitfires stability and the handling under high-speed stalls.

Date: 25.08.1943
Spitfire(s): IX BS118; VIII JF873; VIII JF875; XI MB895
Built: Eastleigh (IX BS118), Chattis Hill (VIII JF873; VIII JF875; XI MB895)

On this day, Lundsten set a new personal record in a number of Spitfire flights. An impressive number of twelve flights—and seven flown in one specific Spitfire. In the morning, he went Chattis Hill in BS118 where he left the Spitfire behind. He flew a Rapide back to Worthy Down the same day for further work. He would now fly VIIIs again, and first up was JF873, which was a second production test. Lundsten wrote 're-fly production test', a slightly Norwegian-English approach to the sentence.

JF875 went through 33 Maintenance Unit and 82 Maintenance before being shipped to North Africa. JF873 had an almost identical life, however this Spitfire went to the United States Air Force on 31 January 1944. It was struck off charge the same year for unknown reasons. Lundsten flew, as mentioned, seven flights in JF875 during the 25 August. The last Spitfire of the day, MB895, an XI, was flown three times. This reconnaissance Spitfire went to Benson just two days after Lundsten's first test flight. It arrived in India in October 1943 and belonged to 681 Squadron until 26 July 1945 when it was struck off charge.

The next day Lundsten flew to RAF Hamble and back with one passenger.

Date: 27.08.1943
Spitfire(s): VIII JF878
Built: High Post

The following day, the 27 August, Lundsten flew to RAF Keevil, in Wiltshire (written as 'Kivill' in his logbook). Then he flew onwards to High Post and then another round trip from High Post to Worthy Down. Only one Spitfire would be tested by Lundsten on this day, this was JF878. JF878 was built at High Post and shared much of the previous fates of VIIIs Lundsten had flown, this one also went to North Africa. On 18 January 1945, JF878 participated in a ground attack where the Spitfire caught fire when the target blew up and crashed—it is not known if the pilot survived. After flying JF878, Lundsten went to Boscombe Down and back. Then to Brize Norton and back. There was lots of flying, but only ten minutes were flown in a Spitfire—there was no flying the next day.

Date: 29.08.1943
Spitfire(s): VIII JF879
Built: High Post

This Spitfire met a tragic fate, with the loss of the aircraft and the death of its pilot in 1944. The loss of JF897 has been thoroughly researched by Italian Matteo Pierro, and it is thanks to this research that the following story of JF897 can be told.

JG879 was lost on 30 March 1944 while flying with 601 Squadron at Marcianaise, Campania, Italy. The pilot flying JF879 was Lt Cornelius Cecil Geldard, called 'Chips'. He was thirty-two years old and originated from South Africa. According to another Italian historian, Vincenzo Cannaviello, woodcutters discovered JF879 in May 1944. It had crashed into the summit of a mountain, and most likely killed the pilot instantly on impact. After a considerable amount of research, Pierro was able to connect JF897 to the right pilot and in fact identify the Spitfire in question. In cooperation with Roy Neighbour, who tracked down relatives to the pilot, the story could be told.

Geldard came from a farm in South Africa called Water Ridenti. When war broke out, he enlisted with his brother Albert in the South African Air Force. He was later assigned to 601 Squadron. This squadron had done their fair share of hard work during the Battle of Britain, and later operated from North Africa and then onwards to Italy after the landing at Salerno.

During the morning of 30 March 1944, the weather conditions were terrible and no operations were being carried out. However, Geldard took off for a simple test flight in JF879. The situation so far is close what Lundsten himself had been doing at North Weald on several occasions; taking Spitfires to the air in poor weather for test flights—when there were no operational sorties planned. For Geldard, this would lead to his untimely death. The reason for the crash is unknown, but Pierro imagines the Spitfire might have had an engine failure due to the horrid weather conditions and then crashed.

Leif Lundsten flew the Spitfire twice on 29 August 1943.

Date: 30.08.1943
Spitfire(s): VIII JF707
Built: Eastleigh

Lundsten flew to Brize Norton to pick up a familiar Spitfire—JF707. He flew it back to Worthy Down, with the flight lasting twenty minutes—no more flying was done during this day.

Date: 31.08.1943
Spitfire(s): VIII JF707; IX EN314; VIII JF953; VIII JF956; VIII JF880; VIII JF881
Built: Eastleigh (VIII JF707; IX EN314; VIII JF953), High Post (VIII JF956; VIII JF880; VIII JF881)

Spitfire EN314 was a IX that was used for considerable amount of trials at Boscombe Down. In July 1943, it was in for major repairs after having been tested with increased tail plane incidence and enlarged elevator horn balance. Lundsten flew EN314 as a production test after these repairs had taken place. EN314 went to South African Air Force in 1947.

JF953 had a less glamorous life. Like several others in the JF series and those that Lundsten flew, it went to North Africa. JF953 also had a spell in the Middle East, before being struck off charge in 1946—JF956 went down the same route. However, this one was damaged by flak and abandoned near Anzio, Italy, on 20 March 1944.

JF880 is a more famous bird, and was photographed a few times while serving with 417 Squadron, Royal Canadian Air Force. The photos were taken during the winter of 1944–45. The squadron was based at Fano airfield, Italy, at this time, and it wore the squadron code AN-U. Additionally, it served with the 31st Fighter Group, USAAF, before they switched to Mustangs. JF880 has also been of high interest to modellers in the past few years, and several 'skins' have been made for the Spitfire. JF880 was struck off charge 14 March 1943.

Lundsten also tested JF880's 'sister', JF881. This one also going to 417 Squadron Italy. Canadian Joseph Hedley Everard claimed a Bf 109 shot down on 14 February 1944 over Anzio. He also claimed a probable on 21 February—this one was also a 109. Everard also claimed a shared Me 262 with 401 Squadron, northeast of Nijmegen, Holland. Everard survived the war, and became group captain in 1961. He flew plenty of jet fighters in many countries, according to Christopher Shores and Clive Williams (*Aces High*, a tribute to the most notable fighter pilots of the British and Commonwealth forces in the Second World War, published 1994). JF881 force-landed at Nettuno, in Italy, in April 1944, which was the time the fighter was last seen. With 417 Squadron, it wore the squadron letters AN-H.

Monthly total of flying ended at 35.45 hours on Spitfires.

25

MB882, The Last of the XII: September 1943, RAF Worthy Down, Chattis Hill, and Eastleigh, Hampshire, and High Post, Wiltshire

As the war went on, the test-flying task at Supermarine—particularly the clearance of the output of production aeroplanes—began to reach such proportions that it was necessary to form a team of RAF and Fleet Air Arm pilots on attachment to the company. Not including those who went to Castle Bromwich to help Alex Henshaw, the list of pilots who were seconded to and served at Supermarine amounted to more than forty. They included men from the Royal Air Force, the Fleet Air Arm, the Belgian Air Force and the Norwegian Air Force, as well as those civilian pilots who already belonged to the company. The service pilots were drawn in the main from Spitfire and Seafire operational squadrons and they were employed principally in the routine testing of production aircraft as they emerged from the factories. At Supermarine they became under my control operationally and under the resident Air Ministry overseer, who was Group Captain, for administrative purposes.

Jeffrey Quill, *Spitfire: A Test Pilots Story*, p. 260

There were two Norwegians serving as Supermarine test pilots during the Second World War. One was Olav Ullestad, originally from 332 Squadron, who served with Alex Henshaw's group of men. He is referred to in Henshaw's book, *Sigh for a Merlin*, as Olaf Ulstad. The other was Leif Lundsten, under Jeffrey Quill, at Worthy Down. He is sadly not mentioned in Quill's book (apart from coming from the Norwegian Air Force), and his death in 1944 seems to have slipped under Quill's radar. In his book, Quill mentions Andy Andrews from 41 Squadron, who was shot down and killed flying a Spitfire XII and noted as KIA in the book. Lundsten, as mentioned, is not listed as killed.

It has not been possible to write about all the pilots who served with me at Supermarine at some time between 1936 and 1946 but what I hope is a full list appears in Appendix II. The contribution made by these men to test-flying task at Supermarine was extremely valuable.

Jeffrey Quill, *Spitfire: A Test Pilots Story*, p. 269

Considering Leif Lundsten was a rather quiet character, it is perhaps understandable why Quill did not write about him in his book, but (for example) dedicated several paragraphs to more colourful characters, like Battle of Britain legend Anthony Bartley. Lundsten's quiet character may also be of a cultural issue (both national and local origin).

Date: 07.09.1943
Spitfire(s): XI MB902; XI MB903
Built: Chattis Hill

Lundsten had the first week in September 1943 off. One can only speculate that he went to London during these times off a flying schedule. On 7 September 1943, a Tuesday, it was back to work. Two Spitfires were on the schedule, both XIs.

The first flights were routine, with two flights at 12.25 a.m. and 12.15 a.m. in MB902. However, from the looks of it, MB903 gave Lundsten a bit of a challenge. It took six flights, with three lasting only five minutes, before he was satisfied. In June 1944, MB902 flew into the ground near Bishops Canning, Wiltshire, in foggy conditions. According to some sources, the Spitfire was serving with 16 Squadron. However, there were no losses on 1 June 1944. There was, however, a loss on 8 June 1944, which shares a striking resemblance to what happened to MB902, but no clear connection can be traced. The pilot was killed in the crash.

MB903, despite its slow start in the hand of Lundsten during this day, had spells with 541 Squadron and 16 Squadron before it was sold in January 1949.

Date: 08.09.1943
Spitfire(s): VII JF707
Built: Eastleigh

This day (8 September) was perhaps one that Lundsten was looking forward to—he went back to North Weald to visit some of his old friends; he was flying in JF707. The Norwegians were quite busy on 8 September; it was the day before Operation Starskey took place. The Norwegians went to

Lille in the morning, providing cover for Marauders. Martin Gran, now in charge of Lundsten's old Blue Section, claimed a 190 destroyed in this sortie. If Lundsten stopped by around noon, he would be in for plenty of familiar faces as the squadrons came back from France at 11.15 a.m. In the afternoon, the North Weald Wing took off once again, this time for Circus S.41. The Spitfires went to Tournai, south-east of Lille, before they turned for home. A third, and last, sortie was due shortly after the second one. The 8th was also the day that Italy surrendered. By this time, the Spitfires were already painted with white and black stripes—which Lundsten may have observed when he was at North Weald this day in September. Taking off from North Weald and flying back to Worthy Down, he also did tank-busting trials with JF707. He also flew to Boscombe Down and back in an Oxford, and then to Farnborough and back.

Date: 09.09.1943
Spitfire(s): Seafire MA970; Seafire LR766
Built: High Post, Westland

On this day, there were more stability tests in Worthy Down's two Seafires, as previously detailed.

Date: 10.09.1943
Spitfire(s): VIII JG171; XI MB906
Built: both Chattis Hill

There were two test flights in JG171 on the 10th. The fighter went to India after the initial production tests. On 10 June 1944, while in India, Pilot Officer J. Bouche came in to land JG171. For some reason he did not manage to deploy flaps—either he forgot or there were technical difficulties. He got JG171 down, but ran into a ditch due to high speed. The ditch did its best to rid the Spitfire of its undercarriage, and succeeded. It was struck off charge a month later. MB906, on the other hand, stayed in one piece until 1947, where no more traces of it can be found.

On 11 August, there were no Spitfire test flights on the agenda for Lundsten, but several flights in Rapides and Oxfords (as well as an unknown aircraft he simply listed as 'bomber'). Stops during the day included Boscombe Down, High Post, Eastleigh, and Hamble. The last flight was from Eastleigh to Worthy Down.

Date: 12.09.1943
Spitfire(s): VIII JF707
Built: Eastleigh

Leif Lundsten flew to North Weald on this day, the only flight of the day. His logbook noted 'intensive flying'. It could be an indication to poor weather, but also intense manoeuvring (a beat up over North Weald?). It took an hour's worth of flying—in other words, this was not a test flight. Pure speculation obviously, but due to the Norwegian's busy schedule during this last stop, he might have decided to come back a later day when things had calmed down a bit. A heavy storm had passed over North Weald at night, which left a lot of ground haze during the day. There was also a lot of low cloud during the entire day, with mist and drizzle, yet Lundsten found his way to the airfield. There was no flying aside from two local flights in the afternoon. So, the weather was suitable for some flying, but not much. The day was perfect to visit old friends in 331 Squadron—it was the only flying he did this day.

Date: 13.09.1943
Spitfire(s): VIII JF707
Built: Eastleigh

There were two hours' worth of flying on the 13th, testing level speeds in JF707.

Date: 14.09.1943
Spitfire(s): VIII JF883
Built: High Post

On 14 September, JF883 took to the air for the first time—a production test. The Spitfire went to India in January 1944. In 1945, Flying Officer T. N. Ghadiok was flying JF883 in a tail chase, when Flying Officer Y. R. Atgey struck the tail of JF883. Both pilots were safe, and Atgey belly landed his Spitfire at Devanahalli. JF883 was struck off charge in December 1946, and it is another Spitfire rumoured to be buried in Burma.

Date: 15.09.1943
Spitfire(s): VIII JG174; VIII JG175; VIII JG177; VIII JF884
Built: Chattis Hill (VIII JG174; VIII JG175; VIII JG177) and High Post (VIII JF884)

A whole ten flights were flown on 15 September, and flying was done in four different VIII Spitfires. On the same day, after he flew the last Spitfire of the day (JF884), he went to Chattis Hill in an Oxford. Then yet another trip to Chattis Hill in what he only described as a bomber.

JG174 went to Australia with the Royal Australian Air Force. The fighter was given a new serial number—A58-332—and flew with 549

Squadron. The sister Spitfire, JG175, naturally went down the same route—to Australia—this one as A58-333. With 548 Squadron it had the squadron letters TS-C. In 1945, it went into storage in Australia, and then was authorised to be scrapped—subsequently ending the life of JG175 in 1948.

For Lundsten, without knowing it, it was a day of full of future Australian Spitfires. JG177, given the Australian serial A58-334, was transferred to 549 Squadron. They were stationed at a civil strip in Darwin, Northern Territory, in October 1944. During the same month, Flight Lieutenant W. B. V. N. Wedd misjudged his approach while landing JG177, and crash-landed onto the runway. JG177 was substantially damaged, but Wedd managed to escape the accident with no injuries.

JF883, another RAAF Spitfire, was given the serial A58-354. Much like JG174, it was authorised to be scrapped in 1946. It was struck off charge in 1948.

After the test flying this day ended, Lundsten had a rest period for five days before he was back flying Spitfires on 20 September.

As mentioned, no flying between 15 September and 20 September, but according to Bjørn Stenstad in 331, often a pilot to be found in Lundsten's former Blue Section, things were happening at North Weald. He wrote the following in his diary on 18 September 1943:

Woke up at seven o' clock. The boys left for a sweep at ten. Parade for A.O.B 11th Group [Air Vice Marshal Hugh W. L. Saunders, 11th Group]. He gave Lundsten and Bjørnstad DFC. Show on again at five, but nothing happened and came back at seven and went straight to Teatch [Thatched House, Epping] and came back to the mess [later on]. Then a dance in Drury Lane. Came back home at two [in the morning] and very tired.

Bjørn Stenstad, 331 Squadron.

According to Stenstad, Lundsten was at North Weald at least for one day (18) September, receiving his DFC.

Date: 20.09.1943
Spitfire(s): VIII JF707; III W3237
Built: Eastleigh, Chattis Hill

There were three flights during the day, and one was rather interesting. First, though, another flight in JF707, with more tank-busting trials. After flying W3237, he flew another forty-five-minute flight in JF707, once again going for tank-busting trials.

A peculiar mark of Spitfire was flown this day—a mark III. W3237 was in fact a converted mark V. It was a planned production version, with a Merlin XX engine, enlarged radiator, stronger wing spar, strengthened landing gear, retractable tailwheel, additional armour, new bullet-proof windscreen, and clipped wings (quite shorter than the normal clipped-winged mark Vs). One was built from scratch (N3297), while the second was Lundsten's Spitfire on this day. This version of the Spitfire did not go into production, but many of its features were incorporated into later marks of Spitfire.

Lundsten's task flying W3237 was to test air and wing temperatures. The Spitfire was still being used in trials well into 1944.

Date: 21.09.1943
Spitfire(s): VIII JF707
Built: Eastleigh

JF707, with the amount of flying Lundsten did in it, could almost be described as his own Spitfire during the first months he was at Worthy Down and Chattis Hill. On 21 September, he did more tank-busting trials—totalling three hours' worth of flying time.

Date: 22.09.1943
Spitfire(s): III W3237
Built: Chattis Hill
Length: 0:10

Transport flight to Eastleigh in one of only two produced IIIs. Lundsten did not fly the Spitfire back to Worthy Down; instead, he flew an Oxford from Eastleigh to Lea-on-Solent, then to Hamble, onwards to Pembroke Walls, and home to Worthy Down (from Hamble he had one passenger with him).

Date: 23.09.1943
Spitfire(s): VIII JF886; IX BS310; XII DP845
Built: High Post, Chattis Hill

Several interesting Spitfires were flown by Lundsten on this day in September. JF886 went to Casablanca and North Africa in the same year that Lundsten flew it, and it was struck off charge in 1946. The other two Spitfires have left a much bigger mark in history.

BS310, a mark IX, was flown by Lundsten for half an hour, testing its combat climb abilities. It was used for comparative climb and level speed performances, using both a four-bladed propeller and a five-bladed propeller. What is interesting is that these trials took place at Boscombe

Down a month later (23 October 1943 to 29 January 1944). However, this cannot be the whole story, as Lundsten flew the Spitfire, testing said combat climb, a whole month earlier. It is not known if he flew it with a four-bladed propeller or a five. From the trials undertaken at Boscombe Down just a month earlier, it was concluded that the IX had no particular advantage in performance if the four-bladed propeller was replaced with a five-bladed one. Later on, after Lundsten had returned to 331 Squadron, BS310 was flown to test the effects of high Mach numbers in dive and recovery, with different engine and propeller combinations. In April 1944, it underwent major repairs before being transferred to 453 Squadron. It went missing near Arnhem on 27 September 1944. The report from the dive trials in BS310 can be found at the National Archives, UK.

DP845, a prototype XII, is one of the more famous Spitfires. It was featured in *The Aeroplane* magazine as early as April 1944. The photos were taken with Clive Gosling at the controls. Quill had first flown the Spitfire in November 1942, a whole two years before Lundsten flew it. The mark XII became Quill's favourite mark of Spitfire, with its spectacular rate of climb and very good low-level performance. In July 1942, almost a year later, Quill would fly DP845 to take part in a demonstration for a small audience of VIPs. Quill wrote of the demonstration in his book.

> Jimmy Bird had no information on what was afoot, so I immediately telephoned Willy Wilson at Farnborough to find out what it was all about. All I could gather was that it was to be comparative demonstration of the low-level speed performance of the FW 190, the Typhoon and the Spitfire
>
> 'How are you going to organise this, Willy?' I asked.
>
> 'God knows,' he said. 'I suppose we shall have to have some sort of race'.
>
> On a reflection the general scheme became clear. The Spitfire was to be a sort of datum pacemaker—Mr. Average Contemporary Fighter. Its job would be to become last, the real excitement of the proceedings being a) by how much it would be beaten by the FW 190 and the Typhoon and b) which of these two bright stars would beat the other and by how much. Outside the tarmac at Worthy Down stood the inoffensive-looking but highly potent DP845. Nobody had said what sort of Spitfire I should bring. Just a Spitfire...
>
> I rang up Joe Smith. 'Joe,' I said, 'about this thing at Farn. I reckon if I take DP845 I will beat the pair of them. Will that upset any applecarts?'
>
> 'You bet it will,' he said. 'Take it'.
>
> At Farnborough I parked DP845 as inconspicuously as I could and walked into Willy Wilson's office. Kenneth Seth-Smith of Hawkers

had arrived with his Typhoon, and together we discussed the plan. We would all three take-off and fly to a point west of the nearby aerodrome at Odiham. We would then head back towards Farnborough in open line abreast at a moderate cruising speed at 1,000 feet. Willy Wilson in the centre with the FW 190 and Seth-Smith and myself on each side of him. At a signal from Willy we could fall open up simultaneously to full power and head for the finishing line at Farnborough, where the assembled VIPs would be waiting.

All went according to plan until we were about half-way between Odiham and Farn and going flat out. I was beginning to overhaul the FW 190 and the Typhoon. Suddenly I saw sparks and black smoke coming from the FW 190's exhaust, and at that moment Willy also saw them and throttled back his BMW engine. I shot past him and never saw him again. The Typhoon was also easily left behind. The eventual finishing order was the Spitfire in first place with the Typhoon second and the FW 190 third.

Jeffrey Quill, *Spitfire: A Test Pilots Story*, pp. 233–234

DP845 went on to become the prototype XII. It was the first Spitfire with the Griffon engine installed. DP845 was based on an Mk II airframe; the airframe was strengthened to cope with the increased power and torque of the new, powerful engine.

Lundsten flew it in September 1943 for thirty-five minutes, listing the flight as 'handling' (written 'handeling').

Date: 24.09.1943
Spitfire(s): XIV JF320; XI MB938; XI MB937; XII MB882; Seafire MA970
Built: Worthy Down (XIV JF320), Chattis Hill (XI MB938; XI MB937; XII MB882), High Post (Seafire MA970)

Another interesting list of Spitfires were flown on this day. At first glance, the serial number JF320 looks to be a VIII. However, it is not. Six VIII airframes were diverted from the production line in 1943 to have Griffon engines installed, unofficially known as VIIIgs. One of these Spitfires was JF320, installed with a Griffon 61 engine. Lundsten did not test fly it, but rather flew another handling flight to get to know this particular mark of Spitfire. At low level, and between 20,000 feet and 25,000 feet, the VIIIs were faster. Above 30,000 feet, the Griffon-engine XIV was faster and had a better rate of climb. The XIV also had a better turn-rate, in addition to good spin characteristics—it simply exited the spin if the pilot removed his hands from the controls. With such good results, the XIV went into production.

It was another first for Lundsten, now having also flown a mark XIV. One could perhaps think that Lundsten did not pick up on the change of mark, especially since the serial number looked to be a VIII, but he did indeed write it down as a XIV in his logbook. He flew JF320 for thirty minutes.

After a quick breather, Lundsten took to the air once again. He took two mark XI Spitfires for their test flights. MB938 had a rather quiet career; it had a spell with Miles Aircraft in 1943, and was struck off charge in 1947.

MB937 was lost at San Severo, Italy, in tragic circumstances. Flight Officer W. E. B. Silva-White, from 682 Squadron, took off at 12.15 p.m. on 23 April 1944 for a photo-recce sortie over the areas of Klagenfurt and Graz. He returned two hours later, reporting trouble with his instruments. At 2.45 p.m. he took off again, this time in MB937. While in circuit, he lost control of the Spitfire. It went into a stall at 300 feet and crashed on the airfield and burst into flames—Silva-White was killed instantly in the accident and MB937 was completely destroyed. The loss of the pilot was deeply felt in 682 Squadron.

Arguably the most historic moment for Leif Lundsten as a test pilot at Worthy Down was his connection to MB882, the last Spitfire XII produced, and perhaps the most photographed Spitfire during the Second World War. On this day in September, he went to High Post to pick up this historic piece of machinery. The task was to fly it to Worthy Down for production tests. He knew it was the last XII ever to be made, and (for once) added an extra comment to his usual remarks and professionalism—'the last Spit XII produced'. Just short of a month after Lundsten first flew MB882, fellow test pilot Clive Gosling flew MB882 in formation with an Oxford between Worthy Down and Keevil. Photographer Charles Brown was seated in the Oxford, taking photographs of the flight. Brown has later become somewhat of a 'founding father' for aviation photographers.

MB882 went to 41 Squadron, who were equipped with XII Spitfires. Most of the XIIs Lundsten flew went to this squadron. MB882 was flown by Flight Commander Don Smith (RAAF) and then Flight Lieutenant Terry Spencer, when Smith was posted to 453 Squadron. In June 1944, the Spitfire was involved in a particularly hairy moment; Peter Cowell flew the aircraft so low over the English Channel that he bounced off the water, shattering all four blades evenly—about halfway down on each—and he barely got back to base. MB882 and Terry Spencer had one of the last Spitfire XII kills of the war when he shot down a Focke-Wulf 190 on 3 September 1944. MB882 took several hits to the tail during the fight. Spencer also shot down several V-1s while flying the Spitfire. It was also in MB882 that he 'tipped' a V-1 instead of shooting it down. Several air-to-air photographs of MB882 can be seen in squadron letters, in other words, after it arrived at 41 Squadron.

High Post Airfield, Salisbury—Birthplace of the last Spitfire XII

The tiny hangar where Spitfires were assembled, and the airfield from which they flew and tested, had to be seen to be believed. Originally intended for use in maintaining the types of aircraft that were used by pre-war flying clubs, the hangar was just large enough to take three Spitfires, providing the first two had their tail ends pushed into the opposite rear corners so that the third could get its tail and fuselage between them, its wings then blocking the other two. If either of the side ones had to come out first, the front one had to be pushed out on to the tarmac apron to give enough manoeuvring space. The push-open sliding doors were just high enough to permit the propellers to clear at the top, as long as the three blades were in the 'Y' position. One side of this little hangar had a brick built lean-to addition, which we housed the armory and the toilets.

For canteen facilities we had to trek over half a mile across the airfield, or along the roadway that ran beyond its boundary hedge, nearly to the Wessex Pyrotechnics factory, where the flying club's little wooden club house was situated. Later on in the war—after I had left in the autumn of 1943—a large new hangar was built across the road and became Jeffrey Quill's Test Flight Headquarters.

C. R. Russel, *My Life at Supermarine*, 1985, p. 109

Most often the pilot would be a RAF pilot seconded to testing Spitfires while 'on rest' from operational flying; in some instances he might well be either French, Polish or Belgian, but whatever his nationality he would have had operational experience in Spitfires and very often in the Battle of Britain. Sometimes we would get Jeffrey Quill himself—our Company's chief test pilot and it was always an experience to see this very expert pilot carry out his test flying—not with any unnecessary aerobatics for display purposes, but smoothly and accurately so that every flying facet and characteristic of that particular aircraft was examined and either found correct or it would be brought in and have whatever adjustments were required to meet the high standard he set.

C. R. Russel, *Spitfire Postscript*, 1994, p. 105

Date: 25.09.1943
Spitfire(s): Seafire III MA970
Built: High Post
More stability tests, this time in Seafire III MA970 (see 22.08.1943). After

the stability test in the Seafire, Lundsten made several flights between Worthy Down and High Post, Chattis Hill, Eastleigh, and Hucknall in other equipment.

Date: 27.09.1943
Spitfire(s): XII MB882
Built: High Post

The only Spitfire flight of the day was a handling and service loading in MB882.

Date: 28.09.1943
Spitfire(s): VIII JG332; XI MB942; XI MB941; VIII JG334; XII EN227
Built: Chattis Hill (VIII JG332; XI MB942; XI MB941; VIII JG334), High Post (XII EN227)

On 28 September 1943, there were three ten-minute flights, each in JG332, a mark VIII. This was then followed with three flights in MB9842, three flights in MB941, and two twenty-minute flights in JG332 and EN227. All of these flights were production tests.

JG332 went to Australia and was given A58-380 as its new serial number. It went into storage 24 May 1946, and was scrapped in September of 1949.

MB942, the second on Lundsten's schedule this day, went to 400 (City of Toronto) Squadron, Royal Canadian Air Force. They were equipped with the PR Spitfire XI in June 1943, and they also flew Mosquitoes during the same period. On the first day of January 1945, MB942 came to an end when it was damaged beyond repair; this was during a German air raid while it was parked at an airfield in Eindhoven. It was written-off on 27 April 1945.

MB941 had a spell with 140 Squadron, a photo-reconnaissance unit, and arrived at their home base a month after Lundsten first flew the fighter. It also had spells with 16 Squadron and 400 Squadron (arriving 14 September 1944), which meant it was reunited with her sister Spitfire, MB942. It was struck off charge in November of 1947.

JG334 went to North Africa, according to some sources. However, author Andrew Thomas mentions JG334 in his book *Spitfire Aces of Burma and the Pacific*:

No 615 Squadron based near Calcutta at Alipore was the first to make the switch [from Hurricanes to Spitfires]. Commanded by 5.5 kill ace Squadron Leader Bob Holland, its first Spitfire arrived on 30th of September 1943. The unit passed on its Hurricanes on to Mohawk IV-equipped No 5 Squadron. No 615 Squadron undertook its first sortie on 2nd of October when Holland (in JG334) flew a height and pressure test.

Spitfire Aces of Burma and the Pacific, 2009, p. 28

JG334 was struck off charge in 1946.

EN227 was another XII Leif Lundsten test flew at Worthy Down. It joined 778 Squadron at Duxford on 28 February 1943. Almost a year later it went to 91 Squadron. In the middle of all this, Lundsten strapped on the XII on 28 September 1943. Perhaps unbeknownst to Lundsten, the Spitfire had already been with an operational squadron—so why was it at Worthy Down? The aircraft had had an engine change—a Griffon III was installed during this period—which may or may not be the reason for its time at Worthy Down.

EN227 also underwent trials with the Royal Navy, which might supply another reason as to why it was at Worthy Down (however, this was done in 1944 and not in the autumn of 1943). Jeffrey Quill gives more insight into EN227 and its Royal Navy trials:

The general characteristics of the Mk XII, from the viewpoint both of performance and handling, made it extremely attractive as a potential naval carrier-borne fighter. In February 1943 two of these aircraft— EN226 and EN227—were fitted with hooks and delivered to the Fleet Air Arm Service Trials Unit at Arbroath for evaluation and aerodrome dummy deck landings (ADDLs). Deck-landing trials were flown by Lieutenant 'Winkle' Brown on 7 March, flying from Machrihanish to HMS *Indomitable*, when he made fifteen landings with EN226. These led to the development for the Fleet Air Arm of the Seafire XV and XVII aircraft, two of their most potent fighters. I also made landings on *Indomitable* in a Seafire II that day, this being my first experience of carrier flying and very challenging I found it. I spent that night aboard *Indomitable* and had a long conversation with Admiral Lumley Lister, Flag Officer Carrier Training, and Commander 'Tubby' Lane who commanded the Carrier Trials Unit in which 'Winkle' Brown was a leading pilot. In the process I began to acquire insights into the problems of naval aviation, and the shortcomings of the Seafire as a naval fighter. I felt sure that a great deal could be done to the Seafire to make it a more practical naval aircraft and I made up my mind I must find out more about the problems.

Jeffrey Quill, *Spitfire: A Test Pilots Story*, 1983, ed. 1998, p. 236

On 29 December 1944, it went to 91 Squadron (as previously mentioned). On 20 January 1944, it was damaged in a collision at Tangmere; Pilot Officer J. T. May landed the Spitfire at the airfield, but collided with Spitfire XII EN606, piloted by Sergeant A. H. Exelby. A third XII, EN615, flown by D. E. Proudlove, which then collided with one or both of the Spitfires (EN227 and EN606). EN606 was written-off, and the other two were repaired.

In June, the same year, EN227 went to 41 Squadron. It was given the squadron letters EB-S and flown by Squadron Leader Chapman. One interesting thing to note is that Norwegian Ingar Helge Knudsen (611 Squadron) flew this Spitfire in July of 1944 for thirty minutes. He borrowed the fighter from Chapman for a quick flight, describing his flight with it as 'Wizard!' Knudsen was most likely the second Norwegian pilot after Lundsten to fly a XII. It is without a doubt the only XII that two Norwegians flew during the Second World War. Knudsen did obviously not know that another Norwegian had flown the Spitfire as far back as September 1943.

EN227 survived the war, but was scrapped on 23 November 1945. Considering the few XIIs produced, one might think EN227 would have been of interest to museums, but this was not the case.

Date: 29.09.1943
Spitfire(s): VIII JG335; VIII JG337
Built: Chattis Hill

On 29 September, normal production test routines were flown, bringing the month to a quick close at Worthy Down—Lundsten flew two more VIIIs on this day.

JG335 went to 601 Squadron, who were based in Italy at the time. On 9 February, JG335s career in the Royal Air Force came to a sudden halt. The Nettuno beach-head battle area was patrolled by eight Spitfires at 12,000 feet to 21,000 feet. Enemy aircraft were reported coming in from the north at 20,000 feet, with two of them spotted at 23,000 feet. They were chased, but no engagements took place. B-25 Mitchells were seen to bomb gun positions on the ground. The eight Spitfires of 601 then returned back to their home base. Sergeant K. R. Henderson, an Australian, was flying JG335 during this sortie; it was not reported what brought him down, but Henderson and JG335 ended up in a field near Nettuno. JG335 was a write-off, but Henderson was uninjured. Henderson had flown JG335 on several sorties in February, but this flight turned out to be JG335s last.

JG337 went to Mediterranean theatre of war. One pilot who flew JG337 was Flying Officer Geoff Bates. He had gotten a posting to ferry Spitfires to Cairo, Sicily, Italy, and Corsica before he was posted back to Britain in 1945. It could very well be that he ferried JG337 to its new home in this area of operations. JG337 got into combat flying with 145 Squadron, and had the squadron letter ZX-T marked on its fuselage. On 19 May 1944, Joseph Scarisbick Ekbery, aged twenty-four from Liverpool, shot down a Focke Wolf 190 flying JG337. The Spitfire was struck off charge in November 1945.

JG337 was the last Spitfire Lundsten tested in September 1943. On 29 and 30 September, he had trips to Chattis Hill and Eastleigh flying an Oxford. He had flown 31.25 hours on Spitfires in September alone. He still did not write down what bomber he had flown, but marked it as thirty minutes of flying. Either he did not know what type it was, or it was a secret not to be written down in logbooks.

26

Spitfire XII to North Weald: October 1943, RAF Worthy Down, Chattis Hill and Eastleigh, Hampshire

Date: 01.10.1943
Spitfire(s): XIV JF320
Built: Worthy Down

Just short of an hour of flying in the Worthy Down-based Spitfire XIV fighter, JF320.

> Design work was put in hand immediately at Supermarine and JF316-JF321 were converted in the works. Changes to the aircraft, generally known as Spitfire Mk VIIIg, were restricted to those essential to enable it to accept the new engine, and I flew the first example (JF361) on 20 January 1943. It had a spectacular performance, doing 445mph at 25,000 feet with a sea-level rate of climb of cover over 5,000 feet per minute, and I remember being greatly delighted with the aircraft. It seemed to me that from this relatively simple conversion, carried out with a minimum of fuss and bother, had come something quite outstanding—another quantum jump, almost on par with the jump from the Mk V to the Mk IX.

Jeffrey Quill, *Spitfire: A Test Pilots Story*, 1983, ed. 1998, p. 237

Date: 02.10.1943
Spitfire(s): VIII JF707; VIII JG269
Built: Eastleigh, Keevil

Two flights in JF707, first more tank busting, and then testing air temperatures. Four flights were then undertaken in JG260, bringing the total amount of time flying the latter up to forty-minutes' worth of flying.

JG269 was transported to Australia and given the serial number A58-378. It was struck off charge in 1948.

Lundsten had to days off test flying, but was back on 5 October.

Date: 05.10.1943
Spitfire(s): VIII JG342; VIII JG343; XI MB945; VIII JG204
Built: Chattis Hill (VIII JG342; VIII JG343; XI MB945), Eastleigh (VIII JG204)

Back in business again, Lundsten tested more Spitfire VIIIs going to Australia. JG342—of the same batch as many of the others he had flown—also went 'down under', and was delivered in February 1944. JG342 and its pilot ultimately met a tragic end. In the morning of 19 April 1944. Three Spitfires of 548 Squadron RAF, took off from Strathpine airfield. Near the airfield and just north Brisbane, Squadron Leader William Henry Alexander Wright, flying JG350, collided with Sergeant Alan Victor Chandler from Chingford, Essex, flying JG342 from 458 Squadron—both pilots were killed. An information sign about the accident has been erected at the corner of Young's Crossing Road and Dayboro Road, at Petrie. Behind it is a rock in which part of one of the aircrafts wiring is embedded.

More on the accident from 548 Squadron ORB:

A section of three A flight machines (F/O Hilton, F/Lt Price and Sgt Chandler) took off at 08:45 this morning and after orbiting the strip, decided to bounce a Spit which had just taken off and was climbing down sun. This section closed to 250 yards at about 2,500 feet and broke away to the right. Red 1 (F/O Hilton) then banked to the left to make sure that Red 2 (F/Lt Price) and Red 3 (Sgt Chandler) were still with him—they were flying line astern—when, to his horror, he saw that Red 3 and the other aircraft had collided. Both kites went into the deck without either pilot getting out. The unknown aircraft was the C.O of the Squadron. We were all dazed at the tragedy—it just didn't seem possible that two good pilots should buy it in such unfortunate accident. Had they bought it on ops, it would have been bad enough, but on a routine practice flight—well it left us numbed. F/Lt Watts assumed the office of Temporary Commanding Officer, and the first thing he did was to call all the pilots of the Squadron together. He told us that the C.O was flat out for building the Squadron into an efficient top line crowd, and that it was up to us to see that we carried on. Although many of us had known S/Lt. Wright for a long time, there is little time for sentiment in war. Its hats off the past, coats off the future. Photographs of the crashed planes are attached. S/ldr W. H. A.

Wright (70834) killed as a result of off flying accident at Strathpine. No 1319672 Sgt. Pilot Chandler A.V killed as a result of flying accident at Strathpine. F/Lt J. A. Aitken appointed adjusting officer to deal with the effects of the late S/Ldr Eright. P/O A. H. Davison appointed adjusting officer to deal with the effects of the late Sgt. Pilot Chandler. P/O W. J. Blooming's appointed Burials Officer for the late S/Ldr Wright.

The funeral for the two pilots, who died in the accident, were held the next day in Brisbane at Lutwyche Military Cemetery with full service honours. Officers and airmen paid their last respects to the CO and Sgt Chandler. Chandler was twenty-two years old at the time of his death, and Wright was aged twenty-six. Lundsten also flew Wright's Spitfire JG350 (see 09.10.1943).

MB945 is another interesting Spitfire. Built at Chattis Hill as a PR XI sometime in the summer of 1943, it was first flown by Leif Lundsten on 5 October 1943. Other sources state that the first flight took place at Benson on 7 October, which is incorrect. It was passed on to the USAAF on 30 October at Mount Farm. Flown by Lt Franklyn I. Van Wart on 1 March 1944, the Spitfire was reported to be lost over the English Channel. This might possibly not be the case, as it was captured by the Germans and flown as part of *Zirkus Rosarius*.

JG343, first flown on this day by Lundsten, was transferred to Australia and given the new serial number A58-344. It was eventually authorised for write-off in May 1945, and scrapped in 1948.

JG204 was a VIII that was extensively flown by Supermarine test pilots, but usually later on than during Lundsten's time as a test pilot. It first flew 23 September 1943, and in 1944 it was used in trials using the F23 wing section. The aim was to improve the pilot's view and reduce drag, but this task was met with little success. It was also used in trials with four cannons installed. It was sold for scrap in 1946. Lundsten flew it from Chattis Hill to Worthy Down, a ten-minute flight. He also flew two passengers from Worthy Down to Chattis Hill after his flight in JG204, but no return flight was listed.

Date: 06.10.1943
Spitfire(s): VIII JG345
Built: Chattis Hill

A whole four flights in JG345, the first only lasting five minutes, and all flights were noted as production tests. JG345 went to Australia marked as A58-381, where it went through several squadrons, including 549 Squadron, before being struck off charge in 1948.

Date: 07.10.1943
Spitfire(s): VIII JG344; XI MB946; VIII JG347; VIII JG344
Built: Chattis Hill

On 7 October 1943, four flights were flown in three Spitfires—Lundsten flew JG344 once again later in the day. JG344 went to India, and, with 81 Squadron based at Imphal, it swung on landing and overturned.

MB946, a photo-reconnaissance Spitfire, went to the United States Army Air Force in November 1943. MB946 was flown by Lt Verner K. Davidson on 29 May 1944, when he flew a bomb-damage assessment flight with the 7th Photo Group. Over Lütkendorf, his camera mounted on the Spitfire recorded oil storage tanks burning from the bombing mission a day earlier. It served with 14th Photo Group, based at Mount Farm, in the spring of 1945. By 1945, the usual blue paint had been stripped to metal, and a standard 12-inch red strike was added to the cowling for identification. This can be seen on photographs of MB946 at this point. The Spitfire was struck off charge in July 1945.

JG347 was another Spitfire destined for Australia. This one was given the serial A58-382. With 548 Squadron, it had the squadron letters TS-M. It was struck off charge in 1948.

Then, as mentioned and for unknown reasons, Lundsten once again flew JG344, which would also be his final flight of the day.

Date: 08.10.1943
Spitfire(s): VIII JG344; VIII JG348; VIII JG347; XI MB947; VIII JG346
Built: Chattis Hill

Over one-and-a-half hours of flying Spitfires was done on 8 October. JG344 was the first up, before Lundsten moved onwards to more VIIIs. He flew JG348 only for ten minutes before he deemed it to be okay; he then flew MB947, a XI, a total of five times in comparison.

JG348 saw combat in India with 81 Squadron. Andrew Thomas wrote:

No. 81 Squadron was in action once again on 25 April (1944), when, shortly before 07:30 hrs, eight Spitfires were scrambled against an incoming raid of around 30 fighters. In the resulting fight, Flt Lt 'Bars' Krohn (in JG348) damaged three 'Oscars' although his fighter was also hit.

Spitfire Aces of Burma and the Pacific, 2009, p. 4

The fighter may have ended its life when it crashed in a paddy field on approach to Kangla. Another flight in JG347 followed (flown the day before) before Lundsten took to the skies in MB947. This Spitfire had spent time with 140 Squadron and 400 Squadron before being struck off charge in 1945.

Back to VIIIs, the Spitfire of the day was JG346. This one also went to Australia, and was given the serial number A58-345.

Date: 09.10.1943
Spitfire(s): VIII JG346; VIII JG350; VIII JG349; VIII JG351
Built: Chattis Hill

Two flights in JG346 before Lundsten felt the Spitfire was fit for operations. JG350 was the second Spitfire involved in the mid-air crash in Australia. This one was flown by Squadron Leader Wright. Lundsten flew both the Spitfires that were involved in this tragic crash (see 05.10.1943).

JG349 went to India, this one was also a part of 81 Squadron. Andrew Thomas picks up the story:

As the fighting on the ground intensified, so the JAAF's aerial offensive was also stepped up a gear, with daily sweeps over the Imphal area by large formations of fighters and bombers. On the afternoon of 17 April, 50+ Ki-43s drawn from the 50th, 60th, 64th and 204th Sentais covered just six Ki-21 'Sallys' in an attack on Imphal. 'Oscars' from the 50th Sentai initially flew a sweep ahead of the main formation, which was heading for Palel. However, before the latter could reach their target they then followed the enemy towards Tamu. Flg Off. Alan Peart, in JG349/FL-D recalled scoring his final kill during this mission. 'We were scrambled from the strip on a clear day, and I think I was leading B-flight's four Spitfires. We climbed hard under instruction from the controller and intersected a large enemy force. There were six bombers at 15,000 ft with covering fighters up to 30,000 ft. We positioned ourselves and then attacked the top cover. At high altitude the Japanese aircraft performed poorly in comparison with the Spitfire, and they rapidly joined their medium cover fighters. This is where the main combat took place. The 'Oscar' I claimed destroyed was badly hit, and it fell out of the sky out of control. The fighter spun, recovered, spun and recovered in that sequence until a gout of flame appeared from the jungle below me. I was assembling my flight for a further attack when a second 'Oscar' came up from underneath me, firing in my direction until he could climb no more—he then stall-turned away.

As we were assembling I only took evasive action, and did not press home this further good opportunity.

Spitfire Aces of Burma and the Pacific, 2009, p. 45

JG351 went to Australia as A58-346, and it was struck off charge in 1948.

Date: 11.10.1943
Spitfire(s): VIII JG351; XI MB948
Built: Chattis Hill

Three flights in JG351, before the rest of the day was dedicated to MB948. MB948 went to the USAAF 14th Photo Reconnaissance Squadron, where it was often flown by Lt John S. Blyth, 14 Squadron, at Mount Farm, UK. The Spitfire had *Oh Johnny* written on the fuselage around the time of D-Day. The Spitfire was recorded in colour film at Mount Farm in 1944. Verner K. Davidson was flying MB948 during this recording. He passed away 7 December 2013 (see 07.10.1943 for more on Davidson). Judging by this, Davidson flew at least two of Lundsten's Spitfires.

Date: 13.10.1943
Spitfire(s): VIII JG353; VIII JG352 (VIII JG353)
Built: Chattis Hill

JG353 went to Australia and was given the serial A58-357. With 54 Squadron, it was given the squadron letters DL-M. Lundsten flew the Spitfire twice this day, and in between these flights he flew JG352.

JG352 also went to Australia, this one as A58-347. In November 1944, the Spitfire crashed into the sea 60 miles off Truscott Airfield, Australia. Its pilot, Flying Officer R. A. H. Palmer, was killed.

Truscott Airfield was named after Squadron Leader Keith 'Bluey' Truscott of 76 Squadron RAAF, who was killed in the Exmouth Gulf in 1943 when his Kittyhawk hit the sea.

Date: 15.10.1943
Spitfire(s): VIII JG352; VIII JG353; VIII JG354; VIII JG373; XI MB950
Built: Chattis Hill

There were a whopping eighteen take-offs and landings on 15 October 1943. First up was another four flights in JG352, and then another round with JG353 before he took JG354 to the air.

JG354 made its mark in history; it was photographed when Air Vice-Marshal C. A. Bouchier, Air Officer Commanding No. 221 Group, RAF, greeted Flight-Lieutenant D. E. Nicholson of Harrow, Middlesex, on completing the last operational sortie by No. 607 Squadron, RAF, prior to its disbandment at Mingalon, Burma. JG354 was Nicholson's Spitfire—JG354 AF-Z. It also spent some time with the RAAF as A58-358

JG373 went to Australia, and was provided with the new serial number A58-394. It crashed on take-off in July 1944 at Livingstone airfield, Australia.

MB950 is a special case. Another Spitfire, PA908, is painted as MB950 and is based in Dayton, Ohio, where it is on display. Some truly fantastic colour photographs exist of MB950 from the Second World War. It served with 14th Photo Squadron at Mount Farm, and was nicknamed *Upstairs Maid*. It is represented widely on the internet with photographs, simulation game skins, and countless profiles. MB950 was struck off charge in September 1945.

A lengthy day of Spitfire flying for Lundsten, all listed as production tests. There was no time to rest though, as the next day brought a new batch of Spitfires that needed to be flown.

Legendary Battle of Britain ace Tom Neill has more on Chattis Hill:

I was soon to learn that Chattis Hill was within 10 miles of Salisbury and therefore in my local area, and that the Spitfire I was expected to fly was a Mark VIII, a type on which I had no experience but one about which I knew a great deal. The Mark VIII, I was aware, was the planned successor to the Mark V, which by 1943 had been totally outclassed by the German Focke-Wulf 190 and relegated to being flown in a supporting role by RAF squadrons not in the front line. To bridge the gap, the Mark IX had been quickly introduced. It was basically a Mark V with one of several more powerful Merlin 60-series engines to be installed. In fact, the Mark IX-b with a Merlin 55—the LF Mark IX, as it was officially referred to—was so successful that the Mark VIII, which was altogether a more modern version of the Mark IX, was only employed in the Mediterranean and the Far East and never used in Britain.

Tom Neill, *The Silver Spitfire*, 2013, p. 50

Date: 16.10.1943
Spitfire(s): XI MB954; VIII JG372; VIII JG375
Built: Chattis Hill

Production tests in one XI and two VIIIs. MB954 went to 16 Squadron in November 1943—it is portrayed in pink camouflage on various websites.

On 18 September 1944, Flight-Lieutenant A. G. Gibb took off from B.48 Amiens Glisy, in France, in MB954. The aircraft crashed after take-off, and Gibb was killed. He is buried in Rouen Saint Sever cemetery.

JG372, like so many of the JG-series, went to Australia, this one as A58-386. However, JG375 went to India. According to John Hamlin and James J. Halley's book *Royal Air Force Training and Support Units*, JG375 was used by No. 1331 CU to train crews for ferrying duties and convert them to new types of aircraft. Lundsten flew JG375 four times on 16 October before he was satisfied with the performance of the Spitfire.

After two very hectic days, Lundsten was on a break from test flying for four days. On 20 October, he flew to Hornchurch and back in an Oxford. From a logbook perspective, there were some interesting bits and pieces coming up, namely testing No. 222 Squadron Spitfire IXs. This more than explains his trip to Hornchurch the same day.

Date: 20.10.1943
Spitfire(s): IXb ZD-J; IXb ZD-G; IXb ZD-K; IXb ZD-C; IXb ZD-T
Built: Unknown

Instead of the almost routinely 'production test', Lundsten was now testing 222 Squadron Spitfires. The subject of these test were on ailerons and reflection. There is nothing in the 222 ORB indicating any testing, and there's no mention of anyone stopping by the squadron on this day. The squadron itself, with Martin Lardner-Burke flying now famous and legendary Spitfire MH434, were very busy doing their trade over the continent, including a search sortie for lost comrades the same day. While Lundsten only lists the squadron letter in his logbook, the ORB only list the serial number.

Date: 21.10.1943
Spitfire(s): XII MB882; IXb ZD-D; IXb ZD-J
Built: High Post, unknown

Having finished most of his trials flying 222 Squadron Spitfires, Lundsten brought MB882 to Hornchurch on 21 October; however, there's nothing in the 222 ORB on this matter. After Hornchurch, he stopped by his old friends at North Weald again. The look of a XII most likely drew a crowd of onlookers.

At North Weald, thick, low cloud and rain put a damper on the morning, and no operations were carried out on the continent. At 10 a.m., when Lundsten was most likely at either Worthy Down or at Hornchurch, 331 and 332 Squadron pilots went out to search for a missing pilot in the Channel. No. 331 located the pilot, while 332 Squadron searched off Bradwell and did not locate anything. The squadron was then released off camp in the afternoon. At North Weald, Major Arne Austeen was in charge of 331 Squadron at this point in time. Austeen had moved to Gjøvik, Norway, in the 1930s, while coincidentally Lundsten was born and bred just half-an-hour's drive south-east of Gjøvik. No. 331 Squadron was therefore in the hands of two men from the same small area of Norway for about eight months' time.

Five days after Lundsten's visit to North Weald, fellow test pilot at Worthy Down, Clive Gosling, flew MB882 on a photo mission. Several photographs were taken of the fighter—still with no squadron letters painted on the fuselage.

Date: 22.10.1943
Spitfire(s): VIII JG380; XI MB956; VIII JG379
Built: Chattis Hill

JG380 went to India with 607 Squadron. It met its end when, on 16 August 1944, Flight-Sergeant Turner, who had been indulging in some aerobatics, was flying along inverted and on righting his aircraft could not get his engine to start after it had cut out while on its back. On attempting to force-land on Baighachi aerodrome, he stretched the glide too much and JG380 went into an incipient spin. It finished up in three separate pieces, while Turner himself got out unscathed—a lucky escape. However, JG380 was a write-off.

MB956 went to USAAF photo-reconnaissance in December 1943, based at Mount Farm, Oxfordshire. The Spitfire was named *Photogenic Virgin*. It was struck off charge on 13 September 1945. What is interesting is Lundsten's unusually long production test flight—thirty minutes flying MB956.

JG379 went to 607 Squadron in India like JG380 had done. It was struck off charge in 1946.

Date: 23.10.1943
Spitfire(s): VIII JG376; XI MB956; XI MB957; VIII JG382
Built: Chattis Hill

Two flights were executed in the previous day Spitfires JG376 and MB956. Then, another two brand-new ones were ready for flying.

MB957 went to 16 Squadron at Northolt. On the day of its demise, it was flown by Jimmy Taylor. Taylor was interviewed by Colin Goodwin in *Pilot Magazine* and his article was published online on 12 December 2013. The following are his words:

Training completed at Dyce, Taylor was posted to 16 Squadron, based at Northolt and on 26 August 1944 took part in his first operation:

photographing Caen airfield flying Spitfire K954. Fifteen sorties later, on 19 November, he took off in MB957 for Rheine, a base for German jets. The weather was fine, the best for a week. Unfortunately, a bearing in the Merlin's supercharger was on its way out. 'During one of my photograph runs there was a loud bang from the engine,' explains Taylor. 'It stopped, then tried to run again. Smoke was pouring out of the exhausts and oil covered the windscreen. I called Melsbroek on the radio and told them I was bailing out'.

Pilot Magazine, 12 December, 2013.

With the Spitfire destroyed, Taylor was captured and sent to Stalag Luft 1 in Barthe, Germany. Lundsten flew MB957 for fifty-five minutes altogether on this day.

JG382 went to Australia as A58-387 with 452 Squadron. It was authorised for write-off on 22 May 1945, and it was scrapped 15 November 1948.

Date: 24.10.1943
Spitfire(s): VIII JG381; VIII JG379; XI MB955
Built: Chattis Hill

JG381 went to the Mediterranean theatre, where it was scrapped in 1945.

After Lundsten's test flying, MB955 was eventually flown to Mount Farm and the USAAF. It was christened *Lease Fleece*. It was sadly lost on 19 September 1944 under the control of Lieutenant Paul Balogh. John S. Blyth also flew the unarmed Spitfire. On 7 July 1944, Blyth flew the Spitfire over Halberstadt Airfield at 30,000 feet. He photographed a visible Heinkel 111-Z on the ground, a twin Heinkel 111, with six engines mounted on the wings.

Date: 26.10.1943
Spitfire(s): XI MB958; XI MB952; VIII JG384; VIII JG385
Built: Chattis Hill

MB958 went to 16 Squadron on 5 November 1943, and was scrapped in 1945.

MB952, another photo-reconnaissance Spitfire, ended up with a quite bizarre and tragic story. With 14 Squadron 7th Photo Group, it took off from Mount Farm, piloted by Belgian Lt Charles J. J. Goffin, a volunteer. His task was to make a sweep over the Siegfried Line, taking photographs. Eye witnesses reported seeing the Spitfire fly low over Reckange-les-Mersch, Luxembourg, when it crashed near the town. Ironically, the brave Belgian volunteer pilot with the USAAF had come down just 80 miles from his own home town in Belgium. This is according to Air Crew Remembered (see Bibliography).

Goffin was aged thirty-one when he perished. His body was eventually brought back to his hometown in Graide, Belgium.

JG384 was lost in Italy during a dive-bombing attack with 417 Squadron. It was flown by Canadian Flying Officer John Raymond Daly from Crystal City, MB. He crashed to the ground south-east of Bologna, Italy. JG385 went to Australia with the new serial A58-448. It was struck off charge on 15 November 1948—two very different outcomes for these similar aircraft.

Date: 27.10.1943
Spitfire(s): XI MB952; XI PA838
Built: Chattis Hill

On 27 October, there was another flight in MB952 (see 26 October 1943). PA838 went to 16 Squadron in November, and it underwent major repairs on 28 June 1945. It was sold for scrap in September 1945. No. 16 Squadron supplied photographs that were instrumental to the planning of the Allied landings in 1944. Essential reconnaissance continued to be given by the squadron until the end of the war. No. 16 Squadron was part of the 2nd Tactical Air Force. Lundsten's second-to-last flight in PA838 clocked in at twenty-five minutes.

Date: 28.10.1943
Spitfire(s): XI PA839; VIII JG385; VIII JG383
Built: Chattis Hill

PA830 was another PR Spitfire. It had spells with 16 Squadron, 400 Squadron, 412 Squadron, and 26 Squadron before it was struck off charge in 1947. Lundsten had already flown JG385 on 26 October. It went to Casablanca in December 1943 and had a spell with 145 Squadron, before it was finally scrapped on 30 June 1944. The squadron took off from their base at Fabrica, Italy, for Pascana Aerodrome on this day. Eleven Spitfires took off, Lieutenant Milboro was to be number twelve, but he hit a bump on the runway and crashed, with wheels up, off the end. Milboro was okay, but the Spitfire was not.

Date: 29.10.1943
Spitfire(s): VIII JG386; XI PA851
Built: Chattis Hill

JG386 went to Australia and given the serial A58-361. It spent time with 452 Squadron and 549 Squadron, and it was struck off charge in 1948.

PA851 was yet another of the XI Spitfires Lundsten flew that went to the USAAF and their operations from Mount Farm, in Oxfordshire. P851 was sadly lost on 23 December 1943, just two months after its first flight in the hands of Lundsten.

Captain Steven A. 'Scotty' Scott, operations officer of the 22nd Squadron of the 7th Photo Group, flew PA851 over Osnabrück and Münster, Germany, on a photo-recce sortie. He had begun the long journey back to the UK when he ran into trouble. His engine died, and he reported that he was gliding at 15,000 feet. Ground controllers kept radio contact with Captain Scott for several more minutes and gave him directions to the nearest place to land. They lost radio contact when his altitude was reported to be at 5,000 feet over the sea. A Walrus was quickly scrambled, and they found a concentrated oil slick on the water at the most likely site of impact—about 10 miles from the coast of Suffolk—he was considerably off course. A reason for the crash (besides his engine having cut) has not been found. Perhaps Captain Scott simply ran out of height and in the end had to unsuccessfully ditch the Spitfire in the sea.

Date: 30.10.1943
Spitfire(s): XI PA842; XI PA840; XI PA851; VIII JG386; VIII JF889; XI PA841
Built: Chattis Hill

Rounding off October, a very busy month, Lundsten would fly a mix of XIs and VIIIs. He would be in the air for about one hour and thirty minutes.

PA842 went to the USAAF in November 1943. John S. Blyth flew it on 4 August 1944 over Watten at 15,000 feet. It was later sold to Heston Aircraft Ltd in December 1945. You can also fly PA842 in Microsoft Flight Simulator—a 'skin' has been made for this Spitfire.

PA840 was lost on 22 February 1944, piloted by twenty-two-year-old Warrant Officer Ronald Lidgate from Cheshire. He was reported missing and believed killed on operations. The Spitfire crashed into the sea 2 miles south of Beachy Head.

PA851 was also flown the previous day (see 29.10.1945). Lundsten flew it again twice on 30 October.

Back to VIIIs, JG386 went to Australia and was given the serial A58-361. It was struck off charge in 1948. JF886 was a familiar sight, as Lundsten had test flown the fighter as far back as 23 September.

JF889 went to India and served with both 92 Squadron and 81 Squadron. It was struck off charge 12 December 1944. Looking at the 81 Squadron

ORB, they had one accident on 16 October 1944 when one Spitfire landed at Minneriya with a dead engine. The pilot was okay, but the Spitfire was damaged. This could have been JF889, as the squadron had few accidents and no operational flying during these months in '44.

Rounding up the day (and the month) in PA481, this Spitfire was later christened *Kisty the 1st* at Mount Farm. John S. Blyth flew the fighter in June 1944 over Nantes, France. He also flew over Dessau airfield in Germany in May the same year, taking photographs from 30,000 feet. It was struck off charge in 1945.

The monthly total of flying ended at 38 hours on Spitfires.

27

Miss Sheila Lee:
November 1943, RAF Worthy Down,
Chattis Hill and Eastleigh, Hampshire

Working on an airfield is vastly different from the confines of a factory workshop. The close contact with the completed product, and the knowledge that was one did, if not done properly, might risk the life of any of the pilots we got to know, induced a form of self-discipline, and of course always, whilst on dayshift, there was flying to watch. Many of our Spitfires were test flown by service pilots who were 'resting' between operational tours of duties.

One I remember vividly was a Belgian—and as mad as a March Hare. I was in attendance on him one day, and while chatting during a minor engine adjustment by our Rolls-Royce representative, he bet me that even if I stood on the battery trolley-acc, he could still come upon me by surprise and force me to jump down. He did too—after throwing the Spit all over the sky he went low below the hump in the middle of our airfield and I expected him to come powering in from the Pyrotechnics works direction [at High Post], but, cunningly, he went further towards Salisbury along the Woodford Valley, then turned in over Old Sarum and hedge-hopped to finally hurtle in over small woods on my left, and so low that had I not jumped, I'm sure the whizzing prop would have decapitated me. When he landed I had to concede that he was the victor, but the final laugh was on him. He reported to the inspector, of vibration in the port wing, and at the Inspector's request I removed the post nose fillet panel to allow him to look inside. As I drew away I noticed a square inch of metal just beyond the first wing nose rib. Lifting it all out I was amazed to find it was eighteen inches long— obviously a riveter's bar and weighing all of two or three pounds.

Poor old 'Belgie', he had been throwing the Spit about with this great lump of metal clattering about loose in the wing. The inspector, quite rightly, had all the access covers and wing doors removed, but despite rigorous search with torchlight, and mirrors on sticks, no damage was found. I hope 'Belgie's' luck held for the remainder of his wartime flying. The 'dolly-bar' was never claimed by any riveter.

C. R. Russell, *Spitfire Odyssey: My Life at Supermarines*, 1985, pp. 111–112

The only Belgian (according to Jeffrey Quill's list of test pilots) was called Pierre Arend. Arend was considerably older than most of his peers, born in 1908, and he had served with several units in England and Burma. He was with Vickers-Armstrongs in the spring of 1943 and went back to operational flying a month before Lundsten went to Vickers-Armstrongs. His luck did indeed hold, and he survived the war, passing away in 1983.

Date: 02.11.1943
Spitfire(s): XI PA841
Built: Chattis Hill
Length: 0:10

A ten-minute production test in PA841. Lundsten had previously flown the Spitfire on 30 October.

Date: 03.11.1943
Spitfire(s): XI PA840; XI PA892; VIII JG387
Built: Chattis Hill

Another short flight in PA840 before taking PA892 to the air. The Spitfire was named *My Darling Dorothy* and was originally assigned to Lt Dan Kraft and named after his sister Dorothy, but was flown (like most of the Spitfires were) by a number of pilots at Mount Farm. It was scrapped in 1946. According to *The Eight Ballers: Eyes of the Fifth Air Force: The 8th Photo Reconnaissance Squadron in World War II* (1999), Captain Walter Eitner flew PA892 on 6 March over Berlin. It was the first time a USAAF Spitfire completed a reconnaissance sortie over the German capital. With PA892 enjoying a long life with the USAAF, she changed her colours in the last stages of war. The unit decided to sacrifice their camouflage blue colour for more speed, remaining cautious about Germany's new jet fighters. PA982 can therefore be seen on different photographs in different colours.

JG387 was sent to Australia and was given the serial A58-388. With 548 Squadron, it had the squadron letters TS-U. It was struck off charge in 1948.

Date: 05.11.1943

Spitfire(s): VIII JF895; VIII JF894; VIII JF898; XI PA843; XI PA844; XI PA845
Built: Chattis Hill

JF895 was, at some point after Lundsten's test flight, ferried by ATA pilot Miss Taniya Whittall. On 24 November 1943, she landed JF895 rather heavy, which resulted in a ground loop. JF895 subsequently went to 92 Squadron. When the squadron was based in Italy, in September 1944, the Spitfire was lost after pilot O. G. Meagher was hit by flak—he crashed at Poggio Berni.

JF984 also went to 92 Squadron in Italy. It got into several dogfights with the enemy, including one on 18 May 1944 when it was flown by Flight Sergeant Peacock. No. 92 Squadron made seven claims during the encounter (six damaged and one destroyed). The Spitfire went missing during a weather recce over the Adriatic Sea on 12 November 1944.

JF898 had a less action-packed career. It was sold for scrap in 1946 after having had lengthy spell in the Middle Eastern theatre of war.

PA843 went to 680 Squadron, but the story behind the fighter from there on is unknown. PA844 went to 683 Squadron and was subsequently struck off charge in October 1945. PA845 went to the Middle East with 680 Squadron, and was struck off charge in September 1946.

In the afternoon, Lundsten flew a Miles Magister to High Post and back, and then stayed at Eastleigh overnight. On 6 November, he flew out from Eastleigh, stopped by Chattis Hill, before ending up back at Eastleigh. The test flights on the 6th and 7th may have taken place at Eastleigh.

Date: 06.11.1943
Spitfire(s): XI PA847; XI PA845; XI PA843; XI PA844; VIII JF898; XI PA846
Built: Chattis Hill

PA847 had a peculiarly short career; on its ferry flight from Porthreath to Gibraltar, it force-landed in Spain where the Spitfire was interned. What happened later is unclear, but the Spitfire was most likely scrapped at some point.

After PA847, Lundsten made two ten-minute flights in PA845, which was first test flown the day before. Another ten-minute flight in PA843, then PA844, and JF898 (also flown the previous day).

PA846 went to India, serving with 681 Squadron, and it was struck off charge 12 June 1945. Lundsten flew the Spitfire for a total of thirty minutes on 6 November, and twenty-five minutes the next day.

Date: 07.11.1943
Spitfire(s): XI PA846
Built: Chattis Hill

Lundsten flew three flights in PA846 before he took off in a Magister alongside a passenger to Chattis Hill, later flying back to Eastleigh. Judging by the logbook, the production test flights for the previous day could have been undertaken at Eastleigh. However, it is difficult to pinpoint his whereabouts as he may have travelled by other means of transportation between Eastleigh, Chattis Hill, and Worthy Down.

Chattis Hill, Hampshire: Spitfire Production Site and Airfield

After the devastating attacks on the Supermarine works at Woolston and Itchen on 26 September 1940, it was decided to abandon the two factories altogether. It was crucial for production to move aircraft production to less obvious sites, in order to make them less vulnerable from attacks by the Luftwaffe. Chattis Hill, Hampshire, was made the new site for the production of Spitfires following the abandonment of Woolston and Itchen.

Chattis Hill was located 2 miles west of Stockbridge, in the county of Hampshire. Chattis Hill could trace its aviation history back to the First World War when it had been used as a landing ground for the Royal Flying Corps. However, the site was not ideal for flying as it was prone to water logging and heavy winds. It was still decided to build more permanent facilities at Chattis Hill, but construction was stopped as the war came to an end. The airfield was then used as storage, but closed in 1919.

The airfield came to life once again when tools and jigs were brought over from Woolston and Itchen. Hangars were built within the shelter of trees, which provided tremendous natural camouflage. The production of Spitfires started in December 1940. The airfield was used for the final erection and test flying of Spitfires. It is likely that Leif Lundsten spent several weeks (if not whole months) at Chattis Hill, flying Spitfires assembled at the site. Initially, Mk Vs were produced, followed by PRIVs from December 1942, VIIIs from spring of 1943, and then PRXIs. A few Griffon-powered XIIs were also produced in the spring of 1943, followed by a larger numbers of XIVs in 1944, and XIXs in 1945. About 1,250 Spitfires were completed at Chattis Hill.

Spitfire production continued throughout the war, but ceased when the Second World War came to an end. Still, some parts for Spitfires continued to be produced at Chattis Hill until 1948. The infrastructure at Chattis Hill was then disassembled, and the old airfield and production site once again returned to nature.

We flew up to Chattis Hill in the following morning, to a find a small grass landing area, apparently an offshoot of the Supermarine

Company, where a small number of aircraft were being assembled and test flown.

Tom Neill, *The Silver Spitfire*, 2013, p. 51

On 8 November 1943, Lundsten was at Eastleigh, flying a passenger in a Magister around the local area—this was his only flight of the day.

Date: 09.11.1943
Spitfire(s): VIII JG563
Built: Chattis Hill

On 9 November, Lundsten performed a twenty-five minute test flight in JG563. This VIII went to India, where it served with both 136 and 132 Squadrons. It was scrapped on 20 September 1945.

Date: 10.11.1943
Spitfire(s): VIII JG318; XI PA848; VIII JG319
Built: Chattis Hill

Lundsten did another round trip to Chattis Hill from Eastleigh before production tests were started. Several brand-new Spitfires were flown this day.
    JG318 ran into trouble with 241 Squadron based at Sinello, Italy, in 1944. On 9 June 1944, the same day Lundsten disappeared off Utah Beach, JG318 was hit by 20-mm flak near Aquila. Second-Lieutenant A. E. Goodman, in JG318, could only watch as his Spitfire was engulfed by smoke. Lieutenant A. R. Lyon led Goodman skilfully back over the enemy lines and explained to him how he should bring the stricken Spitfire down for a crash-landing. Goodman managed to get the Spitfire down, and escaped injuries. Some Italian civilians came over to meet him, and directed him towards the Allied lines. After an hour's walk, he met up with the Allied forces, only to be told he had walked right through a mine-infested area. He was sent further on, but still on foot. After a total of four hours walking in his flying boots, he came the platoon headquarters, where he was received by an officer with a great deal of suspicion. Having identified himself, however, he was delivered by truck to 244 Wing at Venafro. He was picked up by another pilot from his squadron in a Fairchild. As Goodman had just recently been involved in another crash-landing, one would suspect he was put off flying for a while. However, he had lost none of his keenness, despite these hair-raising adventures. Lundsten flew the fighter for fifty minutes altogether.
    PA484 went missing serving with 681 Squadron in Burma. With Warrant Officer William John Cooper, RAAF, it took off from RAF Alipore, south

of Calcutta, *en route* to Cox's Bazar airport, East Bengal, to refuel before continuing on its PR sortie to Namchang. William John Cooper never arrived in PA848 at Cox's Bazar. He was listed as missing, presumed killed on an operational flight. This is according to www.scribd.com/doc/156944140/ Eyes-for-the-Phoenix.

JG319 went to India with 81 Squadron, and it was scrapped in 1946.

Date: 11.11.1943
Spitfire(s): VIII JG320; VIII JG316; XI PA849; XI PA861
Built: Chattis Hill

JG320 served with 151 OTU in Peshawar, India, when it bounced hard on landing on 23 November 1945. The undercarriage collapsed and the Spitfire caught fire; it was registered as scrapped two months later.

JG316 was lost serving with 1 (SAAF) Squadron. On 25 March 1944, it was flown by Ash Homer talongside another Spitfire flown by Derek Cilson. They ran into very bad weather, but managed to climb above it. However, they deviated off their original course in the process. Going down in dense clouds over land was deemed too risky, and the pair headed out to sea. Cilson lead Ash down in a spiral until Ash lost the Spitfire in front of him due to poor visibility. Homer then decided to abort the effort, and baled out of JG316. He got into his dinghy and waited for a Walrus to pick him up.

PA849 had spells with 16 and 4 Squadron. It was sold on 22 August 1947, but no more traces can be found of this Spitfire.

PA861 spent time with 16 Squadron and was damaged on operations in July 1944. It was eventually struck off charge on 23 August 1945.

Date: 12.11.1943
Spitfire(s): VIII JG320; XI PA863; VIII JG323; VIII JG326
Built: Chattis Hill

Lundsten flew two more flights in JG320 before it was declared to be fit for further shipment. Next up was PA863, a Spitfire with yet another tragic end for pilot and aircraft. Serving with 16 Squadron, Flying Officer A. L. Parsall was on his way back to Britain in PA863 when he was hit by flak somewhere in the Calais area. He jumped out of his stricken Spitfire, but no trace was ever found of the pilot. Another fate eerily close to what Lundsten himself would experience in 1944.

JG323 went to India and served with 81 Squadron as well as 132 Squadron before being transferred to the Indian Air Force. It was scrapped in 1947.

JG326 landed with its wheels partly down at Manbur, India, in March 1945, where it was scrapped two months later.

Date: 13.11.1943
Spitfire(s): VIII JG323; VIII JG561; VIII JG567; VIII JG562
Built: Chattis Hill

On 13 November, Lundsten did a twenty-minute flight in JG323, before flying three VIIIs in the 500 serial number range. JG561 went to 273 Squadron at Kyaukpyu, Myanmar (Burma). On 1 February 1945, four Spitfires took off from Kyaukpyu airfield. Sergeant J. Barlow flew JG561 on this sortie. They had been given orders to strike machine-gun positions on the south bank of the Yanbauk Chaung. The Spitfires did excellent work, and the Army was reported to be very pleased with the shooting. All four Spitfires landed safely, but Barlow taxied into soft ground, and JG561 turned over on its back. Barlow suffered a fractured arm and was sent to hospital; what happened to JG561 after this accident is not known.

JG567 became the personal Spitfire of Squadron Leader Bob Day, from 67 Squadron, while in Burma in 1945. The fighter had also spent some time with 607 Squadron (*Spitfire Aces in the Burma and the Pacific*, 2009, p. 94):

No 67's recently appointed CO Sqdn Ldr Bob Day led a section of five Spitfires that were scrambled against a Japanese air attack on shipping around Akyab on 9 January 1945. The enemy formation was compromised of Ki-43s and Ki-84s. Climbing rapidly above the escorts, Day spotted the six Ki-43s led by 64th Sentai CO, Maj Toyoki Eto, and he immediately dived on them. In a brief fight, five were claimed shot down, including two by Bob Day. His final victories took him to 'acedom', all of which were claimed whilst flying Spitfires in Burma. All of Eto's wingmen were killed, while Eto himself had to crash-land his damaged fighter at Myebon. Day received a DFC soon afterwards, but he was then involved in a road accident that ruled him out of further operational flying.

JG567 was finally struck off charge on 31 May 1945.

JG562 also served in India for a long time, with both 136 Squadron and 81 Squadron, before it was scrapped in 1946.

After all those Spitfire flights, Lundsten took the passenger seat in the Magister—going for a visit to Chattis Hill, and then returning to Eastleigh. Then he took the Magister to Feltham (Hanworth Park, now called London Air Park, slightly southeast of Heathrow Airport). Judging by the location of the airfield, and the three days with no flying, it is safe to say that Lundsten was on leave. Landing at Feltham put him within 12 to 15 miles away from his girlfriend, Miss Sheila Lee.

On 16 November, Lundsten flew the Magister again, this time back to Eastleigh with Michael Graham. Whether or not they stayed together during the three days in London is unknown, but they did fly in and out of London together. As for Michael Graham, Jeffrey Quill described him as ebullient and high-spirited while serving as a test pilot with Supermarine. Lundsten dropped off Graham at Eastleigh, before making a round trip to Chattis Hill. He then went on one last Magister flight, flying from Chattis Hill to Worthy Down and back. (The points of departure do not add up, as he landed at Eastleigh and suddenly flew out of Chattis Hill again. However, this information is according to what is written in his logbook.)

From the entries for 13–16 November, it can be concluded that Lundsten was in London. Sheila Lee's apartment in Earl's Court would have been the natural place for him to spend these days.

Miss Sheila Lee

Miss Sheila Lee, most likely a girl of British origin, moved into 262 Earl's Court Road, London, at some point in 1942 or 1943 (first registered in the 1943 phone book). It is not known of what age Miss Lee was, or where she originated from. Sheila Lee was a relatively common name at the time, and women of this name have been traced to places such as York, Bramley, Kettering, Liverpool, Ecclesall, and Sunderland within the years 1915–1926. It could very well be that Lundsten's Sheila Lee was one of these girls.

In the census of 1911, 262 Earl's Court Road was a house containing one (and most likely a rather wealthy) family. In the 1930s, advertisements started appearing in *The Times* where 262 Earl's Court was offered to tenants as apartments. The house had been converted from one big house to two or more flats. It is advertised as the following:

> High class MANSION FLAT; 2nd floor; lounge hall, 2 reception, 4 bedrooms each fitted lavatory basin, hot and cold, bathroom and admirable domestic offices. Fair war-and-tear agreement, five years unexpired. Rent £275 per annum inclusive.

During the 1930s, the house had one tenant in the name of Alan G. Bruce, who wrote to *The Times* and spoke fondly of fencing as a sport that did wonders for your health—if one had a partner to fence with.

As for Sheila Lee, traces of one can be found living in Colindale before 1943, which places this person very close to RAF Hendon if one was to consider anything aviation-related.

In June 1944, Leif Lundsten was engaged to Miss Sheila Lee from 262 Earl's Court Road. It is not known when Lundsten got engaged, but many of his fellow pilots either married or got engaged before D-Day. On Lundsten's official records, someone has handwritten: 'Engaged: Miss Lee. FRO 0409 (*underettes hvis noget nytt*/informed if any news)'. Considering this, it appears that the information about Miss Lee was added after Lundsten's disappearance.

Miss Sheila Lee, if telephone books are to be trusted, lived in the same apartment until 1960—still going by the name Miss Lee, meaning that she did not marry until the 1960s. From 1960, her name disappeared from the phone books, and no traces are to be found. One Miss Sheila Lee attended a wedding in Liverpool later in the 1960s, but it remains unknown if it was same person.

'I didn't know the neighbours,' was one reply given to numerous requests for Miss Lee during research for this book—it was the closest by date. The reply came from Jennifer Ware, a local resident.

I lived in Earl's Court Sq., just around the corner, in the '40s but I was a child and did not know the neighbours.

Jennifer Ware, E-mail conversation with the author, 2014

Unfortunately, it appears that this lost-love will never be found—vicars have asked their churchgoers about the name, a Harrods manager got involved after a request for a Sheila Lee (though not the right one) was sent to him, local MPs have also entered into the fray, giving tips and information of where to ask next, and several requests have been posted on the internet. So far, all of these efforts have been fruitless.

'We [Leif's brother Bjarne and his son Morten] thought about contacting Tore på Sporet [equivalent to Heir Hunters on BBC] about her in the 1990s, but we never got around to it,' Morten wrote in 2013. Since then, Leif's brother has passed away—never having been able to find his brother's love.

Date: 16.11.1943
Spitfire(s): VIII JG325
Built: Eastleigh

Back from three days stay in London, Lundsten flew JG325. Notice how it was manufactured at Eastleigh, while most of the Spitfires Lundsten had flown in the past month or so had been built at Chattis Hill. Apart from this, JG325 had a long, but relatively quiet life. In 1944 it arrived in India and was quickly transferred to the Indian Air Force. It was scrapped as late as 1947.

Date: 17.11.1943
Spitfire(s): VIII JG325; XI PA860; XI PA867
Built: Eastleigh, Chattis Hill

On this day, there were several more flights in JG325, which was first taken to the air the day before. PA860s claim to fame happened when it collided with a Hurricane of 4 Squadron during taxiing at Akyab airfield, in India, on 3 March 1945—the cause of the collision was poor visibility. Flying Officer Hyder, in the Hurricane, and the pilot of PA860 walked away from the scene across a spreading pool of aviation spirit (Geoffrey Thomas, *Eyes for the Phoenix*, 1998). PA860 lost its entire right wing in the collision. Photos can be seen in the book mentioned above. PA867 went to 682 Squadron, and it was struck off charge on 18 October 1945.

Date: 18.11.1943
Spitfire(s): VIII JG327; XI PA860; XI PA865
Built: Eastleigh (VIII JG327), Chattis Hill (XI PA860; XI PA865)

JG327 ended its career in the most bizarre fashion—it collided with a steam roller while taxiing at Imphal airfield in 1944. However, the exact date of the accident remains somewhat unclear. The Spitfire was struck off charge in July.

Between two flights in brand-new Spitfires, Leif flew two flights in PA860 (first flown the day before), clocking in at thirty-five minutes of flight time.

The last Spitfire for the day, PA865, went to India. It had a spell with 681 Squadron before being scrapped in June 1946.

Date: 19.11.1943
Spitfire(s): VIII JG404; VIII JG405
Built: Chattis Hill

Lundsten flew three flights in JG404 and one flight in JG405, and both Spitfires went to India a month later. JG405 served with 81 Squadron before the Royal Indian Air Force claimed the Spitfire for service. Interestingly, Lundsten performed both test flights on the same day, and when the Spitfires were struck off charge it was again on the same day—30 January 1947.

After flying the two Spitfires, Lundsten flew from Eastleigh to Chattis Hill and back. This is another indication that Lundsten was flying Spitfires out of Eastleigh at this point (today known as Southampton International airport).

Date: 20.11.1943

Spitfire(s): VIII JG500; VIII JG621; VII JG404
Built: Chattis Hill

Lundsten started the day with two more return flights to Chattis Hill from Eastleigh before test flying two new Spitfires and doing another two ten-minute flights in JG404.

JG500, like the previous day's Spitfires, went to India with 607 Squadron, where it was scrapped on 31 July 1947. JG621 also went to India, but had a more violent end to its career; serving with 273 Squadron, on 30 May 1944, it collided with JG565 and was written-off.

Date: 21.11.1943
Spitfire(s): VIII JG406; XI PA850; VIII JG621
Built: Chattis Hill

Lundsten flew another two flights to Chattis Hill and back in the morning. Another India-bound Spitfire, JG406 arrived in the spring of 1944 and was scrapped on 30 August 1945. PA850 took another route and arrived in Gibraltar on 5 January 1944. It served with 680 in the Mediterranean theatre from May 1945. No. 680 Squadron was formed in February 1943 as a photo-reconnaissance squadron; they had a variety of aircraft at their disposal between 1943 and 1946 (Hurricanes, Spitfires, Mosquitoes, Beaufighters, and Lockheed Electras). PA850 was scrapped on 29 August 1946.

Date: 22.11.1943
Spitfire(s): XI PA850; VIII JG621
Built: Chattis Hill

Lundsten had another four flights to do in the Spitfires—PA850 and JG621—from the previous day.

I considered the extended wing tips on the early Mk VIIIs entirely unnecessary. The aeroplane was not, in my view, a specialised high-altitude machine; it was an air-combat fighter with excellent all-round performance and destined for theatres of war where it would have to operate in a wide variety of circumstances. The extended win tips did nothing for it except increase the lateral damping and spoil the aileron control. I complained incessantly to Joe Smith about them and did my best to get rid of them. Eventually—thank the Lord—when the Merlin 66 engine was brought in on the Mk VIII, we reverted to the standard wing-tip configuration. We then had an excellent aeroplane which was very pleasant to handle and with performance as good as the Mk IX, with many other advantages added on.

Alex Henshaw, *Spitfire: A Test Pilots Story*, 1998, p. 221

Date: 23.11.1943
Spitfire(s): VIII JG621; XI PA850; VIII JG500
Built: Chattis Hill

Lundsten undertook more flying in JG621, PA850, and JG500 on 23 November. JG500 seems to have caused lots of headaches as Lundsten flew four flights at five minutes each, and then a final one at ten minutes before he was satisfied.

Eastleigh airfield was originally developed as an Aircraft Acceptance Park for the RFC in 1917. As such it was provided with a number of hangars, when then passed to the US Navy when they arrived in 1918. The airfield closed in 1920 and the hangars were used for migrant accommodation. Purchased by Southampton Corporation, the site was redeveloped as a municipal airport, which was officially opened in November 1932. The RAF arrived in the summer of 1935 and established four FAA Squadrons on 1 October. The airfield was transferred to the Admiralty in 1940. It was re-established post-war as Eastleigh Airport, and major investment in the 1980s saw the emergence of the rebranded Southampton Airport.

Mike Phipp, *Wessex Aviation Industry*, 2011

Date: 24.11.1943
Spitfire(s): VIII JG621; VIII JG481; VIII JG478; VIII JG604; XI PA862
Built: Chattis Hill

Lundsten had yet another flight in JG621 before moving on to three VIIIs and one XI, which were test flown on 24 November 1943. JG481 was sent to Australia, flying with the RAAF as A58-406. It was scrapped in 1948.

JG478 was one of the Spitfires that went to India. On 27 May 1945, Flight-Lieutenant D. M. Finn of 81 Squadron took JG478 up for night flying. During the flight he may have gotten lost; he was unable to find his airfield, and landed on a road instead. Although he got down alright, he ran into a ditch. His undercarriage collapsed and the Spitfire was scrapped shortly thereafter. JG604 went to the RAAF as A58-409, and was scrapped on 15 November 1948.

PA862, the only XI for the day, went to the Middle Eastern theatre of war in June 1944. It might have been marked up with the squadron letter 'W', and it served with the South East Asia Command (SEAC).

Date: 25.11.1943
Spitfire(s): VIII JG604; VIII JG478; VIII JG481; VIII JG484; VIII JG607
Built: Chattis Hill

First up was another ten-minute test flight in JG604. JG481 was also taken up for flights for a total of twenty-five minutes.

First flown two days before Lundsten got his hands on it, JG478 was eventually sent to India. First serving with 273 Squadron, it also moved on to 81 Squadron. On 27 May 1945, still in India, Flight-Lieutenant D. M. Finn force-landed JG478 on a road while lost. He hit a ditch and the undercarriage collapsed near Mysore, India—the Spitfire was scrapped due to the incident.

JG484 is a special case, it was one of the few Spitfires Leif Lundsten flew during the war that is still in existence. The Spitfire was delivered to No. 6 MU (not far from Chattis Hill) on 1 December and then taken onwards to No. 215 MU (at Dumfries), where it was dismantled, crated, and sent to Australia—as was done with all Spitfires sent there. It was delivered to the RAAF and given the new serial A58-408, and then allocated to 54 Squadron as 'DL-T' on 19 May 1944. It stayed with 54 Squadron until it needed the attention of No. 7 RSU (Repair and Salvage Unit) on 18 June 1945. After these repairs, it was sent to an Aircraft and Repair Depot. Parts from another Spitfire, MD238, were authorised to make the necessary repairs and TLC. It was then authorised for write-off (like all of Lundsten's Spitfires going to Australia were at some point) and subsequently scrapped on 15 November 1948—at least that was the official version.

Spitfire Survivors (2010) tells a different story:

This Spitfire project first came to the attention of UK historians when the Australian Woman's Weekly journal ran a follow up story to its 'Spitfires down the mineshafts at Oakey' article of 1980. The story featured several photographs of Bill Martin and Lester Reisinger inspecting a Spitfire being rebuilt for the Oakey Aviation Museum. Strategic positioning of components and the two men gave the impression of a well advanced project. In fact it was just a Merlin engine on its stand with a top cowling draped over it and a propeller spinner hung on the front. To the rear were a firewall top, top tank cover, a propped up windscreen and with the two men obscuring the 'rear end' the illusion was complete. Follow up correspondence with the Bill

Martin elicited the serial MV321, which is believed to have come from a stencil on the inside of an engine cowling. The components were later dispersed, with the principal parts being acquired by Noel Smoothie of Ningi, Queensland. In February 1993 Peter Arnold inspected the parts at Nigel Smoothie's property, the firewall top being of particular interest. There, and unbeknown to the owner, following the removal of a fabricated mounting bracket, the faded stencil marks JG484 could be clearly read, the paint under the bracket being totally fresh. With quite a number of these top firewalls inexplicitly being in existence this was the first to have a factory-applied identicity stencil in this position.

G. Riley, P. Arnold, and G. Trent, *Spitfire Survivors*, 2010, p. 232

Since Peter Arnold's visit in 1993, Smoothie has parted with the project. Alec Wilson of Yunta, South Australia, is said to be the current owner of the project, and the Spitfire is waiting its turn to be restored to flying or static condition.

JG607, thought to have been flown for the first time on 24 November and not 25 November, went to Australia as A58-410. It served with 452 Squadron and 457 Squadron. Lundsten flew another fifteen-minute flight in JG607 the following day.

Date: 26.11.1943
Spitfire(s): VIII JG607; VIII JG485; VIII JG609; XI PA864
Built: Chattis Hill

Lundsten had a fifteen-minute flight in JG607, which he first flew the day before. Next up were three test flights in JG485. JG458 went to Australia and the RAAF, and was given the serial A58-417. The next Spitfire on the list, JG609, also went to Australia as A58-451. It was put into storage in 1945, and scrapped in November 1948. The only XI for the day, PA864, had a long service with 541 Squadron before it was transferred to 8 OTU in 1944. It was struck off charge on 30 May 1946.

Finished with the days Spitfire flying, Lundsten flew to Eastleigh from Chattis Hill with one passenger on board. The interesting aspect of this flight is the aircraft; in his logbook, Lundsten wrote 'Monock' or 'Monack'. The style of his writing suggests that he was unsure of spelling as he wrote it differently than his usual writing style. The aircraft in question could very well be the Miles M.17 Monarch, a two-seat cabin monoplane of low wing configuration, developed in the 1930s. A number of them were used for experimental purposes, which puts them on the right spot for Lundsten having access to such aircraft. Leaving Eastleigh the next day (staying the night), he flew back to Chattis Hill in a Miles Magister on 27 November.

From Chattis Hill, he flew to Feltham the next day for another stay in London. Speculating, considering the absence of any flying into London until his first flight to Feltham on 13 November, it could indicate that his relationship to Sheila Lee had not been for long, and that they met in 1943. It might very well be that he was not in a position to fly to Feltham until he became a trusted, skilled test pilot. Lundsten was back in action at Chattis Hill on 30 November after three days with Miss Lee in London. He flew via Eastleigh back to Chattis Hill on 30 November.

Date: 30.11.1943
Spitfire(s): VIII MD228; VIII JG612
Built: Chattis Hill

Leif Lundsten first flew MD228 from Chattis Hill on this day. It was originally intended to be one of a batch of Mk Vs, but the order was amended and later built in Salisbury as a VIII. It was delivered to No. 82 MU at Lichfield, on 25 December 1943, where it was packed and sent to Australia on board the SS *Hindustan*—it left the UK in February 1944. Like the previous VIIIs Lundsten flew that were shipped to Australia it was provided with a new serial number—MD228 became A58-445. It went through several repairs in Australia before it was stored from 1 October 1945. It was then scrapped in 1948, but parts were recovered from a farm near Oakey, Australia, in the 1970s.

> Eventually passed on to Bob Eastgate in Melbourne, MD228 was identified by the fading witness marks of the serial which had been stencilled on the upper frame 5 firewall panel, this being only one of two instances in current knowledge where an RAF serial has been located here. The parts were stored initially at Essenden and latterly at Point Cook with anticipation of restoration at some point in the future.

> Gordon Riley, Peter Arnold, Graham Trent, *Spitfire Survivors*, 2010, p. 232

Over seventy years after its first ever flight, MD228 became one of the few Spitfires that Lundsten flew that are still in existence today.

JG612 had a quite different life than MD228; it was first listed as flown the day before (29th), and Lundsten flew the Spitfire on 30 November, and the fighter went to India and 17 Squadron. On 4 November 1945, the engine cut during a search; the pilot crash-landed JG612 at Mukkdaw Chaung, and it never flew again.

After flying JG615, Lundsten flew to Eastleigh from Chattis Hill in a Miles Magister. He stayed the night at Eastleigh, and test flew one Spitfire there the next day.

The monthly total of flying ended at 30.50 hours on Spitfires, 12.15 on Magister, and 0.15 in the Monarch.

28

A Christmas with Sheila: December 1943, RAF Worthy Down, Chattis Hill, and Eastleigh, Hampshire

Date: 01.12.1943
Spitfire(s): VIII JG610; VIII JG612; VIII MD224
Built: Chattis Hill

If Lundsten's logbook is to be trusted, the test flight in JG610 was undertaken at Eastleigh, and not Chattis Hill. The fighter was listed to have first flown 29 November 1943, and Lundsten was not the first pilot to fly the Spitfire. The fighter was transferred to India where it stayed for the duration of its career until it was struck off charge in 1946.

Once he was finished with JG610, Lundsten took the Magister and flew back to Chattis Hill where he flew two more Spitfires before the day was over. One of them was JG612 from the previous day.

MD224 was also flown a few days before Lundsten's first flight in the fighter. This one went to India and the famous 152 (Hyderabad) Squadron. It was struck off charge in 1945.

Date: 02.12.1943
Spitfire(s): XI PA869; VIII JG610; VIII JG568
Built: Chattis Hill

PA869 was sent to 16 Squadron on 3 January 1944 and stayed with the squadron until October the same year. With 34 WSU, the Spitfire was taken up for a flight on 18 June 1945, which was to be its last; the engine failed, and the pilot decided to do a wheels-up landing at Sandley, near Gillingham. The airframe was a write-off, and the Spitfire was scrapped just a month later.

The second flight of the day was another one in JG610, and the third and last of the day was in JG568; this Spitfire was sent to India and 273

Squadron. It then went on to 132 Squadron, stationed at Vavunlya, in Sri Lanka. For 132 Squadron, March 1945 was a quiet month with little flying and from time to time, very poor weather that meant the airfield was unserviceable. On 11 March, the weather was good enough for practice flying (which the squadron had also done the two days prior to 11 March), and a tail-chase was scheduled to take place. Pilot Officer Anthony Keith McGregor Paton (nicknamed 'General') from Denbigshire, in Wales, was flying JG568 on this occasion. A new member of the squadron, he had only joined 132 Squadron on embarkation to India in the UK, but he had already become very well-liked by his fellow pilots and members of the squadron. During the tail-chase that took place, Paton crashed in the jungle near the airfield. It was concluded that JG568 spun into the ground. Seven officers left the following day to bury Paton at Liveramentu cemetery. He was only twenty-three years old at the time of his death.

Date: 03.12.1943
Spitfire(s): VIII JG568; XI PA871; XI PA866
Built: Chattis Hill

Lundsten performed two ten-minute flights in JG568, before he changed to a XI, PA871. This Spitfire spent time with 400 Squadron where it was photographed at RAF Buckeburg, Germany, in snowy conditions in 1945. It was struck off charge on 15 September 1945.

PA866 had spells with 61 Squadron and 683 Squadron. With the latter based in Italy, it went on a PR sortie on 19 May 1944 piloted by Flying Officer P. J. R. Brocklehurst who set out to cover points near Trento, but did not return. The squadron scrambled to make enquires about their pilot, but they could only conclude that he was missing in action. It was Brocklehurst's seventy-seventh sortie since he joined the squadron in Malta at the beginning of July 1943. He had a fine record of accurate and determined flying and had never come back without achieving as least part success. With clouds and bad weather closing in on the squadron the next day, the CO of the squadron took off anyway to enquire at Bastia for news of their missing pilot. The only thing that he got out of his attempt at information was to be chased by friendly fighters.

This would more than often be the last of information about yet another missing pilot, but *The Daily Telegraph* listed late 2014 that one P. J. R. 'Jim' Brocklehurst of 683 Squadron had passed away peacefully at home, aged ninety-two. Brocklehurst had survived—the Spitfire, however, had not.

There was widespread fog and rain over England on 3 December 1943.

Date: 04.12.1943
Spitfire(s): XI PA866; XI PA888; VIII JG534; VIII MD233; VIII MD237;
VIII MD234
Built: Chattis Hill

On 4 November 1943, fine weather blessed the day's flying objectives.
Lundsten had not flown as many Spitfires in a very long time. The day would
be packed with flying, and at the end of the day Lundsten had flown 1.45
hours' worth of test flights.

PA866, another PR Spitfire, operated with No. 400 (RCAF) Squadron
from April 1944. It was damaged on 12 May 1944, but was repaired, and it
was struck off charge a year later.

JG535 became one of the few Spitfires Lundsten flew that was caught on
film. It was flown by Leif Lundsten on this day and was sent to 6 MU on
22 February 1944. It was received by RAAF on 20 June 1944, and given
the new serial number A58-484. It spent a short amount of time with 457
Squadron, but spent most of its war-time career with 452 Squadron as well
as 607 Squadron.

The aircraft was one of the Spitfires flown by Acting Group Captain
Clive Robertson Caldwell. It was also flown by Flg Off. J. R. Andrew of
607 Squadron at Mingaladon, Burma, in 1945. Andrew was twenty-three
years old, had become an ace over Italy the year before, and had joined 607
Squadron in Burma. Most sorties in 1945 consisted of ground-attack sorties
in support of the Army, as well as escorting transport aircraft. Andrew flew
JG534 for the first time during a C-47 drop over Burma on 10 June 1945.
He would only live for fifteen more days before he did not return from
operations (flying a different Spitfire).

It was with 607 Squadron that the Spitfire was caught on tape during the
disbandment of the squadron on 31 July 1945. The caption read as follows:

Flight Lieutenant Donald Nicholson, pilot of Spitfire Mk VIII JG534
AF:Z, climbs out of his aircraft after completing the squadron's
final sortie. Nicholson greeted by AVM. Bouchier. A jovial-looking
Bouchier given a mug of tea. The WAS(B)s distribute tea and slices
of cake. Spitfire VIII AF:C MV208 taxiing with two more Spitfires
behind. A staff car arrives and AVM Bouchier and an Air Commodore
get out. Bouchier informally addresses the men of the squadron
standing on the bonnet of a jeep. He shakes hands with one of
the airmen.

Colonial Film

MD233 had a less glamorous career; it went through 6 MU and 82 MU in the UK, before it arrived in India on 16 March 1944, and was struck off charge on 16 February 1945.

MD237, also going to the Indian theatre, met a rather violent fate when it hit a bank on approach to the airfield at Chittagong, Bengal, and broke its back—it is not known if the pilot was hurt. The Spitfire was struck off charge on 7 February 1945.

MD234 went to Australia and was given the serial A58-421. It served with 549 Squadron and was subsequently struck off charge as late as 1948.

Date: 05.12.1943
Spitfire(s): VIII MD244
Built: Chattis Hill

Two flights in MD244, which was the only Spitfire Lundsten flew this day. MD244 went to India and was struck off charge in 1947. It is rumoured to be part of the batch of Spitfires David Cundall thought could be buried in Burma. The lack of flying can be connected to the weather as England suffered considerably foggy conditions on 5 and 6 December.

Date: 06.12.1943
Spitfire(s): VIII MD244
Built: Chattis Hill

Just one flight of the day, it was once again in MD244. Due to the fog, Lundsten stayed on the ground for the rest of the day.

Date: 07.12.1943
Spitfire(s): VIII MD239; VIII MD240
Built: Chattis Hill

MD239 went to India with 155 Squadron, and was scrapped in 1947. MD240 went the same way, serving with 273 Squadron and the Royal Indian Air Force. There was no flying on 8 and 9 December.

Date: 10.12.1943
Spitfire(s): VIII MD240; VIII MD239
Built: Chattis Hill

Flying both MD240 and MD239 once more.

Strong winds on 10 December kept flying restricted, but Lundsten took MD239 and MD240 up for one flight each.

Date: 11.12.1943
Spitfire(s): XI PA886; XI PA885; XI PA887; XI PA884; VIII LV644
Built: Chattis Hill

PA886, an XI, went to 400 Squadron in January 1944; it survived the war, and was sold for scrap to International Alloys in 1949. Not counting the survivors to this day, this Spitfire was one of the longest surviving Spitfires that Lundsten flew. It was first flown on 7 December, but with another pilot.

PA885 had a very different fate. Serving with 542 Squadron, twenty-six-year-old Neville Roy Maslen Clark from Australia took off in PA885 on 28 May 1944 for a PR sortie to Dortmund. No trace of him was heard and overdue action was taken. Clark had not been with the squadron very long. Unconfirmed reports state he went missing over Meerlo, close to the Siegried Line. Clark was buried/commemorated at Jonkerbos War Cemetery, in the Netherlands.

PA887 was damaged beyond repair while with 400 Royal Canadian Air Force, based at Eindoven in the Netherlands. This happened on 1 January 1945 during *Unternehmem Bodenplatte* (Operation Bodenplatte), a large operation undertaken by the Luftwaffe to cripple Allied air forces in the Low Countries. The operation achieved some surprise and tactical success, but was ultimately a failure. A large amount of Allied aircraft were destroyed, including PA887, but most were replaced within a week. It was the last large-scale strategic operation mounted by the Luftwaffe in the Second World War. Note that Lundsten only flew the Spitfire for a mere five minutes before turning to the next in line.

PA884 had spells with several squadrons and units, including 4 Squadron. It was flown by several pilots, one of them was F/L G. Collinson from 4 Squadron in 1944. On 14 March 1945, Collinson was intercepted by a Me 163, which made several attacks on him from above. He managed to avoid the attacks by turning into the Me 163 and passing underneath him.

With the last XI flown for the day (PA884), Lundsten turned to another VIII waiting to be flown. This one being LV644. The Spitfire went to Australia as A58-453. With 548 Squadron, it was marked up as TS-A. It was struck off charge on 15 November 1948.

Date: 12.11.1943
Spitfire(s): VIII LV644; XI PA889; VIII JG566
Built: Chattis Hill

Thirty-five minutes flying LV644 on 11 November was not enough—Lundsten flew the Spitfire for another thirty minutes on this day, too.

PA889 had a long service with 400 Squadron. It was damaged a few times during operations, and was repaired on site on 10 August 1944. It was eventually struck off charge on 20 December 1945.

JG566, a VIII, went to Australia as A58-449, arriving Down Under on SS *Miss Clu* on 18 April 1944. In August the same year, it suffered damage to its propeller after a taxiing accident. After the war was over, it was allocated to ground instruction, but not flown. It was then approved for conversion to an instructional airframe in 1947. As late as 1951, it was converted to components that made it the last Spitfire VIII held by the RAAF. Alongside PA886, it was one of the longest-lasting survivors flown by Lundsten (unfortunately, they have not survived to this day, but it beat PA886 by two years).

Date: 13.11.1943
Spitfire(s): VIII LV657; VIII LV649; VIII LV647; VIII JG613; XI PA884; XI PA887
Built: Chattis Hill

With the weather staying mainly cold and dry, flying opportunities increased. A good number of fifteen flights took place on 13 December 1943. LV657, the first Spitfire of the day, became the personal aircraft of Group Captain B. Walker, DSO, with the RAAF as A58-454. It had served with 548 Squadron and 54 Squadron before getting scrapped in 1948.

LV649, later given the serial A58-425, arrived in Australia on SS *Ajax* in April 1944. It suffered a landing accident at Gorrie airfield on 7 August 1943, flown by O. W. K. Eldrid. It was approved to be dismantled for components two months later.

Re-serialled as A58-452 for the RAAF, it went into storage on 8 September 1944, just under a year after its first flight. It was scrapped in 1948.

Finishing off a very hectic day, Lundsten flew several more flights in PA884 and PA887. Even with the weather being kind, but cold, Lundsten did not fly any more Spitfires until 17 December. His time as a test pilot was slowly coming to an end, but there was still a few more months until he would return to 331 Squadron. By now plans were starting to sketch out. These plans eventually placed Leif Lundsten at the forefront of the Norwegian D-Day campaign.

Date: 17.12.1943
Spitfire(s): XI PA889; XI PA852; PA891; PA890; PA855
Built: Chattis Hill

A low pressure moved east over the British Isles, but flying continued unscathed at Chattis Hill. Lundsten took PA889 up once again (first flown by the Norwegian on 12 December) followed by PA852. PA852 was also flown by F/L G. Collinson from 4 Squadron. His sortie in PA852 took place on 15 March 1945, but his target was covered in clouds. The Spitfire disappeared from the records in 1947.

PA891 also served with 4 Squadron when they were based at Gatwick. According to the Gatwick Aviation Society, PA891 suffered an accident on 12 May 1944 when Flight-Lieutenant B. A. J. Draper returned with hydraulic failure and ran off the runway. The pilot was uninjured and the Spitfire repairable (www.gatwickaviationsociety.org.uk/history_wartime. asp). PA891 was scrapped as late as in 1949.

PA890 served with 681 Squadron, which operated a detachment of PR Spitfires out of Ton Son Nhut outside Saigon during December 1945 to January 1946. The chances are high that the Spitfire was photographed here by Col. Donald Winder, who served with III Amphibious Corps. The Spitfire was damaged in March 1945, and later scrapped.

PA855 was with 542 Squadron at Benson when on 25 February Flying Officer G. W. Puttick was flying homewards after a PR sortie over France. He had not even crossed the coast of France when he ran out of petrol. His height was considerable, and he managed to glide back to England. He did not make it all the way to Benson and crash-landed in an orchard near RAF Manston. PA855 was severely damaged, and Puttick received slight head injuries. But, it was indeed a lucky escape. He was still alive and in one piece, but PA855 was a write-off.

Date: 18.12.1943
Spitfire(s): XI PA890; IX PA891; VIII LV666
Built: Chattis Hill

Leif Lundsten had three short flights in three different Spitfires on this day. PA890 and PA891 were flown on 17 December, while LV666 was a new bird; it was put on board SS *Masir* on 8 February 1944, and arrived in India on 25 March 1944—it was struck off charge three years later. LV666 most likely met the usual faith of Spitfires in the area, by dropping a large concrete block from a crane over the airframe. It is, however, rumoured to be one of the Spitfires buried in Burma since there is an uncertainty as to whether the concrete-block action did take place.

Date: 19.12.1943
Spitfire(s): VIII LV666; VIII LV669; XI PA855
Built: Unknown

Picking up where Lundsten left off on 18 December, he flew a twenty-five-minute flight in LV666, then a twenty-minute flight in LV669. LV669 went to India and served with two squadrons—607 and 152 (Hyderabad) squadron. It was struck off charge on 19 July 1945. Lundsten then had several flights in PA855, which brings the total of flying in PA855 to over an hour.

Date: 20.12.1943
Spitfire(s): XI PA893; VIII LV669; VIII LV658; VIII MD245; VIII LV654; XI PA895
Built: Chattis Hill

PA893 is a special case, as official records list it as lost during a sortie over Arnhem in September 1944. However, sources have discovered that PL893 can be found in 683 Squadron ORB well into January 1945. What eventually happened to PA893 remains unclear. As with a lot of Spitfires, LV658 went to India and 81 Squadron, where it was scrapped in 1947.

MD245 had an almost bizarre end to its career in the RAF. When based at Tabingaung, India, in 1944, it was flown by Flight-Lieutenant J. L. Briggs on a patrol with 607 Squadron. He ran into some trouble on coming back from this mission, suffering a burst tyre on landing, which caused him to swing towards some parked aircraft of 155 Squadron and a patrol bowser. To avoid them, he swung his Spitfire around, but the strain was too great and caused the port leg to collapse. He ended up stationary on one side of the airfield. Sergeant H. Handsley in MD245 came in following Briggs, and crashed into the ambulance that was crossing the airstrip to give aid to Briggs. MD245 turned over on its back, but Handsley survived with a lacerated scalp—a miraculous escape. The Indian ambulance driver was less fortunate, and was killed in the incident. A medical orderly (LAC Moore) had to have fourteen stitches, and received a concussion. Briggs went on leave just a few days later.

LV654 also went to 607 Squadron in India, and it was scrapped 30 January 1947. The final Spitfire of the day, PA895, went to 682 Squadron and the Mediterranean theatre in 1944, where it was scrapped 31 January 1946.

Date: 21.12.1943
Spitfire(s): VIII LV654; VIII LV673
Built: Chattis Hill

Spitfire LV673 went to 615 (County of Surrey) Squadron in India. While based at Charra, India, tragedy struck on 23 May 1945. A storm had been developing throughout the day, and by the late afternoon it came in. Roofs were torn from buildings, with many of them destroyed, and the squadron itself suffered immeasurable damage to their Spitfires. When the storm finally dissipated, the squadron saw that five of their Spitfires had been blown into each other and lay in a heap, another was in a ditch, and the Harvard had been blown 150 yards into the bushes. The wing commander's personal Spitfire was undamaged, but had moved 200 yards from its original position. There would be no more flying from Charra, as the squadron moved to Cuttack. It is possible that LV673 was among the Spitfires damaged in the storm and therefore was not flown again.

We are getting out of this!

615 Squadron ORB, 29.05.1945

Date: 22.12.1943
Spitfire(s): VIII LV673
Built: Chattis Hill

Before its likely demise in the storm in India, Lundsten took LV673 up for something quite different than his regular test flying. Taking off from Chattis Hill after two regular fifteen-minute flights, Lundsten took LV673 to Eastleigh. Going south-east, he passed the village of Hursley, and, for some reason, Lundsten decided that Hursley would be the perfect place for a good old-fashioned beat-up. There were no airfields at Hursley in 1943, so why Lundsten chose it for his little air show is anyone's guess—friends in the village perhaps? Blowing off some steam? After finishing his show, he set out for the rest of the short journey down to Eastleigh. He landed there and stayed the night, and he flew LV673 back the morning after.

Date: 23.12.1943
Spitfire(s): VIII LV673; XI PA854; VIII LV671; XI PA911; XI PA853; VIII LV659; VIII LV676
Built: Chattis Hill

There was no rest for Lundsten before Christmas; he had to fly seven Spitfires, changing from VIIIs to XIs throughout the day. Staying the night at Eastleigh, Lundsten took off for Chattis Hill (which must have been early morning 23 December 1943). This day has a special meaning to Norwegians—'Little Christmas Eve', as Norwegians celebrate Christmas on 24 December. Decorating a Christmas tree and making cookies would be far from Lundsten thoughts, as he had a day of extensive testing ahead of him. He arrived at Chattis Hill about ten minutes later for his first test of the day in PA854. Unfortunately, PA854 was shot down by a friendly Spitfire IX while somewhere in the Mediterranean theatre on 7 April 1944.

LV671 went to India and served with 67 Squadron and 607 Squadron. On 10 January 1945, the Spitfire was flown by Sergeant F. Moran, who, on returning from a patrol, crashed it during landing at Taykkuon—LV671 had run off the landing strip and cartwheeled. Moran got out of LV671 in one piece, but suffered a nasty concussion. He was admitted to hospital and LV671 was scrapped for good a month later.

PA911 first went to the Mediterranean, and then onwards to the Middle East, where it was scrapped on 26 June 1946. Little is known about PA853; it was damaged or destroyed while on operations in March 1944, and no more traces have been found of this Spitfire.

LV659 arrived in India in March 1944 and served with 154 Squadron. It was then transferred to 152 (Hyderabad) Squadron and finally to 273 Squadron. While with 273 Squadron, it might have been given the squadron letters MS-X. It was struck off charge in 1946.

LV676 served with 81 Squadron in Sri Lanka; on 27 August 1944, Flight Sergeant Howling took LV676 up for its last flight. Howling was on a low-level cross-country exercise when LV676s engine cut. At very low altitude, Howling had little time to decide on his next action, although he chose the only viable option—he baled out after informing the CO of his problem. He left LV676 at 800 feet and fell into the branches of a tree in the dense Sri Lankan jungle. He managed to cut himself free and started to walk home, and, after following tracks for an hour, he sighted a native and persuaded him to guide him to the main road where he was picked up and brought back to Lieutenant Commander Reynolds. Reynolds later took off in a Tiger Moth to locate LV676, but only succeeded in locating the remains of the parachute. LV676 was not found and abandoned in the jungle near Giritale.

Date: 24.12.1943
Spitfire(s): VIII LV672; VIII LV732
Built: Chattis Hill

Christmas Eve 1943 was Lundsten's final day of test flying before some well-deserved holiday. LV672 was given the new serial A58-538 and delivered to the RAAF during July 1944. The Spitfire served with No. 8 Operational Training Unit at Parkes, New South Wales, where it suffered a ground collision with a Wirraway in May 1945. It was subsequently converted to components and written-off.

LV732 served with 607 Squadron in India; on 11 April 1946, it swung on take-off and crashed at Samuneli—it was registered as scrapped a month later.

Finishing up with the Spitfires, Lundsten flew a Miles Magister from Chattis Hill to Feltham for his Christmas holiday. He brought fellow test pilot Flight-Lieutenant Clive Gosling (the man behind the controls of Spitfire XII MB882 in the now-legendary air-to-air photographs) as a passenger. Landing at Feltham, they parked the Magister and went into London. Lundsten more than likely travelled to Earl's Court Road and Sheila Lee, and Gosling perhaps went to visit his own family. It was finally Christmas, and Lundsten wouldn't be back flying Spitfires until 30 December.

Date: 30.12.1943
Spitfire(s): XI PA859; XI PA858; VIII LV737; XI PA857
Built: Chattis Hill

On 28 December 1943, Lundsten headed back to Feltham together with Clive Gosling, and took off towards Chattis Hill—the flight lasted forty minutes. Back at Chattis Hill, it was back to the regular testing of Spitfires straight from the assembly line.

PA859 went through plenty of action during the war. With 541 Squadron, it was damaged by flak on 26 March 1944, and Category 'B' damaged on 26 March 1944; however, there is nothing in the 541 ORB detailing this specific incident. Several pilots were, however, both before and after this date, subjected to heavy flak over enemy territory. PA859 stayed in operational service until the end of the war, when it suffered from engine failure during landing near Celle, Germany, in April 1946. The pilot, P. F. Griffiths, force-landed the Spitfire, and it was scrapped shortly thereafter. It is uncertain whether Griffiths survived or not.

PA858 has its own story to tell. Alex Walker flew an operational flight over Italy in this Spitfire on 1 August 1943. The following story comes via Scottish Saltire, Aircrew Association, at www.aircrew-saltire.org/lib003.htm:

August 1st '45 was an average sort of day which belied the fact that I was about to be bombarded by hailstones at a very high altitude. Taking off from San Severo, I soon ran into cloud over Ancona. Pre-flight Met Reports had not given any real hint of foul weather. I decided to climb over the cloud but it was still there at 33,000 ft and since it was quite thin and light, I descended and continued to fly through it. I felt quite a bit of turbulence as I came down, and suddenly it became very dark. There was a thunderous crash as loud as a cannon shot with lots of gravel in it. The din was terrific and the turbulence was indescribable. The wings fluttered fiercely and the changes from positive to negative G and vice-versa were sudden and most violent. I realised I was being subjected to a bombardment of hailstones of enormous size. The whole picture was lit up by vivid flashes of lightning. Had I not been well strapped in, I'm certain I would have been severely injured by the sharp, erratic, violent movements of the aircraft.

I could not keep my feet on the rudder pedals and the stick was quivering and quite rigid. I reasoned (if you could call it that) during those hectic seconds, that any attempt to turn the aircraft in those conditions might well damage the control surfaces and make matters much worse, so I held tight and waited. Then the canopy came adrift and slammed back with a final blast of noise and it was over. The whole thing took two or three minutes.

I knew my kite had taken quite a beating so I called base and put them in the picture then called for a Q.D.M. and returned to base very, VERY gently. My plane and I attracted quite a crowd at dispersal. PA858 would no longer be considered a very good paint job, but the new aerofoil section of the wings was somewhat different. PA858 looked like the toes of my son's first pair of school shoes! This was hardly surprising, but the main attention was centered on the pros and cons of whether the plane could have flown at all!

There are two ways of constructing a paper aeroplane. One is to fold the paper into a streamlined dart to glide unaided through the air; the other way is to scrunch the paper into a ball and chuck it. The leading edges of the wings were no longer those famous shapely sections, but had become hammered back to a square face of some six or seven inches. The same applied to the fin, and to a lesser extent the tail planes. The spinner also attracted much attention. It had been so hammered into the constant speed unit that all the details of the gears looked as if 'shrink wrapped'. The cooling fins in all radiators were flattened but I don't recall any rise in temperature on the way back—perhaps they were full of ice? I was interviewed by an investigation officer at the time, but cannot really remember much about him, save the fact that he seemed rather sceptical of my account of the various altitudes involved. On consulting 'SPITFIRE–The History' page 400, I read that the plane was SOC (struck off charge) on 19/10/45. I have often wondered if I should contact them with all the above detailed information on events leading up to PA858 being S.O.C.?

LV737 first went to India and them Burma, where it suffered an engine failure and crashed at Kalewa airstrip on 30 March. It was scrapped 28 December 1944.

PA857 served with 4 Squadron, and Flight-Lieutenant G. Collinson was among the many other pilots that flew it by late 1944. The Spitfire suffered damage in November 1945, and was subsequently scrapped. With PA857 set the final flight of the day, this ended Lundsten's test flying for 30 December 1943, the second last day of 1943.

Date: 31.12.1943
Spitfire(s): XI PA857; VIII LV738; VIII LV661; VIII LV678; XI PA857
Built: Chattis Hill

Finishing and starting the day in the same Spitfire (PA857), the last day of 1943 would give Lundsten plenty of work. LV738 went to India and the Royal Indian Air Force. On approach to Samungli airfield, 17 October 1944, the Spitfire's engine stopped causing it to crash just short of the runway. Too damaged to repair, it was scrapped a few months later. LV661 was also India-bound, where it served with 136 and 132 Squadron. It was scrapped 7 January 1945.

LV678 was ferried to 9 MU at RAF Cosford on 31 December, the same day as Lundsten's test flight. No. 9 MU's role was to store, maintain, modify, repair, and ultimately issue aircraft to operational units. LV678 was sent on from 9 MU to 222 MU at High Ercall on 1 January 1944—No. 222 MU was a storage unit. LV678 was then sent to RAF Masirah, which is an island off the coast of Oman and was used as a staging airfield for aircraft destined for deployment to the Far East. LV678 arrived in India on 15 Feb. '44 and was issued to 81 Squadron on 20 March '44. It ended up with 155 Squadron and was struck off charge on 28 Sept. '44. The Spitfire has also been offered in a plastic 1:72 scale-model kit by AZ Models, portraying Flying Officer 'Witt' Witteridge of 155 Squadron in September 1944.

Author Thomas Andrew wrote:

In September 1944, 'Witt' Witteridge was allocated LV678/DG-C as his own aircraft, which his groundcrew decorated with the Chindit badge in honour of their XIVth Army colleagues. They also made some modifications to the fighter, including removing the rear view mirror, outboard machine guns, ballast in the tail, armour plate behind the pilot's seat and the emergency canopy lock. They also polished the wing leading edges, prompting Witteridge to comment it was 'Quite a boy racer!' It certainly made its mark on the enemy, as on 25 September Witteridge intercepted and destroyed a high flying Ki-46. Then, on 7 October, Flg Off 'Babe' Hunter was flying LV679 when he shot down another 'Dinah' while on 5 November Witteridge destroyed a Ki -43 'Oscar.

Spitfire Aces of the Burma and the Pacific, 2009, p. 91

Finishing the day in another flight in PA857, Lundsten looked back on an extremely eventful year—and unbeknownst to him, it was his last full year of life. From serving as flight-leader with 331 Squadron, claiming several fighters shot down, to testing a very high number of Spitfires, the year had been extraordinary, even for a Spitfire pilot in the Second World War. He flew 32.40 hours of Spitfires in December, which means that he on average flew a bit over an hour each day.

There would be little time to celebrate the New Year, as Lundsten would strap on a Spitfires once again on the very first day of 1944.

Monthly total of flying ended at 32.40 hours on Spitfires and 1.30 on the Miles Magister.

29

'You Took Off Up a Hill'
January 1944, Chattis Hill and Eastleigh, Hampshire

Date: 01.01.1944
Spitfire(s): XI PA896; XI PA900; VIII LV681; VIII LV742
Built: Chattis Hill

There was plenty to do on the first day of 1944, and January was Lundsten's last month as a test pilot. There is not much available information about PA896; although, it is known that it served with 681 Squadron before being scrapped in 1946.

PA900 served with 39 Reconnaissance Wing in 1944. Aviation enthusiast Larry Seath made a D-Day skin based on PA900 for simulation game *IL-2 Sturmovik*, which can still be downloaded online. The Spitfire was scrapped in September 1945.

LV681 went to India and served with 20 Squadron from 20 March 1944. On 6 November 1944, an unknown pilot landed the Spitfire at Don Muang, with its wheels still retracted. It would be the final flight of LV681 as it was scrapped shortly thereafter.

Following 1 January's flying, Lundsten had three days off. A low pressure was also active over southern England at the time, which might indicate poor flying weather over Hampshire.

LV742 went to 615 Squadron in India. On 10 August 1945, sixteen Spitfires took off from Deragon flying to Baigachi, located to the east of Calcutta. *En route* to their destination, the formation of Spitfires flew straight into a violent monsoon storm, which wreaked havoc on the unlucky squadron. Eight Spitfires were lost and four pilots killed, including their experienced and popular leader, David McCormack, DFC & Bar—he had been in charge of 615 Squadron from February 1944. He had already finished one tour with the squadron between May 1941 and March 1943, and had also been flying Hurricanes with 615 (Churchill's Own) Squadron on escort and low-level operations. The squadron was rendered non-operational on the spot. The tragic incident was somewhat hushed-up in the years to come. McCormack was well-regarded as a leader, and a memorial window was unveiled at St Augustine's in Yarraville, Melbourne, in 1946.

Date: 04.01.1944
Spitfire(s): VIII LV755
Built: Chattis Hill

LV755 had a rather glamorous career with the RAF and was flown by several pilots. One of them was Wilfred Arthur Goold, an Australian with 607 Squadron based at Imphal. On 11 May 1944, he shot down a Japanese 'Oscar'.

> Goold went for two Ki-43s flying in line-astern, but his targets successfully evaded. Pulling up, he then got in behind another 'Oscar' and shot up its tail before the enemy pilot also wildly evaded. Goold then went for a third fighter that he succeeded hitting in from 300 yards as it banked sharply to the left. This machine went down in trailing flames from its cowling, and the fighter was seen to crash south of Bishenpur. Goold had just scored his fifth kill.

Andrew Thomas, *Spitfire Aces of Burma and the Pacific*, 2009, p. 48

However, on 30 May 1944, LV755 was hit by Spitfire VIII JG379 while taxiing at Imphal, and was scrapped following this incident.

Date: 05.01.1944
Spitfire(s): VIII LV744; VIII MD214; VIII LV680; VIII LV747; XI PA894
Built: Chattis Hill

Like many of Lundsten's recently flown VIIIs, LV744 also went to the far-east, serving with 615 and 607 Squadron before being scrapped in 1947. MD214 went the same route, being struck off charge in 1945.

LV680 suffered an almost comedy type of fate; Flight Sergeant A. H. Milne of 136 Squadron was ordered to take-off from RAF China Bay, Sri Lanka, on 23 January 1945 for a routine practice scramble. Milne proceeded to taxi into a roll of runway netting, which was between him and the runway, causing considerable damage to his aircraft. It was stated that the removal of this obstruction had been requested earlier in the week, but it was obviously not executed like planned. The Spitfire was scrapped under a month later.

LV747 ended up in much more tragic circumstances. It was most likely flown by Barrett Christison of 166 Wing, based at Bangladesh. The Spitfire crashed during an air test, and Christison was killed.

PA894 became another victim to Operation Bodenplatte while serving with 400 Squadron at Eindhoven. Attacked by the Luftwaffe while parked at the airfield, the Spitfire almost fully burned to the ground. In John Manrho and Ron Pütz publication *Bodenplatte*, from 2004, there are two poor-quality photos of PA894 on fire.

Date: 06.01.1944
Spitfire(s): XI PA898; VIII LV747; VIII MD216
Built: Chattis Hill

PA898 served with 681 Squadron, and it was scrapped in 1947; however, not much else is known about this XI Spitfire. MD216 served with 155 Squadron in the Far East before it was scrapped in 1946.

More about Chattis Hill

A windy hill above the River Test does not sound like the ideal spot for an airfield.

Ian Philpott, *The Birth of the Royal Air Force*, 2013, p. 243

At Chattis Hill there was an old racecourse, and you took off up a hill which was part of the gallops. The most exciting thing I experienced happened there; one day I went into the operations room and found on our books a page and a half of Spitfires marked P1W ... Priority One aircraft were urgent, you moved them before everything else. And 'W' was even worse, because it meant you had to go and sit there, wherever the plane was, and wait 'til you got it wherever it was supposed to go. Of course, this coincided with the most ghastly spell of weather! The cloud was absolutely deck. There was no way you could take-off. So we dutifully went over by car to Chattis Hill, where they were, and sat there. Then they rang P and said, 'Haven't you moved those Spitfires yet?'

I said, 'Have you looked out of your window?'

'We haven't got any windows,' they said. This was 41 Group at Andover.

I said, 'Well, I have got a window and I can't even see the far side of the aerodrome, which isn't very far away.'

'Well, they are absolutely vital! You must get them off!'

I said, 'We cannot get them off!' But I went over, my aircraft happened to be the one tied down on the tarmac. I said, 'I think the cloud is lifting. Quick! Quick! Run it up!' and I leapt into it.

They said, 'I don't think it is, dear.'

I said, 'Yes, yes, I think I can see a little bit of a rise. We'll go off a bit lower than the proper height'. And I ran it up and took off straight into the cloud! So I fell out of the sky again, as quickly as I could, back on to the aerodrome. There was no way.

Max Arthur, *Lost Voices of the Royal Air Force*, 1993

Another time, I was taking off in a Spitfire from Chattis Hill when the undercarriage refused to fully retract. It was jammed in the halfway up position. I tried all sorts of manoeuvres to get it to move. No luck. The best option was to land back at Chattis. As I came down, I could see a fire engine and ambulance waiting by the side of the landing area. They knew I was in trouble, watching me making the manoeuvres and they shot off a green flare, which told me all preparations were ready for a forced landing. Which was, I suppose, a sort of comfort. I managed to make a forced landing. It was a slithery stop, which unfortunately resulted in some damage to the plane.

Jacky Hyams, *The Female Few: Spitfire Heroines of the Air Transport Auxiliary*, 2012

Date: 07.01.1944
Spitfire(s): VIII LV679
Built: Chattis Hill

Just one Spitfire flight on 7 January 1944 in LV679—it was sent to the Far East and was scrapped on 11 August 1944 after suffering damage.

Lundsten flew a Miles Magister from Eastleigh to Chattis Hill and back on this day. Then he flew another Magister flight from Eastleigh to Chattis Hill. This may indicate that part (or more) of his flying over the last few days had been done at Eastleigh.

Date: 08.01.1944
Spitfire(s): XI PA897; VIII LV746; VIII MD218
Built: Chattis Hill

PA897 had its first flight on 29 January and served with 4 Squadron as a PR Spitfire before being registered as scrapped in 1947. LV746 went to India and then perhaps to Burma; it is among the Spitfires Lundsten flew that is rumoured to be buried in Burma. MD218 went to the same theatre and served with 136 Squadron for a time, as well as the Royal Indian Air Force. It was struck off charge on 31 October 1946.

After Lundsten's test flying on 8 January, he had a long break from flying; however, his whereabouts during the next few weeks is impossible to know, as he did not register any flying during these days. He was not back flying at Chattis Hill until 20 January.

Date: 20.01.1944
Spitfire(s): XI PA899; VIII MD297; VIII MD299; VIII MD279; VIII MD278; VIII LV726; VIII MD298
Built: Chattis Hill

Leif Lundsten was back in the cockpit on 20 January, and flew seven different Spitfires on this day. PA899 served with 4 Squadron before it was transferred to 16 Squadron a month after D-Day. On 9 September 1944, Flying Officer J. Wallace took PA899 on its last flight. Wallace did not return from the sortie, and was noted as missing from a PR sortie over Holland—he was later confirmed as killed in action.

MD297 went to Australia as A58-458, and, serving with 457 Squadron, it received the squadron letters ZP-R. On 17 July 1945, the Spitfire crash-landed at Morotai Island, in Indonesia. It was scrapped in September 1945. MD299 also went to Australia, this one as A58-460. It had spells with 457 Squadron and 54 Squadron before being scrapped in 1948.

Little is known about MB279, other than serving with 136 Squadron before being scrapped in 1946. MD278 went the same way and on the same dates, also serving with 136 Squadron (but also with 132 Squadron) before being struck off charge in 1946. LV726 was part of the same batch and served with 615 Squadron before being scrapped in 1947.

MD298 went to Australia as A58-459 and served in 457 Squadron. It was authorised for write-off in May 1946 and was finally struck off charge in 1948.

Date: 21.01.1944
Spitfire(s): VIII LV745; XI PA926; XI PA906; XI PA907; XI PA903; VIII MD302; XI PA929
Built: Chattis Hill

Yet again seven Spitfires were test flown on the same day, with the majority of them XIs. LV745 ran out of fuel and belly-landed near Kohat, Pakistan, on 22 June 1945, and it was scrapped a month later.

PA926 went to the Far East serving with 681 Squadron, and it was struck off charge in June 1945. PA906 met almost the same fate as PA926, also going to 681 Squadron and scrapped 31 December 1946. PA907 was the third Spitfire going to 681 (all test flown by Lundsten on the same day), this one was struck off charge on 31 October 1946.

PA903 followed a different path of wartime service; it served with 400 Squadron from 11 February 1944, and then served with 16 Squadron— PA903 was regularly used on low-level sorties with this outfit, before it was scrapped in 1946.

MD302 served with 607 Squadron in Bengal and Burma. On 15 April 1945, it was flown by Flying Sergeant Gonner from RAF Dwehla, Burma. On one of the first patrols of the day, MD302 developed engine trouble and appeared to be losing petrol rapidly. After trying to rectify this from 2,000 feet, Gonner baled out at 500 feet and landed safely about 50 yards away from MD302, which was on fire, with ammunition exploding all around. Gonner managed to make his way back to base unharmed, but the Spitfire was lost.

PA929 has a particularly interesting history. While with 16 Squadron, based at RAF Northolt, it took off from its base on 8 June 1944, flown by Flight Lieutenant Michael Adian McGilligan, originally from Ireland, aged twenty-five. On returning from his sortie, McGilligan lost control of PA929 or suffered oxygen failure, which resulted in him losing consciousness and the Spitfire crashing at Bletchingley, Surrey. The young Irishman flying the Spitfire lost his life in the violent crash. In 2012, Wings Museum excavated the crash site and discovered several components from the Spitfire. (More information about the dig can be seen at www.wingsmuseum.co.uk/spitfire_ xi_PA929.htm).

Date: 22.01.1944
Spitfire(s): XI PA929; XI PA907; VIII MD332; XI PA904
Built: Chattis Hill

PA907 went to the Middle East and served with 681 Squadron before it was struck off charge 31 October 1946. MD332, Lundsten's first and only VIII of the day, collided with Spitfire VIII LV663 during landing at Cox's Bazar, in Bangladesh, on 7 January 1945—it was struck off charge five days later. Another aircraft from 683 Squadron's Spitfires that Lundsten took for a test flight was PA904—it was struck off charge on 18 October 1945.

Date: 23.01.1944
Spitfire(s): VIII MD332; VIII MD330; VIII MD303
Built: Chattis Hill

MD330 served with 67 Squadron at Akyab, in Burma; in February 1945, the Spitfire ran into an accident after it swung on landing. Its undercarriage collapsed and the Spitfire was scrapped a month later. MD303 served with 607 Squadron in the same area of operations as MD330, and had a spell with 607 Squadron before it was scrapped in 1947.

For Lundsten, there were no flying on 24 January except for a Magister flight to Boscombe Down from Chattis Hill, and he did not go back to Chattis Hill until 26 January. Flying commenced once again on 27 January, and Lundsten was now at the very end of his time as a test pilot, with only five days remaining before he would be posted.

Date: 27.01.1944
Spitfire(s): XI PA909; XI PA908; XI PA905; VIII MD334
Built: Chattis Hill

After his stay at Boscombe Down, Lundsten was back flying several Spitfires. His stay may have been prolonged due to heavy wind and rain, but from 27 January a high pressure prevailed, which made flying easier. PA909 was another 683 Squadron Spitfire, however, little else is known about the Spitfire except that it was scrapped on 18 October 1945.

Just a few days before returning to operational duties, Lundsten did a test flight in PA908—which can arguably be regarded as the most famous Spitfire that he ever flew. PA908 is the only Spitfire that Lundsten flew that is still a complete aircraft. The first flight is not recorded in official records, but Lundsten did fly the Spitfire on 27 January. A Merlin 63-powered Spitfire was delivered to RAF Benson just shortly after Lundsten's test flight. It was then transferred to No. 1 OADU (Overseas Aircraft Dispatch Unit) in March 1944. The Spitfire eventually made its way to 681 Squadron at Alipore, in India, with the squadron letter 'E' on its sides. The same squadron still had the Spitfire in their ranks until mid-1945 in Mingaladon, Burma, before it was transferred to the Indian Air Force in December 1947—at some point it was used as an instructional airframe. It was acquired by a Canadian syndicate in the early 1980s and shipped to Vancouver in 1985. An amazing coincidence then occurred:

As a result of considerable local publicity John Bradford, who had flown Spitfires with the RAF during World War II, checked his flying logbook and, to his amazement, found that he had flown PA908 on a six-hour mapping mission over enemy territory in Burma in February 1945. He had also logged an air test in '908 on a later date.

Spitfire Survivors: Then and Now Volume 1, 2010, p. 536

Restoring the Spitfire to airworthiness proved too costly for the Canadians, and they decided to sell PA908 to US Air Force Museum at Wright-Patterson AFB, in Dayton, Ohio. It was moved to their restoration facility, but remained in storage for several years. Pete Regina worked on the Spitfire at his facility in Van Nuys, California, and it was decided to paint the Spitfire as MB950, which operated from Mount Farm, Oxfordshire. Interestingly, Lundsten also test flew this Spitfire during his tenure at Worthy Down and Chattis Hill. PA908 is still on display in Dayton as MB950. The museum have been notified of PA908's small, but important Norwegian connection.

MD334 had a considerably less famous career; it served with 81 Squadron and the RIAF before it was struck off charge on 30 May 1946.

Date: 28.01.1944
Spitfire(s): VIII MD333; VIII MD335; XI PA934
Built: Chattis Hill

When MD333 served with the RIAF, its undercarriage collapsed during a landing at Hmwabi, Burma, on 31 January 1946. This happened almost two years after Lundsten had flown it, and it was struck off charge five months later. Little trace can be found of MD335s career, but this Spitfire too had a spell in India before being struck off charge on 31 May 1945 (same day as MD333).

PA934 went to 681 Squadron in 1944. At some point it had a 'Snake' written on the fuselage and was photographed with this during the time in service. It was struck off charge in 1947.

Date: 29.01.1944
Spitfire(s): XI PA931; XI PA930; XI PA928; XI PA939; VIII MD335
Built: Chattis Hill

PA931 was a PR Spitfire that stayed in Britain with 4 Squadron; it flew photographic reconnaissance sorties, mainly in support of the 21st Army Group and the First Canadian Army until VE-Day. The Spitfire might have been scrapped in the Gatwick area in 1947. On 23 February 1945, PA931 was lost somewhere over the Adriatic Sea on a PR mission to Udine. Flown by Flying Officer Bernard Lawrence Sims, it never arrived back to its base at Peretola Airfield in Florence, Italy.

PA928 served with 681 Squadron in the Mediterranean theatre before being struck off charge in June 1945. PA939 was a Spitfire that had a long career. After the regular stop at Benson, it was transferred to 400 Squadron until April 1945, when it served with 16 Squadron. It also had a spell with BAFO Communications Wing in 1945 before being sold in 1947, with the likely outcome of being scrapped.

The last Spitfire of the day, MD335, had already been flown a few days earlier.

Date: 30.01.1944
Spitfire(s): VIII MD335; XI PA910
Built: Chattis Hill

There was another flight in MD335 before switching to a new bird, PA910. The PR Spitfire was sent to 682 Squadron and then 40 Squadron (South African Air Force). It was struck off charge in 1947.

Date: 31.01.1944
Spitfire(s): VIII MD338; VIII MD339; VIII MD337; XI PA912
Built: Chattis Hill

Spitfire VIII MD338 was one of the rare survivors of the Spitfires that Lundsten flew at Chattis Hill. Although it did not remain in one piece (like PA908), the history of MD338 is still of importance. Listed by Leif Lundsten as test flown on 31 January 1945, the official records puts MD338 as assembled at Keevil and not Chattis Hill, before it was delivered to 6 MU Brize Norton on 30 January 1944 (one day prior to Lundsten's test flight at Chattis Hill). There is nothing in Lundsten's logbook that indicates him being at Brize Norton on this day, which means the fighter might have been flown to Chattis Hill. The whereabouts of MD338 remains then somewhat in question during those last days in January 1944. In February, it was shipped to Australia on board SS *Elanafaire*, and it arrived Down Under on 9 May 1944 where it was provided the serial number A58-467 and coded 'ZP-S'.

> On 6 November 1944, Flight-lieutenant L. A. Leeming, who flew the aircraft nine times on operations, took off in MD338 at 09:20 hours for some shadow-shooting practice and aerobatics over Shoal Bay N.T but after some aerobatics the fuel pressure system failed causing the engine to stop. Leeming force-landed on the beach at Shoal Bay at 11:00 hours but with a battery flown in and some assistance from an Army Observer Unit the aircraft was able to get airborne at 17:10 hrs and return to base before the tide came in.
>
> *Spitfire Survivors*, 2010, p. 239

MD338 was later scrapped—it was cut up and buried at Gorrie, Northern Territory. In 1978, a group excavated the remains of a Spitfire, and, after some early confusion concerning the serial of the Spitfire, it was later concluded that it was MD338 they had found. In 1999, the remains were transferred to Alec Wilson in Yunta, Australia, for long-term restoration.

MD339 also went to Australia, this one as A58-429 on SS *Clan MacIver*, and arrived on 11 March 1944. It served with 452 and 54 Squadron before it was authorised for write-off in 1946, it was later scrapped in 1948.

MD337 was given the new serial A58-462 and arrived in Australia in May 1944. On 19 July 1945, it ran off the airstrip at Darwin due to very strong winds. It was scrapped a few months later.

PA912 would be the last Spitfire Leif Lundsten would test fly before heading to Milfield. It served as a PR Spitfire with 542 and 400 Squadron before it was sold to Ministry of Sound in 1947, and more than likely scrapped some time thereafter.

When Lundsten touched down at Chattis Hill on 31 January, most likely sometime in the afternoon, he would look back at a having test flown Spitfires in the hundreds during the past six months. His return to operational flying was not far away.

The monthly total of flying ended at 30.50 hours.

30

'Those Guys Must Really Be Blind' February 1944, Fighter Leader School, RAF Milfield, Northumberland

RAF Milfield opened as a Class 'A' (heavy bombers) airfield in 1942. It ultimately served as a training base for British and Canadian pilots, who were learning to fly Hawker Hurricanes. In 1942, the Fighter Leaders' School operated from the airfield. The school had been operating from Aston Down and Chedworth, in Gloucestershire, as well as Charmy Down, near Bath, but due to the high concentration of air activity and its high incidence of wet weather as well as the three moves, it was decided to change plans. Strategies for the invasion of Europe had already been established and the ideal dates had been set. Milfield had already served as a Hawker Typhoon OTU and produced a large number of capable ground-attack pilots destined for the large amount of new Typhoon squadrons needed. Milfield was now training squadron leaders, experienced men from the previous years of hard fighting. These leaders would learn to operate their squadrons from primitive airstrips, in close support of the Allied ground troops that were quickly progressing into Europe and Germany.

Milfield assembled aircraft, weapons, instructors, and scientists. The latter were at work analysing the results of different weapons used on a variety of targets, an assortment of approaches, different weights of bomb, and variously timed fuse settings—all of these tests were flown by the pilots. The final results were passed on as a bulletin to 2nd TAF Squadrons.

Leif Lundsten had most likely already been chosen by the Norwegians to serve a prominent role in the invasion of Europe, leading his former squadron 331 into action. When he was told of his new assignment, he already knew what was coming and what he was destined to do.

Not far from Milfield lay Goswick Sands Bombing and Air-to-Ground Gunnery Ranges, a very comprehensive air-to-ground range in the 1940s. After flying from Milfield for about five to seven minutes, Leif arrived over Goswick. There were also other ranges for practice bombing and strafing that were a bit closer to Milfield.

Date: 22.02.1944
Spitfire: IX, FN-Y MJ827/MH828
Built: Castle Bromwich
Length: 1:40
Where: North Weald–Milfield

On 22 February, after a well-deserved rest for twenty-one days, Lundsten took off from North Weald in Spitfire IX, FN-Y (MJ827 or MH828), to Milfield, in Northumberland.

MJ827 was used by Squadron Leader Arne Austeen on this day, during a morning sortie. The squadron was back 11.45 a.m. If Lundsten (unlikely) used the Spitfire, he must have departed after this sortie had taken place. Flying up to Milfield, the fighter was back into action with Austeen behind the controls just two days later, which means someone flew the fighter down to North Weald again.

MJ827 was transferred to 403 (Canadian) Squadron later on, and the 'Y' letter was painted on new arrival, MK121, instead.

On 9 June 1944, at 8.20 p.m., 403 (Canadian) Squadron took off for an evening patrol over the invasion beaches, flying to Omaha beach. They would be positioned just north-east of the Norwegians, who were over Utah beach at approximately the same time. The weather was horrible, and visibility was down to 800 feet. Unfortunately, possibly due to this poor visibility, they Navy opened fire at the Canadians—the Norwegians were still over Utah beach at this point. The Canadians immediately removed themselves from the shelling area and made contact with 'Research', who told them that they could once again return to the area and that it would now be safe. No. 403 went in 'line astern', with their navigation lights on; however, it did not give the results they had wished for. Yet again, the Navy opened fire, letting the Canadians have it a second time. After calling 'Research' again, 403 pulled out to be given the 'okay' to return. On this third attempt, the Navy reacted in the same way, but by now the Canadians had run out of luck. Flight Lieutenant E. C. 'Bill' Williams was hit in MJ827, and disappeared through the low, thick clouds. Another pilot was also wounded, although he managed to get back to Tangmere. Two other Spitfires were also damaged.

It is possible that the first Spitfire Lundsten flew after coming 'home' to North Weald, on 22 February, had just suffered an almost identical fate to his own on the same day and at the same time, except for one crucial difference—the pilot had survived. Bill Williams had managed to crash-land his stricken Spitfire near Valognes, France. However, he was severely wounded in the crash, and taken to hospital in Cherbourg as a prisoner. He was later freed on 27 June when the Allies took the hospital.

The other possibility is that Lundsten flew Austeen's former FN-Y, MH828, to Milfield as it was not needed at North Weald, with Austeen flying MJ827. MH828 might have stayed with Lundsten at Milfield for the duration of his stay. MH828 was transferred to 80 Squadron on 29 May 1944 and eventually sold for scrap as late as 28 August 1950. Based on Lundsten's referrals to 'A' and 'B' IX models in his logbook, it might indicate on MH828 was the right Spitfire. Arne Austeen had himself flown this Spitfire to Milfield for his course between 2 February and 19 February 1944.

[...] those guys [Navy] must really be blind because of all the aircraft that have been seen most in this show, the Spit certainly has.

403 Squadron ORB.

Settled at Milfield, Lundsten practised dive bombing in Spitfire Vbs between 24 February and 11 March 1944 before returning to North Weald on 13 March 1944.

At Milfield he flew nine or ten different Spitfire Vbs previously used by 165 Squadron, including squadron letters P, N, T, C, D, L, T, S, and five flights only listed as SK. The total flying time flying in Spitfire Vbs was 18.35 hours. Not included is a flight in a P-47 Thunderbolt, which he flew on 11 March 1944. It was a 1.10 hours flight, getting to grips with the American fighter-bombers. It was his last flight from Milfield before returning to North Weald in either MH828 or MJ827 (MH828 as mentioned was the most likely candidate). The flight down to North Weald lasted one hour and fifty minutes. He then took charge of 331 Squadron leading up to D-Day, and he would have led them into Europe had he survived.

31

Squadron Leader:
March 1944, 331 Squadron,
North Weald, Essex

Back at 331 Squadron, things had changed since Lundsten left the Norwegians during the summer of 1943. Luftwaffe were seldom seen in the skies over the Channel any more, as the Allies had managed to get the upper hand in air superiority. As Lundsten knew from his time at Milfield, the squadron would now add bombing and other ground targets to their list of tasks as part of 2nd Tactical Air Force. From 15 March, Major Leif Lundsten led the squadron, but there was no time for celebrations or formal parades as the squadron was heavily involved in Army co-operation exercises, although it was under poor weather conditions.

Date: 15.03.1944
Spitfire: IX, FN-Y MK121
Built: Castle Bromwich
Length: 0:55
Where: North Weald–East Grimstead–North Weald; North Weald–Gatwick–North Weald

No. 66 Squadron, now part of 132 Airfield (former North Weald Wing), wrote in their ORB about the sortie of the day:

> It was intended that 66 and 331 Squadron should dive bomb and that 332 Squadron should strafe the target, but weather was unfavourable for bombing, and all three squadrons strafed the target.
>
> No. 66 Squadron ORB.

Another sortie was done in the Gatwick area in the afternoon, with a third north of Uxfield. It is unclear if Lundsten participated in the sortie to Gatwick or to Uxfield.

Meanwhile, among the pilots of 331 Squadron, a sigh of relief went through the ranks when Leif Lundsten took over the squadron; Arne Austeen had had his work cut out for him from the day he took charge of the squadron. He had to replace arguably the most popular officer and leader in the entire Norwegian air campaign in the Second World War—Rolf Arne Berg. It was a battle that Austeen could not win, and he suffered during his time with the squadron. No. 331 pilots had been complaining (though perhaps quietly) for a while about Austeen's ability to lead, especially in regards to navigation. Some even criticised his poor English vocal skills. Lundsten, a former 331 pilot and a friend of Berg from the Kjeller days, was greeted with open arms.

> Major Leif Lundsten became a popular leader. He was a very capable pilot and had our absolute trust. As a leader he was steady and calm, his reactions proper and quick. He was very easy and confident to deal with. But, one discovered quickly he did not come from Oslo's west side—he was a solid farmer from Østre Toten. We were all happy when he took charge from Austeen.

> Annæus Schjødt, 331 Squadron pilot, *Spitfire Saga*, 2014, p. 126

Schjødt, not having any former relations to Lundsten, had quickly caught on to Lundsten's dialect and background (mentioning a farming history). However, Lundsten had never been a farmer, nor had his parents (although his father came from neighbouring farming village of Kolbu, Østre Toten and his mother from a farm in Bøverbru). It was perhaps just a way of explaining Lundsten's attitude and personality.

> There was a sigh of relief through all of us at the end of the month when major and Squadron Leader Austeen was posted. Lundsten, previously commanding B-flight, had already arrived, and became our new CO. All of us relaxed instantly, and we noticed change at once. Sweeps were once again a pleasure to do. No profanities when we come home from sweeps about that 'cross-over' being so and so horrible. It had been a poor month for 331, the worst since I arrived, so we had some catching up to do.

> Odd Roald, 331 pilot, *Spitfire Saga*, 2014, p. 126

Date: 19.03.1944
Spitfire: IX, AH-Z MH846
Built: Castle Bromwich
Length: 0:30
Where: North Weald local

On 19 March, there was an air test in a 332 Squadron Spitfire (most likely MH846), which flew its first operational sortie with 332 Squadron in February 1944. On 30 September 1944, while serving with 64 Squadron operating out of Bradwell Bay, it ran into trouble. Flown by Flight Sergeant Recile, the squadron was escorting Boston bombers to Holland. On the return journey, MH846 developed engine trouble, and Recile was forced to land the Spitfire 4 miles south-west of Eindhoven. Recile got out of the Spitfire, and was quickly surrounded by soldiers and women. He ended up in a military hospital, and was slightly wounded—the Spitfire was beyond repair.

Date: 20.03.1944
Spitfire: IX, FN-O MJ732; IX, FN-Y MK121; IX, FN-D MJ583
Built: Castle Bromwich
Length: 1:40, 1:00, and unknown
Where: Unknown

Final day of the Army co-operation exercise, mainly spent dive bombing. MJ732, after a spell with 33 MU, in August 1944, was transferred to 414 Squadron. On 5 January 1945, it was hit by flak and abandoned during a tactical reconnaissance sortie.

MK121 would end up as Lundsten's personal Spitfire until the fatal sortie on 9 June 1944. The Spitfire arrived at 331 Squadron around the same time as Lundsten, and was flown on a few sorties by Squadron Leader Austeen while he was still in charge. For some reason, it left 331 on 8 June 1944 and arrived at 421 Squadron not long after. In early 1945 it went to Cunliffe-Owen, primarily a repair and overhaul service located near Southampton. It was sold to the Royal Netherlands Air Force in 1946 and received the squadron letters H-18.

No. 331 Squadron was MJ583s only operational squadron during the war. It was transferred to 84 Group Support Unit in July 1944; however, nothing is recorded after this move. Lundsten used the Spitfire to fly to Eastleigh, then onwards to High Post and back to North Weald. His business is not known, but it's easy to assume he was there in connection to his time as a test pilot. Two days later, he went to Stapleford and then Thorney and back to North Weald in an Auster.

Date: 23.03.1944
Spitfire: IX, FN-B MJ567
Built: Castle Bromwich
Length: 2.10
Where: North Weald–Beauvais–North Weald

This was the first sortie over enemy territory for Lundsten since his return to North Weald, and his first as squadron leader. The mission would take them almost to Paris supporting bombers. When south of Beauvais, the bombers turned port and proceeded to Neufchâtel where they turned starboard and then to target, arriving there fourteen minutes late. Intense, accurate flak was reported, but everyone came back in one piece.

On this occasion, Lundsten flew FN-N; this may have been a 331 Spitfire that would later be damaged in an operation on 27 April 1944 at RAF Bolt Head (before being repaired on site). The Spitfire was later sold to the Turkish Air Force in 1947.

Date: 24.03.1944
Spitfire: IX, FN-Q MJ732; IX, FN-Z (TBC)
Built: Castle Bromwich (TBC)
Length: Unknown
Where: Unknown

There were two test flights on this day, with one in MJ732 and one in what appears to be a new Spitfire with 331. However, for March 1944, the author of the ORB decided to skip the serials when writing, which makes it quite difficult to locate the correct Spitfires at times—FN-Z ended up as one of these that were difficult to identify. The previous FN-Z, which was serving with the squadron, was lost with Otto Treider, who lost his life on 9 February 1944 (MK129).

Date: 26.03.1944
Spitfire: IX, FN-Y MK121
Built: Castle Bromwich
Length: 2:05
Where: North Weald–IJmuiden–North Weald

Nos 331 and 66 Squadrons provided support to B-26 Marauders going IJmuiden, in Holland, on the 26th. Heavy flak was experienced, but Luftwaffe did not show up to fight. It would be the last operational sortie from North Weald before the Norwegians moved to their new home at Bognor Regis, in Sussex.

Date: 31.03.1944
Spitfire: IX, FN-Y MK121
Built: Castle Bromwich
Length: Unknown
Where: North Weald–Bognor Regis

The move to Bognor Regis was obviously in connection to the planned invasion of Europe, and was just a small part in a large-scale movement of fighter squadrons in preparation for the big day. The Norwegian's two-year stay at North Weald ended with all Spitfires departing by air, and the ground crew by lorries and other transport vehicles. Leif Lundsten led his squadron over the airfield as a 'last goodbye' and then set course for Bognor Regis. They knew they would not be back, and the pilots and crew all understood why they moved closer to the English Channel.

32

No-ball Target and Royalty on the Same Day: Bognor Regis, West Sussex

That night we slept under canvas for the first time. The squadron tents had been put up in a quiet corner of a green field. We slept two in each tent on folding beds, quite comfortable. The Norwegian Air Force had fitted us with extremely pleasant double sleeping bags. We arranged for ourselves for the night, and then went down to the mess which had been installed in a farm building previously used as a cattle stable.

Egil Ulstein, Spitfire pilot, *Spitfire Saga V*, 2014, p. 186

Bognor Regis was a very different airfield from the one at North Weald, with two runways crossing each other—it served as a temporary airfield, constructed specifically for the invasion of Europe. The Norwegians had to adapt to a very different life under much more Spartan living conditions—Bognor Regis was only the first step, Europe would come later. All men, like Ulstein described above, would sleep in tents with a few exceptions. The main house on nearby Morells Farm became the Officer's Mess, and the stable was to become a cinema. Breakfast was served from field kitchens every day, but some made their own arrangements, collecting eggs from nearby farms. Many would rent a bath in a private house to keep clean, or go to a hotel once or twice a week depending on pay. Like at North Weald and Epping, the Norwegians smoothly established connections with the locals, and were regularly invited for tea on Sundays. North Weald Wing, now operating under the new name of 132 (N) Airfield, had its own flying control, operating from a truck, mobile hangars, a field hospital, an operating room, and doctors. The British 66 Squadron also operated from Bognor Regis, alongside 331 and 332 Squadrons.

Date: 04.04.1944
Spitfire: IX, FN-Y MK121
Built: Castle Bromwich
Length: 0:45
Where: Bognor Regis local

In the morning of 4 April, bad weather engulfed 132 Airfield at Bognor Regis, but the weather cleared up enough in the afternoon for a squadron formation, led by Lundsten. An unknown English civilian tells more in *Spitfire Saga V* (2014).

> Their immaculate flying skills had to be seen to be believed, formation flying of the highest order. We were very well aware of their presence, as after the squadrons returned from their sorties, they would circle overhead, then breaking away they would line up to land, passing just over the tops of the trees opposite our cottage lowering their undercarriage and throttling back their engines. Exciting times for us children!
>
> *Spitfire Saga V*, 2014, p. 198

Date: 05.04.1944
Spitfire: IX, FN-Y MK121
Built: Castle Bromwich
Length: 0:50
Where: Bognor Regis local

Lundsten was practising night flying on 5 April, and the airfield was still soft from the torrential rain on 4 April, which made flying difficult. However, this did not last for long, and the squadrons were no longer 'trapped' in Bognor Regis.

Date: 08.04.1944
Spitfire: IX, FN-Y MK121
Built: Castle Bromwich
Length: 1:05 (from Manston)
Where: Bognor Regis–Manston; Manston–English Channel–Bognor Regis

No. 331 took off for Manston in the afternoon to refuel and give support for twenty-four Bostons on Ramrod no. 710 to France. A rendezvous was accomplished over the English Channel, but owing to bad weather, the formation returned to England. Lundsten did not list how much time he had spent airborne, but the ORB indicates that it was at least 1:05 from Manston and back to Bognor Regis, via the Channel.

Date: 11.04.1944
Spitfire: IX, FN-Y MK121
Built: Castle Bromwich
Length: Unknown
Where: Bognor Regis–English Channel–Bognor Regis

Lundsten and 331 Squadron participated in exercise 'Trousers', doing convoy patrols from 1.20 p.m. to 9.25 p.m., with the last Spitfire landing at 11.20 p.m. However, once again Lundsten did not list his time in the air. This particular exercise continued the following day.

Date: 12.04.1944
Spitfire: IX, FN-D MJ583
Built: Castle Bromwich
Length: Unknown
Where: Bognor Regis–English Channel–Bognor Regis

Exercise Trousers continued on this day, with convoy patrols from the early morning until 4.20 p.m. There were no incidents during this exercise.

MJ583 arrived with the Norwegians in January 1944. It was regularly flown by Ragnar Dogger of 331 Squadron, but was later flown by Martin Gran and Kjell L'Abee-Lund (who also shared the destruction of a Bf 109 near Caen 20 June 1944). Five days prior to this, Dogger had shot down a Fw 190 flying the same Spitfire. The fighter was transferred to No. 83 Group Support Unit in the summer of 1944. It is not known when the Spitfire was scrapped.

In the next few days, the pilots were photographed quite extensively. It was expected that the Norwegians would suffer considerable losses during the invasion, and the photographs were connected to these expected losses. The Norwegians also painted their country's flag on the Spitfires' noses.

Date: 14.04.1944
Spitfire: IX, FN-D MJ583
Built: Castle Bromwich
Length: 1:10
Where: Bognor Regis local

On 14 April, the squadron practised their formation flying over the local area of Bognor Regis.

Date: 15.04.1944
Spitfire: IX, FN-Y MK121
Built: Castle Bromwich
Length: 0:20
Where: Bognor Regis local

MK121, most likely away for a few days for service, was flown by Lundsten once again on this day. Having vast experience in testing Spitfires, he took MK121 up for a twenty-minute test flight. Again, the rain poured down over the airfield, and following the flight on 15 April the airfield became unserviceable, due to the heavy downpour.

Date: 19.04.1944 to 23.04.1944
Spitfire: IX, FN-Y MK121
Built: Castle Bromwich
Length: 0:30
Where: Bognor Regis local

Lundsten has written 'S-test' in his logbook, and he flew one service test a day in MK121, ending these on 23 April—the flights from the 19th lasted thirty, forty, forty-five, and thirty-five minutes, and on 23 April he took an aircraft on a test for fifty minutes. Lundsten's flying on this day may have been connected to the testing of the 'FRANKS' suit—designed to reduce the pressure from G-force when flying. The ground crews filled the suits up with water, and the pilots flew off to test them; however, the tests ended shortly after take-off, with a most unsatisfactory result.

Date: 25.04.1944
Spitfire: IX, FN-Y MK121
Built: Castle Bromwich
Length: 1:20
Where: Bognor Regis–Neuchâtel–Bognor Regis

Twelve Spitfires led by Wing Commander Rolf Arne Berg took off at 9.55 a.m. for Ramrod 793. Their mission was to bomb construction works in the Neuchâtel area of France—it would be the first bombing experience of enemy occupied territory made by the Norwegians. They dived down from 10,000 feet and released their bombs at 400 feet. Intense, light, accurate flak was experienced by the last section over the target, but all aircraft returned safely at 11.15 a.m. Their target had actually been V-bomb installations, so-called 'No-ball targets'. There were no bomb sights installed in the Spitfires, which led many pilots to believe (and correctly so) that the damage done to the ground targets was rather minimal.

Back from operations, Crown Prince Olav and his entourage arrived at the airfield. He held a speech and stayed with the Norwegians until late at night, visiting a local pub in the process. The Norwegians expressed in their tales of the night much respect and admiration for Crown Prince Olav. In the middle of all the partying, the Germans decided to bomb the area (RAF Tangmere took the brunt). The Crown Prince stayed at the airfield for the entire night, at one time having to thrown himself to the ground due to a German bomb falling quite close.

Date: 26.04.1944
Spitfire: IX, FN-X MJ217
Built: Castle Bromwich
Length: 2:00
Where: Bognor Regis–Le Touquet–Bognor Regis

Lots of hungover pilots took off for Ramrod 793 in the morning to the Le Touquet area, supporting seventy-two Marauders bombing the St Ghislain marshalling yards. A few pilots noticed how the flak had increased over the area since their last visit, and Wing Commander Berg and his number two were both hit by flak, but landed at Manston in one piece.

MJ217 arrived at 331 Squadron as FN-X, in February 1944. It previously served with 66 Squadron and 165 Squadron, and, against all odds, it found its way back to the Norwegians and the Royal Norwegian Air Force following the end of the Second World War. It was lettered as AT-T while at Gardermoen, in Akershus (now Oslo Airport). MJ217 stayed with 331 Squadron until Sergeant Holter-Sørensen crashed the Spitfire during take-off from Gardermoen.

Date: 27.04.1944
Spitfire: IX, FN-Y MK121
Built: Castle Bromwich
Length: 1:50, unknown
Where: Bognor Regis–Le Touquet–Bognor Regis

On 27 April 1944, two patrols were carried out over the Channel. All returned to base without incident, except for Bjørn Bjørnstad from 331 who crash-landed at RAF Bolt Head. Lundsten was part of the subsequent aid provided to the pilot and the damaged Spitfire at RAF Bolt Head, flying the Auster on a return trip to the airfield.

Date: 28.04.1944
Spitfire: IX, FN-Y MK121
Built: Castle Bromwich
Length: 2:00
Where: Bognor Regis–Fécamp–Bognor Regis

Fighter Roadsted to Fécamp harbour, France, for a bombing sortie. It was an eventful sortie, even though the results were observed to be poor—some bombs had hit the town by mistake.

No. 331 Squadron pilot Christen K. Gran mentions the sortie in *Spitfire Saga V*:

Even before we crossed in over Fécamp the German heavy flak opened up at us. We were at 10,000 feet. A voice came through the radio: 'Going down!' It sounded like a threat. The first four fighters rolled over on their backs and dived straight down, released their bombs at 4,000 feet and disappeared out to sea. Then the next four fighters. The light flak joined in on the game, and fired deadly explosives. It was like a grey carpet of grenades almost covering the target below us. Then it was our turn. The target under the left wing. Over on my back, straight down now! Aim for the target. The tracer from the anti-aircraft guns lit up towards us. 'Fire back at them', I thought. From all six guns. It all played out in amazing speed, an inferno of grenades and a volume out of this world. Insane!

4,000 feet. Press the trigger and the bombs left the aircraft towards its goal. Noise on the radio. 'Jesus Christ', I hear someone gasp. 'I don't want to go down in that hell! I don't want to die yet!' Someone had forgotten to turn off their transmitter. In a flash I saw the result of the bombing. Several houses along the wharf. Mattresses and other stuff had been thrown out the windows. A small boat had capsized. Mission completed.

Spitfire Saga V, 2014, p. 232

Date: 29.04.1944
Spitfire: IX, FN-Y MK121
Built: Castle Bromwich
Length: Unknown
Where: Bognor Regis–English Channel–Bognor Regis

Lundsten participated in two of seven patrols on this day. His monthly total of flying ended at 10.45 hours in Spitfires and 4.00 in the Miles Magister.

On 3 May 1944, Lundsten took the Auster and flew to Feltham and then returned the same day. It is the second last (at least recorded) visit Lundsten made to Sheila Lee in London.

33

All the Way to Paris and Back: May 1944, 331 Squadron, Bognor Regis, West Sussex

Date: 04.05.1944
Spitfire: IX, FN-Y MK121
Built: Castle Bromwich
Length: 1:15
Where: Bognor Regis–English Channel–Bognor Regis.

'Exercise Fabious' was on the agenda on 4 May 1944, a major event held along specific English coastal areas in connection to the forthcoming landings in Normandy. No reaction from the Germans was detected, perhaps to some surprise considering the scale of the convoys.

Date: 05.05.1944
Spitfire: IX, FN-Y MK121
Built: Castle Bromwich
Length: Unknown
Where: Bognor Regis–Cambrai–Bognor Regis

Twelve Spitfires, led by Lundsten, took off for Ramrod 821, supporting twenty-four Bostons to Cambrai marshalling yards. No enemy activity was detected, either from the air or the ground. The squadron then turned for home, and crossed the coast over Dunkirk. Everyone arrived back at Bognor Regis in one piece.

Date: 07.05.1944
Spitfire: IX, FN-Y MK121
Built: Castle Bromwich
Length: Unknown
Where: Bognor Regis–Lille–Reims–Paris–Bognor Regis

Ramrod 843 was filled with drama, and the loss of a pilot—the first to be lost on a sortie while Lundsten was in charge. The Ramrod would take them to the outskirts of Paris, which meant they even caught a peak at the Eiffel Tower in the distance.

Twenty-four Spitfires took off from Bognor Regis at 6.16 p.m. They quickly gained height, but then went on the deck going straight towards the French coast, just north of Boulogne. At Lille, they turned south towards Paris. On their way to the French capital, the Norwegians flew straight over a French castle full with Germans lined up outside. The squadron decided to continue on instead of attacking them. When the Norwegian approached Moiselles airfield, their luck was up. They were as low as they possibly could be at this point; however, when they flew over the airfield they were met by a wall of flak. Knut Bache, Lundsten's number two during the attack on the Junkers 88 in May 1943, was hit. The Spitfire, by some reports, exploded in mid-air and went down just outside the airfield boundaries. Shortly after Bache went down, Bjørn Bjørnstad (also of 331) hit a power cable head-on, which almost severed the spinner of his Spitfire. Bjørnstad left the squadron and headed for home with a rough running engine—he had been very lucky. A few days later he would take command on 80 Squadron, leaving Bognor Regis.

The Norwegians then faced Paris. No. 331 Odd Knut Roald wrote in his diary (via *Spitfire Saga V*):

> Our Sqdr. Cmdr Lundsten got something on his mind when we passed the Paris suburbs and discovered the church clocks running an hour late.

Spitfire Saga V, 2014, p. 238

> We roared over the German positions. In the corner of my right eye, I saw him [Knut Bache] being hit by the flak. Parts of the engine cowling fell off, the aircraft weaved, hit the ground and exploded. Knut must have been killed instantly, as the only allied pilot during this sortie.

Birger T. Johannessen, Spitfire, *Norsk Jagerflyger i kamp*, 2004, p. 74

The Norwegians proceeded to follow the River Seine on their way back. They were apparently so low that the German soldiers looked down on them from the banks of the river when they passed.

When they finally got back to Bognor Regis, many of them, according to Tidemand Johannessen who participated in the sortie, had a couple of strong drinks. Johannessen's ground crew later showed him a bag of four dead birds, taken out of the oil cooler of his Spitfire—they had indeed been flying low.

Date: 08.05.1944
Spitfire: IX, FN-Y MK121
Built: Castle Bromwich
Length: 1:25, 1:15
Where: Bognor Regis–Ault/Cayeux–Bognor Regis; Bognor Regis–St Omer–Bognor Regis

No-ball targets were on the agenda once again; however, Lundsten still does not use the term No-ball, but rather bombing—he first used the term on 11 May. The first sortie was a mission between Ault and Cayeux, with a midday take-off from Bognor Regis. Over the target, the Norwegians released their bombs on target and observed several hits. Without losses or incidents to their own, the Norwegians arrived back at Bognor Regis at 1 p.m.

For the second sortie, Lundsten led 331 Squadron (332 did not participate) at 5.25 p.m. on Ramrod no. 846, going just west of St Omer. The Norwegians hit their target once more, but while they got away safely, they observed a B-25 Mitchell and a P-47 Thunderbolt going down over Caen and Cayeux. They were back on the ground at 6.40 p.m.

> Without alcohol we would never have managed to loosen the tension when we came back to base after the last sortie of the day. The alcohol wiped out the events and made sleep possible. Sleep was needed to be in good shape for the next day, new sorties to be done. I dare to say that if we did not have had access to alcohol, we would have been out of the game in short time. Broken down.
>
> Helner Grundt-Spang, *Den hemmelige kampen*, p. 67

Date: 09.05.1944
Spitfire: IX, FN-Y MK121
Built: Castle Bromwich
Length: 0:50
Where: Bognor Regis–Cap Gris Nez–Bognor Regis

On Ramrod no. 856 to Calais, the Norwegians provided support to thirty-six B-26 Marauders on their way to Cap Gris Nez, bombing costal targets as part of the invasion plans. The task was carried out without incidents.

Date: 10.05.1944
Spitfire: IX, FN-Y MK121
Built: Castle Bromwich
Length: 0:55, 0:55, 1:10
Where: Bognor Regis–Bradwell Bay; Bradwell Bay–Bognor Regis; Bognor Regis–Unknown French target–Bognor Regis

The Norwegians left Bognor Regis for Bradwell Bay, to position themselves for Ramrod no. 859. Two 331 Squadron Spitfires were hindered from participating due to technical difficulties. Judging from Lundsten's logbook, he split his flying to Bradwell Bay and back into two, and added a third flight after this one. It could indicate that Lundsten was one of the pilots that suffered from difficulties, and had to return to Bognor Regis without going on the sortie. If this is the correct assumption, Lundsten only led 331 Squadron on their second sortie this day—Ramrod no. 863 was to France (it is not clear where the Norwegians went, except that they crossed the coast just south of Cayeux). The target was reached at 4.05 p.m., and the squadrons successfully bombed it. They arrived back at Bognor Regis at 4.45 p.m.

Date: 11.05.1944
Spitfire: IX, FN-Q MJ732; IX, FN-T MJ728
Built: Castle Bromwich
Length: 0:35
Where: Bognor Regis–Manston; Manston–Valenciennes–Bognor Regis

The change in Spitfire for Lundsten might be another indicator he did not participate in the first sortie on 10 May 1944. On this day, he used two different Spitfires for his sorties—MJ732 and MJ728. The squadron took off again from Manston at 11.10 a.m. for Ramrod no. 867, bombing the Valenciennes marshalling yards. Inaccurate flak from the Calais area was reported, but otherwise no opposition was met in the air, and they all returned safely back to base. The Norwegian ground crew also spotted the B-24 Liberator that crashed in Chichester, killing three civilians on 11 May, often called 'The Chichester Bomber'.

Date: 12.05.1944
Spitfire: IX, FN-Y MK121
Built: Castle Bromwich
Length: 2:00, 1:50
Where: Bognor Regis–Ramburges–Bognor Regis; Bognor Regis–Douaui–Bognor Regis

On 12 May, there were more No-ball targets, and Lundsten was back to flying his regular MK121. This mission was Ramrod no. 874, and, with Lundsten in charge, the squadron took off at 8.55 a.m. They arrived over the target at 9.30 a.m., and dived down from 10,000 feet. Exceptional bombing was observed, with very good results, before they left the area for the return home. No enemy fighters were seen, but some inaccurate heavy flak was experienced on their return flight to Bognor.

The second sortie of the day, Ramrod no. 878, took Lundsten to Douai, just south of Lille. More flak was experienced on the way out of France, but once again everyone was alright when back at Bognor Regis—arriving around 6 p.m. The Norwegians later reflected upon the lack of German fighters, and concluded that they must have left Northern France and Belgium altogether.

Date: 13.05.1944
Spitfire: IX, FN-Y MK121
Built: Castle Bromwich
Length: 1:40
Where: Bognor Regis–Béthune–Bognor Regis

The mission of the day was Ramrod no. 881, which targeted the Béthune railway marshalling yards. Lundsten later crossed out Béthune and wrote Merville instead. Bombing was yet again successful, although one Spitfire, during take-off from Bognor Regis, lost a 500-lb bomb. Fortunately, it did not go off (if it had exploded, there would have been many casualties), and it was found that it had not been armed. The pilot in question had apparently released it himself by pulling the wrong handle (he thought he retracted his undercarriage).

From this point, the Norwegians had a few days off operational flying following some very hectic days. Lundsten used the time off for a visit back to High Post.

Date: 14.05.1944
Spitfire: IX, FN-Y MK121
Built: Castle Bromwich
Length: 0:30, 0:30
Where: Bognor Regis–High Post; High Post–Bognor Regis

Lundsten flew a return flight to Vickers-Armstrongs, High Post. The weather was fairly poor, but not bad enough to prevent any flying from taking place. It is unknown what Lundsten's business at High Post was; perhaps he was picking up some personal items, tying up loose ends, or simply visiting old friends?

Lundsten was not back into the air until 19 May. However, there were several incidents that took place on the ground during these days. On 16 May 1944, two British soldiers dressed up as Germans visited the camp. The idea was to test everyone's reaction to the unfamiliar uniforms. Lundsten, as well as several others pilots, were photographed by H. P. Mellish, 132 Airfields official photographer, during the visit by 'the Germans'.

On 17 May (the National Day of Norway), games, drinking, small and large accidents, and other incidents were an extremely common occurrence. A boxing game was arranged, as well as a football match. Disappointingly, it was pouring down with rain, which dampened the celebrations. Plenty of pilots and ground crew were drinking and having a good time—some also took a nightly bath. Leif Lundsten, who was driving a car at some point, collided with another car; he was rumoured to be driving rather fast and wild somewhere around the vicinity of the airfield. The other individual, apparently not present to explain what happened, left the incident unsolved. Station Commander Helge Mehre took note of the incident, and was not pleased.

Date: 19.05.1944
Spitfire: IX, FN-Y MK121
Built: Castle Bromwich
Length: 1:15
Where: Bognor Regis–Abbeville–Bognor Regis.

Ramrod no. 896 was the mission on this day, and it was to a No-ball target about 10 miles east of Abbeville. Lundsten led 331 Squadron over the Channel, while Rolf Arne Berg led the wing. They crossed the French coast at Ault at 7.45 p.m. at 13,000 feet. The squadron proceeded to drop their bombs from 4,000 feet due to thick cloud over the target—only four hits were observed. There was no flak, and (once again) no enemy fighters, permitting everyone to return safely at 8.30 p.m.

Date: 20.05.1944
Spitfire: IX, FN-Y MK121
Built: Castle Bromwich
Length: 2:20, 1:15
Where: Bognor Regis–Le Tréport–Bognor Regis; Bognor Regis–Le Grand Verdret–Bognor Regis

On 20 May 1944, two Ramrods were flown to No-ball targets in France; one was in the early hours of the day. Their task was to attack railway installations at Le Tréport. The bombing results were observed to be good. Moderate, but inaccurate flak was experienced during the mission, with heavy flak over target. Fortunately, everyone was back safely at 11.15 a.m.

Lundsten took off again at 4.30 p.m., to participate in Ramrod no. 904—bombing the Le Grand Verdret junctions. Bombs were dropped from 4,000 feet, due to 5/10 clouds and very thick haze up to 7,000 feet. All Spitfires were back at Bognor Regis at 5.45 p.m.

Leif Lundsten did not participate during the next day, 21 May 1944. Instead, he took the Auster to Feltham together with Birger Tidemand-Johannessen. It is the last recorded trip into London and Feltham, which could also be the last time Sheila Lee saw her fiancé alive. Considering Lundsten was not back to operational flying until 24 May, it is also a possibility that Tidemand-Johannessen went along for the ride to Feltham to fly the Auster back to Bognor Regis after dropping Lundsten off. However, these are just educated guesses.

Date: 24.05.1944
Spitfire: IX, FN-Y, MK121
Built: Castle Bromwich
Length: 1:45, 1:55
Where: Bognor Regis–Évreux–Bognor Regis

Nos 331 Squadron and 66 Squadron, led by Wing Commander Berg, participated in Ramrod no. 914 to Évreux airfield on the 24th, supporting Boston bombers. Several hits were observed on buildings, and on the runway itself, and one B-25 was hit, but managed to struggle home. Everyone was back at base at midday.

The day was not over yet, as Lundsten and co. set out once again in the evening. They took off at 6 p.m. for a No-ball target 10 miles east of Abbeville, officially called Ramrod no. 918. The Norwegians approached the target from south-east, and dived down from 10,000 to 4,000 feet. All but one bomb fell in the target area. Lundsten turned 331 Squadron for home, landing back at Bognor Regis at 7.55 p.m.

All bombs hit the target but one (amazing, but true). No Germans as usual.

331 diary via *Spitfire Saga V*, 2014, p. 257

Date: 25.05.1944
Spitfire: IX, FN-Y MK121
Built: Castle Bromwich
Length: 1:45, 1:55
Where: Bognor Regis–Évreux–Bognor Regis

More No-ball targets were on the agenda for the 25th. This time, the target was about 15 miles north-east of Rouen. When the Norwegians approached the target, they spotted a hole in the cloud that made bombing the target a lot easier. Due to the clouds in the area, it was hard for anyone to spot the results of the attack.

Date: 27.05.1944
Spitfire: IX, FN-Y MK121
Built: Castle Bromwich
Length: 0:35, 1:45
Where: Bognor Regis–Manston; Manston–Cambrai–Bognor Regis

Twelve Spitfires from 331 Squadron took off from Bognor Regis and headed for Manston to refuel and attach their bombs for Ramrod no. 927—to bomb the Cambrai railway station. Two 331 Spitfires failed to take-off from Manston due to engine trouble, but the rest of the Norwegians reached Cambrai at 6.05 p.m. Lundsten led 331 Squadron in a dive from 15,000 to 5,000 feet, before they dropped their load. No flak was observed, and once again no Luftwaffe, and 331 Squadron concluded the bombing to be of very poor quality—most bombs ended up west of the target. The Norwegian crossed the coast at Neufchâtel-Hardelot, two Spitfires from 331 left the formation for Ford due to low fuel, and nine landed at Bognor Regis at 7.17 p.m.

Date: 28.05.1944
Spitfire: IX, FN-Y MK121
Built: Castle Bromwich
Length: 1:15, 1:35
Where: Bognor Regis–Forêt d'Hesdin–Bognor Regis; Bognor Regis–unknown No-ball target–Bognor Regis

The last two sorties of May 1944 took Lundsten to Forêt D'Hesdin, 20 miles south-east of Le Touquet—this was Ramrod no. 993. The other sortie was to the Becry rail junction and station area.

For the first show of the day, the Norwegians left Bognor Regis at 9.40 a.m. They bombed from 4,000 feet, but could not observe any significant results. They turned back towards Bognor Regis, without having seen either flak or German fighters.

No. 331 was at full force for the last sortie of the day, with twelve Spitfires. The operation was carried out according to plan, and target was reached at 4 p.m., however, two of the pilots did not manage to release their bombs. A warehouse took a direct hit, but the Norwegians were unsure if some of their bombs had exploded as they only observed small dust clouds.

It is unclear how many hours were done in Spitfires in May 1944.

34

Into the Fire:
June 1944, 331 Squadron, Bognor Regis, West Sussex

Date: 02.06.1944
Spitfire: IX, FN-Y MK121
Built: Castle Bromwich
Length: 1:31
Where: Bognor Regis–Neufchâtel-en-Bray/Yvetot–Bognor Regis

Trafford Leigh-Mallory visited Bognor Regis on 1 May. The day after, 331 Squadron was back in the air and once again led by Leif Lundsten. The Norwegians took off from Bognor Regis 5.29 p.m., for a ground-attack sortie to Neuchâtel/ Yvetot-area. They crossed the French coast at 12,000 feet, and attacked a convoy of lorries, with the railroad at Yvetot also receiving some damage. Satisfied with their results, Lundsten turned for home and landed at Bognor Regis at 7 p.m.

This was the final sortie for Lundsten to France before D-Day, mainly due to a great deal of very poor weather. On 3 June 1944, the Spitfires at Bognor Regis were painted with white and black invasion stripes on the wings and fuselages. They painted them at night.

Not many days now until the invasion starts. Everything is ready and set to go at the airfield. All our aircraft are painted with big black and white stripes so we won't mistake our own aircraft when we get to it. There will be so many allied aircraft in the air, which will make it hard to spot the Germans, but these shiny white stripes should make it easier. We have not been allowed to fly outside the coast today, probably so the Germans won't get the same idea. I can imagine the Germans on the other side not feeling too well tonight, that is if they are stupid enough to not know what is coming.

No. 331 Squadron pilot Kjell Wilhelm Tvedt's diary via *Spitfire Saga*, 2014, p. 265

On 4 June 1944, the airfield was unserviceable due to poor weather, which meant there was no flying. It was indeed a 'quiet before the storm'.

On 5 June 1944, the command and operational personnel gathered at Morell Farm, to be briefed about the coming invasion. Leif Lundsten, as squadron leader, had most likely already been told what would happen—the invasion was about the start. Rolf Arne Berg was so keen on going that he was upset when he could not brief the men—the task was given to the Station Commander, Helge Mehre.

Date: 06.06.1944
Spitfire: IX, FN-Y MK121
Built: Castle Bromwich.
Length: 1:50, 1:30, 2:00
Where: Bognor Regis–Utah Beach/Beachhead–Bognor Regis

Leif Lundsten did not fly the first sortie this important morning, but stayed on the ground while Nils Ringdal led the squadron. It is unknown why Lundsten did not fly the first sortie, but there had been plenty of heated discussions about the roster for the first sortie over the beaches. Everyone wanted to be part of the invasion and the first to be over the beaches. Perhaps Lundsten, as squadron leader, stepped down from the first sortie since no one else would give in. The wing was led by Rolf Arne Berg.

Well, this is it boys.

Helge Mehre via *Spitfire Saga V*, 2014, p. 270

That night, only a few people at Bognor Regis Airfield could fall asleep; they all heard and saw the massive armada of aircraft passing over head. The sight was so spectacular that no one forgot about it for as long as they lived.

Coming home after their first sortie on 6 June, many pilots expressed surprise at the lack of anything German in the air. They had expected a massive show, a final show-down with the Luftwaffe. They more than likely expressed this surprise to a waiting Leif Lundsten, urging to take part in the invasion in FN-Y, MK121. He would finally be on his way at 12.15 p.m.

For the second sortie (Lundsten's first), Werner Christie from 332 Squadron led the wing. He told of that second sortie:

We flew out from Bognor Regis and stayed on deck before we as usual climbed upwards to gain altitude. We were all given free seats on the balcony for the invasion. I've never before been so happy to be in the Air Force than I was that day. It was impressive to see allies force in the air, on the ground and on the sea. I also got to see the Mulberry's by the French coast. At one point, I saw a warship being hit. It broke in two pieces, and sunk in a V-sign. We thought the invasion day would be the big show-down with the Germans, that they would show up *en masse*, and we would get our hands full fighting. But, it didn't happen.

Werner Christie via *Spitfire Saga V*, 2014, p. 279

The unbelievable cruelties made a lasting impression on us fighter pilots. At the same time, there was something distant about it all—we flew so high the engine covered up the sound of everything. It looked like a silent film, something totally unreal.

Birger T. Johannessen, *Spitfire norsk jagerflyger i kamp*, 2001, p. 79

Kjell Wilhelm Tvedt also participated in the second sortie that day. He wrote in his diary:

We started op. 12:15 and set course. Lundsten lead the squadron. Ringdal leading yellow and myself blue section. We passed just off Isle of Wight, and flew straight towards France. Already the sea was full of ships and boats in all shapes and sizes. There were clouds at 4000 feet, but visibility very good. After 25 minutes flying we hit the coast just at the right place, and I saw something I will never forget. Hundreds, thousands of ships were anchored off the coastline and kept unloading soldiers and weapons...

Kjell Wilhelm Tvedt's diary via *Spitfire Saga V*, p. 282

During the first sortie, one 331 Squadron pilot, Arvid Steen, received a puncture just before take-off. The ground crew changed the tyre in record time, but Steen was already behind the others—Lundsten was leading the squadron—Steen took off anyway and tried to catch up, which he did. Some noticed Steen catching up, and thought he was a German. 'Break' was called on the radio, but the misunderstanding was quickly solved.

...after landing at Bognor Regis, I was called in to Major Leif Lundsten's office who yelled at me for flying across the Channel all alone. It was idiotic, he said. Later on that same day, Ole Georg Eidsvis (pilot, 331

Sqd) came over to me and explained; 'Lundsten had to yell at you, but he personally thought it was all right.'

Arvid Steen via *Spitfire Saga V*, 2014, p. 285

Lundsten's second sortie took place from 4.30 p.m., and the same route was flown. Wing Commander Rolf Arne Berg led the Norwegians down to St Catherine's Point, Isle of Wight, then he headed straight towards Cherbourg before changing course by about 20-degrees port. Over the beaches, 331 Squadron split into three sections, with four Spitfires in each section.

On the fourth sortie (Lundsten's third), former squadron commanders Wilhelm Mohr (332) and Helge Mehre (331) participated. Patrolling over the beachhead, some pilots raised concerns about the huge shells fired from the battleships off shore, which passed above them. However, once back from the final sortie of the day at 10.30 p.m., many pilots felt that it was a very anti-climactic mission, as the expected armada of Luftwaffe fighters never appeared. The sights on the beaches, the ships, and the scale of the invasion left a lasting impact on everyone taking part on 6 June 1944. The day had been long and tiresome, and they would yet again be up in the early hours the next day for more patrols. The success of the invasion was still unsure.

Date: 07.06.1944
Spitfire: IX, FN-Y MK121
Built: Castle Bromwich
Length: 1:55, 2:00, 2:00
Where: Bognor Regis–Utah Beach/Beachhead–Bognor Regis

They all had short night's sleep before Lundsten and the boys from Bognor Regis made their way over the coast of Normandy for the second day of the invasion—D-Day plus 1. They performed the same type of operations, mainly patrols over the beachhead. Lundsten flew three out of a total of four sorties on this day.

Early start today once again to get the aircraft ready. The Germans doesn't send up even one aircraft, so there's not much excitement going on here. The army have proceeded ten miles inwards. The pilots are in the air *circa* eight hours a day so it takes a hard toll on them, and obviously they need better maintenance after each trip.

Ragnvald Myhre via *Spitfire Saga V*, 2014, p. 288

The Norwegians flew lower over the coastline on this day, and they spotted about 2,000 gliders towed by Lancasters, Halifaxes, and Stirlings. Most of them flew over Bognor Regis before the Norwegians had taken off, but the squadrons caught up with them over the French coastline. The Norwegians also patrolled slightly further inland on 7 June. Although they were subject to shellfire from the ground, no one was hit. However, 332 lost Egil Bernhard Olufsen on the first sortie of the day. He was hit by flak and crash-landed on a road not far from the coast—he died later on in an English hospital. In total, 150 landings were accomplished at Bognor Regis throughout the day, with no incidents. Lundsten participated in the first, third and fourth sortie of the day, with the last landing at 10.30 p.m. Once again, there was little time for sleep, though a few managed to get some before the squadrons took off once more at 7.15 a.m. on 8 June. The next day, Lundsten would disappear.

Date: 08.06.1944
Spitfire: IX, FN-Y MK121
Built: Castle Bromwich
Length: 2:00
Where: Bognor Regis–Utah Beach/Beachhead–Bognor Regis

The Norwegians gradually flew further inland each day. On 8 June, they flew over St Mere-Eglise towards Montebourg—beyond the western invasion front—when they spotted artillery firing on the troops at Utah beach. A group from 332 attacked the artillery, and one pilot was hit (Bjørnestad, 332 Squadron). Luckily, he managed to bale out of the Spitfire and survive—he was the second Norwegian Spitfire lost following the invasion.

The Norwegians also spotted Spitfire Vs with clipped wings. Their manoeuvring led them to believe that they were German-flown captured Spitfires. No attacks were made, and they last saw the Mk Vs head in a north-westerly direction.

Lundsten participated in the first and second sortie of the day, one less than the two days before. Did MK121 develop some sort of trouble, which excluded him from the third and possibly fourth sortie of the day?

35

Fall of Night:
9 June 1944, 331 Squadron,
Isigny Sur-Mer/Utah Beach, France

Date: 09.06.1944
Spitfire: IX, FN-M MK966
Built: Castle Bromwich
Length: 1:00
Where: Bognor Regis–Utah Beach/Beachhead–Bognor Regis

The serial of Lundsten's Spitfire during his last sortie has been hard to identify. Some sources claim it was FN-Y, MJ827, but his logbook, filled in and concluded by someone else due to the tragic circumstances, listed it as FN-W (with no serial). The ORB listed it FN-M (again, with no serial). After extensive research (including the confusing event with MJ827, which happened at the exact same time, see 22 February 1944), it is with some certainty that Lundsten flew FN-M, MK966. MK121 was not used, perhaps due to technical issues, and it was later transferred to 421 Squadron. So, Lundsten had to fly a different Spitfire for the only sortie of the day. He chose FN-M—M for Major.

The flying was limited due to horrible weather conditions all day. Low clouds and heavy rain stopped any operations over Normandy until late in the evening. Some Spitfires had been left by the Norwegians at Tangmere the night before, and were picked up by their pilots during the day. The Norwegians did not strap in before 9 p.m., with take-off set at 9.15 p.m. It was a sortie filled with misunderstandings, miscommunications, trigger-happy sailors, poor flying conditions, and fading daylight.

The wing set course for their regular patrol area over Utah beach, St Mere-Eglise, and Isigny Sur-Mer. The wing was led by Werner Christie from 332 Squadron, and Lundsten led 331 Squadron as usual.

When over Normandy and the Channel, they were under FDT 216 (Fighter Direction Tender 216), based on a ship between Utah and Omaha beach. It was essential to locate effective radar and communications close to the Normandy beaches during the critical days from D-Day, at least until mobile land-based radar and communications units could take over—a period of around three weeks.

No. 132 Wing crossed the French coast at 3,500 feet south-west of St Iles Marcouf at 9.45 p.m. The first event, which led to the disapperance of Lundsten, was a report given to the Norwegians about six enemy fighters flying very low to the south. The Norwegians went down on the deck to chase the enemy down. They gained some altitude north of Isigny, in order to avoid balloons in the area (Lundsten spotted them just in time), and then dived down again on the other side. It was not long until they were fired upon by shore-based flak, north-east of Isigny. The controller (FDT 216) was informed of the enemy fire upon the Norwegians. On the deck, in poor weather, they were ordered to turn around and get out again the same way they came in, as the controller thought it could be a German flak position they had just encountered—they did as they were told.

They crossed out over the coast from 1,000 to 1,500 feet, but it was not an ideal height. According to some witness accounts, the shelling first opened up from the Americans in the west by Omaha beach. It didn't take more than a few seconds before the entire fleet opened up at the Norwegians. The incident could even be connected to the Canadian Spitfires over Omaha, who were shelled at approximately the same time.

Lundsten (as well as Christie) were exposed to the shelling as they were flying in front. On FTD 216, LAC Leslie Armitage wrote a diary about the events that happened on 9 June 1944.

At 9 p.m. he wrote:

> Air-raid warning, terrific barrage, 2 hostiles reported down. All clear sounded 21:30. Tried to have a shave, having one when air raid warning sounded. Action stations until 23:30. Germans bombing beaches and shipping.

Lundsten was then hit by the inferno coming from the Navy ships. The witness accounts, mostly from *Spitfire Saga V*, each have their own versions of the situation. However, most agree Lundsten was hit, screamed profanities at the Navy before informing the rest he would gain height before baling out. One pilot (Ulstein) later thought Lundsten went 'straight into the sea'.

> Major Lundsten was hit and went straight into the sea, but not before he managed to shout 'You bloody bastards!' over the R.T.

Egil Ulstein via Spitfire Saga V, 2014, p. 297

Lundsten was on my right side, less distance than usual battle formation, maybe about 200 meters. Then I heard him say over the R.T: 'Faen ta Navy'en [author edit: loosely translated to 'Fuck the Navy.']. He gave the others the correct course to base, and then said he would bale out.

Werner Christie via *Spitfire Saga V*, 2014, p. 296

Suddenly, Major Lundsten came on the radio: 'I am hit! Going to bale out!'
According to 331 Squadron pilot Arvid Steen, no one saw Lundsten getting hit due to the massive barrage. Steen saw him disappear into the clouds above, trying to gain altitude.

Red 2, Sgt. Steen last saw Major Lundsten weaving like mad and with smoke pouring out of the aircraft. Then he disappeared into the clouds.

331 ORB.

...he was so calm over the R.T that the panic became less amongst those of us in the middle of the inferno. No one knows what happened to Lundsten, but we are all hoping for the best.

Odd Knut Roald via *Spitfire Saga V*, 2014, p. 297

Many of us literally shit in our pants that day, myself included. I had never been more scared in my entire life. Squadron Leader Leif Lundsten was shot down. He managed to give us the correct course for home before his Spitfire crashed and took his life. It was an experience that shook all of us, of how pointless it was that our popular and skilful Squadron Leader had been killed by our own; and not the least the fact that he thought of his boys and gave us the right course for home while his Spitfire was on fire. Only one in four shells was a tracer, the others we naturally never saw at all.

Birger T. Johannessen, *Spitfire norsk jagerflyger i kamp*, 2001

Bob Winsjansen, a sailor on the USS *I* (positioned off Utah Beach), recalled little from the event:

...and I was at Utah Beach during the invasion of Normandy. I only remember a plane that was shot down on June 6. From what I understand, it was a German that was flying a rebuilt British plane. He did not survive. I do not remember Spitfire planes on 9 June.

E-mail conversations with the author 17 December 2014.

The incident has later been blamed on the Royal Navy; however, the ships off Utah Beach had a mix of American and British ships involved.

Back at Bognor Regis, the Norwegians were upset and angry. Upset over losing their popular leader, not to German flak or fighters, but to their own guns. Angry because their own Navy had just shot down their leader for no reason. The Navy, US or British alike, was not popular at Bognor Regis that night, or in the months that followed. However, many pilots had hopes Lundsten was alright. If he had managed to gain height, as he said he would, he would have good chance of surviving. Following D-Day, the chance of rescue was perhaps not as good as one might think. With so much going on, a 'minor incident' of a mistaken 'enemy aircraft' getting shot down might not have made much impact. Considering Canadian 'Bill' Williams' impressive survival story, when he set course for Normandy and survived a crash-landing on the same night, it seems unlikely Lundsten managed to do the same. Lundsten either did not manage to get out of the Spitfire or was killed in a possible ditching-attempt, or he did bale out and something happened in the jump itself. If he jumped out and landed in the sea, he was not found due to the poor weather conditions. Baling out of a Spitfire can be tricky; as an example, it killed Kåre B. Anthonsen just two days later when his parachute got tangled up in the tail of his Spitfire—he was killed.

Major Lundsten shot down by our own Navy later in the day, June 9 1944. He is believed to have baled out, but nothing certain is known.

Rolf Arne Berg, logbook.

Lundsten's course for home action would stick as a gallant and heroic act from a stricken leader, fighting for survival, thinking of his pilots until the very end. However, Kjell Wilhelm Tvedt later said it was him who gave the course for home—intended for a new pilot in the squadron (Kåre A. Anthonsen) on his first sweep that evening, perhaps to calm him down after having gone through one of the worst 'baptisms of fire' one can imagine. Tvedt was later reluctant to speak up about the incident, since he did not like to take anything away from their very popular leader's post-war reputation. The story stuck, and was later retold in several books through the years.

On 12 June 1944, Helge Mehre wrote in his diary: '...nothing new about Lundsten'. There was no news in the months, years, or decades to come. Major Leif Lundsten, aged twenty-six, had disappeared forever.

After the loss of Lundsten, I decided to never again fly over the ships off the invasion beaches. It took us ten minutes extra time to fly around them.

331 Squadron Leader Martin Gran via *Spitfire Saga V*, 2014, p. 326

My grandmother used to say; 'I can't believe Leif is gone. I can't believe he is gone. I just can't believe it'.

Erna Johansen, conversation with the author in 2015

Appendix:
Lundsten's Spitfires

Mk I

X4622

Mk II

P7366, P7377, P8729, P7886, P7388, P7616, P7929, P7759, P8199, P7963, P7384, AB794

Mk III

LR766, MA970, W3237

Mk V

AD509, BL821, BL891, AR328, AB794, AR297, EN786, P8707, AR296, BL897, BM295, EP769, BM408, BL862

Mk VII

BS299

Mk VIII

JF275, JF320, JF676, JF836, JF707, JF842, JF841, JF621, JF846, JF872, JF873, JF875, JF878, JF879, JF953, JF956, JF880, JF881, JG158, JG164, JG171, JF883, JG174, JG175, JG177, JF884, JG332, JG334, JG335, JG337, JG269, JG342, JG204, JG345, JG344, JG347, JG348, JG346, JG350,

JG349, JG351, JG353, JG352, JG354, JG373, JG372, JG374, JG375, JG380, JG379, JG376, JG382, JG381, JG384, JG385, JG383, JG386, JF889, JG387, JF895, JF894, JF898, JG563, JG318, JG320, JG316, JG323, JG526, JG561, JG767, JG562, JG325, JG327, JG404, JG405, JG500, JG621, JG406, JG481, JG478, JG604, JG484, JG602, JG485, JG609, MD228, JG612, JG610, MD224, JG568, JG534, MD233, MD237, MD234, MD244, MD239, MD240, LV744, JG566, LV657, LV651, LV647, LV613, LV666, LV669, LV659, MD245, LV654, LV671, LV676, LV672, LV732, LV737, LV738, LV661, LV678, LV681, LV742, LV755, MD214, LV680, LV747, MD216, LV679, LV746, MD218, MD297, MD299, MD278, MD279, LV726, MD298, LV756, MD302, MD332, MD330, MD303, MD334, MD335, MD336, MD338, MD339, MD337

Mk IX

BS466, BS467, BS470, BS137, BS388, BS471, BR594, BR982, BS125, MA225, LZ920, BS118, EN684, EN314, BS310, LZ917, MJ567, MK121

Mk XI

EN684, EN683, MB889, MB902, MB903, MB906, MB838, MB937, MB942, MB941, MB945, MB946, MB947, MB948, MB949, MB950, MB954, MB956, MB957, MB955, MB958, MB952, PA838, PA839, PA851, PA842, PA841, PA840, PA892, PA843, PA844, PA845, PA897, PA846, PA848, PA849, PA861, PA863, PA860, PA867, PA865, PA850, PA862, PA864, PA869, PA871, PA866, PA858, PA686, PA885, PA987, PA884, PA889, PA887, PA852, PA891, PA890, PA855, PA856, PA893, PA895, PA911, PA853, PA859, PA857, PA896, PA900, PA894, PA898, PA899, PA926, PA906, PA907, PA903, PA929, PZ904, PA909, PA908, PA905, PA931, PA930, PA928, PA939, PA910, PA912

Mk XII

MB863, MB875, MB889, MB877, MB895, MB902, MB903, MB906, DP845, MB882, EN227

Mk XIV

JF320

Bibliography

Oral sources

Gundersen, Olav. Conversations with the author in 2011
Johansen, Erna. Coversations with the author in 2015
Lundsten, Roald. Conversations with the author in 2011
Lundsten, Bjarne. Conversations with the author in 2011

Books

Brown, P., *RAF Southend*, (2012)
Darling, K., *Supermarine Seafire*, (2008)
Gran, M., *Vi Flyr*, (1965)
Goodwin, C., *Pilot Magazine*, 12 December 2013
Grundt-Spang, H., *Den hemmelige kampen*, (1971)
Guhnfeldt, C., *Nattjager*, (2004); *Spitfire Saga I and II*, (2009); *Spitfire Saga III*, (2011); *Spitfire Saga IV*, (2013); *Spitfire Saga V*, (2014)
Hamlin, J., and Halley, J. J., *Royal Air Force Training and Support Units*, (1988)
Heglund, S., *Høk over Høk*, (1995)
Henshaw, A., *Sigh for a Merlin*, (1979)
Hyams, J., *The Female Few: The Spitfire Heroines of the Air Transport Auxiliary*, (2012)
Neill, T., *The Silver Spitfire*, (2013)
Nyerrød, K., *En av de mange*, (1997)
Phipp, M., *Wessex Aviation Industry*, (2011)
Philpott, I., *The Birth of the Royal Air Force*, (2013)
Price, A., *The Spitfire Story*, (2011)

Quill, J., *A Test Pilots Story*, (1989); *Flight Magazine*, (October 1953)

Ree, M., *Våre jagerflygere i kamp*, (1962)

Russel, C. R., *My Life at Supermarine* (1985); *Spitfire Postscript*, (1994)

Riley, G., Arnold, P., and Trent, G., *Spitfire Survivors*, (2010)

Rønhof, K., *Vi fløy for friheden*, (1991)

Sarkar, D., *Ace of Aces: The True Wartime Story of Johnnie Johnson*, (2012)

Stanaway, J., *The Eight Ballers: Eyes of the Fifth Air Force: The 8th Photo Reconnaissance Squadron in World War II*, (1999)

Shores, C., and Williams, C., *Aces High: A Tribute to the Most Notable Fighter Pilots of the British and Commonwealth Forces of WWII*, (1994)

Tidemand-Johannessen, B., *Spitfire: en norsk jagerflyger i kamp*, (2001)

Thomas, A., *Spitfire Aces of Burma and the Pacific*, (2013)

Thomas, G., *Eyes for the Phoenix*, (1998)

Taylor, J., *Pilot Magazine*, (December 2013)

Other sources

Meteorological Committee. Monthly weather report of the meteorological office (August 1943–February 1944)

Leif Lundsten official service records

Ware, Jennifer. E-mail communication 8 February 2014

Lundsten, Morten. Email communication 2012–2013

Winsjansen, Bob. E-mail communication 2014

Pierro, Matteo, about JF879

Operational Record Books

1 (South African) Squadron

124 Squadron

130 Squadron

132 Squadron

136 Squadron

145 Squadron

152 Squadron

16 Squadron

19 Squadron

222 Squadron

229 Squadron

273 Squadron

308 (Polish) Squadron

310 (Czechoslovak) Squadron
331 (Norwegian) Squadron
332 (Norwegian) Squadron
400 Squadron
403 Squadron
41 Squadron
417 Squadron
453 Squadron
542 Squadron
548 Squadron
549 Squadron
601 Squadron
607 Squadron
611 (Canadian) Squadron
615 Squadron
66 Squadron
682 Squadron
683 Squadron
719 Squadron
74 Squadron
76 Squadron
81 Squadron
81 Squadron
91 Squadron
92 Squadron

Logbooks

Berg, Rolf Arne
Elkington, Tim
Haave-Olsen, Reidar
Knudsen, Ingar Helge
Lundsten, Leif
Nordmo, John
Sognnæs, Helge
Endresen, Per Svanøe

Combat reports

Leif Lundsten, 15.02.1943, 26.02.1943, 12.03.1943, 16.04.1943, 04.05.1943, 08.05.1943
Fredrik Eitzen, 12.03.1943
Knut Bache, 08.05.1943
331 Intelligence Report, 08.05.1943

Websites

www.airshowspresent.com/chattis-hill.html
www.602squadronmuseum.org.uk/
xm424.com
aircrewremembered.com/goffin-charles.html
www.afleetingpeace.org/
www.airshowspresent.com/chattis-hill.html
www.scribd.com/doc/156944140/Eyes-for-the-Phoenix
announcements.telegraph.co.uk/deaths/184443/brocklehurst
www.colonialfilm.org.uk/node/2304
www.gatwickaviationsociety.org.uk/history_wartime.asp
www.aircrew-saltire.org/lib003.htm
www.wingsmuseum.co.uk/spitfire_xi_PA929.htm
www.nationalmuseum.af.mil/
www.combinedops.com/FDT%20216%20Diary%20of%20a%20Veteran.html
There is a reconstructed film of the Circus 267 and Scramble sorties at goo.gl/E6KboQ (*made by Knut Åshammer*)